BETWEEN THE BUDDHA AND THE NEW TSAR

BETWEEN THE BUDDHA AND THE NEW TSAR

Urban Religion and Minority Politics at the Asian Borderlands of Russia

Kristina Jonutytė

CORNELL UNIVERSITY PRESS   ITHACA AND LONDON

Copyright © 2026 by Cornell University

All rights reserved. Except for brief quotations in a review, this book, or parts thereof, must not be reproduced in any form without permission in writing from the publisher. For information, address Cornell University Press, Sage House, 512 East State Street, Ithaca, New York 14850. Visit our website at cornellpress.cornell.edu.

First published 2026 by Cornell University Press

Librarians: A CIP catalog record for this book is available from the Library of Congress.

ISBN 9781501786051 (hardcover)
ISBN 9781501786068 (paperback)
ISBN 9781501786082 (pdf)
ISBN 9781501786075 (epub)

GPSR EU contact: Sam Thornton, Mare Nostrum Group B.V., Mauritskade 21D, 1091 GC, Amsterdam, NL, gpsr@mare-nostrum.co.uk.

To all those struggling for their basic freedoms and peace in Buryatia and beyond

Contents

Preface	ix
List of Acronyms and Abbreviations	xiv
Note on Transliteration, Translation, and Local Language	xv
Introduction	1
1. Buryats in Russia: From "Aliens" to Model Soviets to Complex Modern Identities	38
2. Buryat Buddhism: Politics and Identity of a Minority Religion in Russia	59
3. Urban Buddhism in Buryatia: Continuing Expansion Encounters Fragile Diversity	78
4. Being a Pillar: Buddhist Counseling	107
5. Buddhist Imperfections: Religious Giving and Belonging	129
Conclusion	149
Acknowledgments	155
Notes	159
References	167
Index	181

Preface

It is the summer of 2022, and I am writing these words from my home in Vilnius, Lithuania. Russia began waging a full-scale war against Ukraine just months ago, on February 24. It seems that the world has changed in the intervening time—it certainly has for myself and my friends, colleagues, and interlocutors in Buryatia. Today, we find ourselves at odds, in opposite camps of this war. As citizens and residents of Russia, people in Buryatia are—at least technically, if not necessarily politically and personally—on the side of the aggressor. I, as a Lithuanian citizen based in Europe, am much closer to Ukraine. While Lithuania is not officially engaged in warfare as of this writing, this post-Soviet northeast European state on the shore of the Baltic Sea is among Ukraine's staunchest allies, on the levels of military and humanitarian support, as well as in discourse and policy.

In fact, Lithuania also figures prominently in Russian state propaganda, described as "fascists," "Russophobes," and one of the closest allies of Ukraine. Russia's politicians and propagandists have long used *Pribaltika*, the Baltic states, as a figure of speech, a metonym for an enemy just across the border. From the Russian imperial perspective, *pribalty* are people who were once "our own" (Rus., *nashy*) but have since been dazzled by Western propaganda and lost their moral and cultural compass. Just like Ukraine, Lithuania was once part of the Russian Empire and later the Soviet Union, and Russia's imperialists have had a hard time letting it go and acknowledging its sovereignty and right to political will, in this case a Euro-American orientation.

Unlike Ukraine, Lithuania was able to conjure firm Western support and was accepted into NATO and the European Union relatively early in the post-Soviet period, in 2004. It seemed to many in Lithuania that the Russian past was long gone and a (surely much idealized) "Western" future lay ahead. But Russia's annexation of Crimea and the war in eastern Ukraine since 2014 has brought back the collective trauma and the realization that the empire may well return—or at least attempt to do so. In response Lithuania has reinstituted (partial) compulsory military conscription for young men and has since more than quadrupled its military expenditure: rising from 0.8 percent of the GDP in 2013 to 3.91 percent in 2025, with recent calls to raise it to 6 percent.

But it is not just government spending that changes when neighboring enmity is on the rise. Tensions in society have been growing as well, and distaste for anything Russian has indeed become more prominent in response to Russia's military aggression on a neighboring sovereign country. Anthropologist Neringa Klumbytė (2022) has referred to this as "radical sovereignty": a type of "radical politics where national unity supersedes individual interests, rights of a particular group are prioritized over others, patriotism and militarism define the everyday." She notes that such radical sovereignties as those in Lithuania or Ukraine may indeed arise in contexts marked by war, occupation, violence, and trauma. Since February 2022, these processes and sentiments have understandably swelled. On the one hand, there are tangible measures in Lithuania by the state and various institutions, including academic ones, to cut ties with Russia, for instance, by terminating all collaborations with the country or exchange with it, as well as discontinuing imports. On the other hand, reverberations of the war may at times mean antagonism toward any Russian citizen regardless of their political views and biographies.

All this certainly places me, a Lithuanian researcher of one of Russia's ethnic minorities, the Buryats, in a peculiar position. Buryats are Russian citizens, and as such, they are also Russia's soldiers, officials, and journalists, and they form part of the various arms of the Russian regime. Buryats, like other Russian soldiers, fight in Ukraine on the Russian side, killing Ukrainian soldiers and civilians and destroying the country's infrastructure. Among those who are not physically at war, many Buryats, like other inhabitants of Russia, consume the pro-government media, and it provides much of the basis of their knowledge and interpretation of current events. According to its narratives, Russia is on a noble mission to save its Slavic kin from "fascists" in Ukraine, and Lithuanians, just like Ukrainians, are clear-cut enemies and a threat to their country.

However, anthropologists take pride in establishing and maintaining close relationships with their interlocutors and more broadly with the region they study. This is perhaps not very surprising, given our long-term fieldwork and involvement in the everyday life of our research participants. This closeness was etched into me from day one of anthropological training. I remember pondering why the lecturer of my introductory undergraduate anthropology course repeatedly called his Indonesian research participants "friends" (in fact, it seemed like the word "informants" that was often used in anthropological texts at the time did not exist to him). I, too, left Buryatia after yearlong fieldwork in 2016 with many friends and a lifelong connection with the region.

These personal entanglements were already problematic during my fieldwork, which started after Russia's 2014 annexation of Crimea. I decided to nonetheless carry out my research project on issues of minority religion—issues that already appeared important in increasingly authoritarian Russia. But since February 2022, this means I have suddenly found myself "in bed with the enemy." Given Lithuania's position as one of the ultimate enemies in contemporary Russian propaganda and given the small size of this country in a strategically important position to Russia (it separates Kaliningrad from Belarus and Russia), it is not a stretch to imagine that Buryats—together with other Russian soldiers—could have invaded Lithuania like they invaded Ukraine. In times of war, empathy, compassion, and attempts to understand those on the other side in terms other than black-and-white seem to many to be redundant, repugnant, and even suspicious. Buryats, like other Russians, were now *orki* (a term derived from the name of humanoid monsters in the *Lord of the Rings*), *rashisty* (a blend of the words *Russia* and *fascist*), *rusnia* (a variation of a derogatory name for Russians) in much of Lithuanian public discourse.

But I knew Buryatia well—I had researched it for eight years by the time the full-scale war started and had lived in Ulan-Ude for thirteen months. My time there was certainly not all rosy, and I had encountered hostility, verbal abuse, and threats of physical harm, much of it on the grounds of my being a foreigner from Europe. But having intimately known the region, I knew that this was not the whole picture. Many people I knew in Buryatia wanted no part of this war, and some firmly, even openly, opposed it.

As the war continued into the summer of 2022, some Buryats in Russia and in diaspora bravely took part in antiwar activities and oppositional movements. Some, while unequivocally opposing the war, feared repressions and kept quietly to themselves. Yet others had complex feelings and reactions or supported the war for varying reasons. In no way were all Buryats, or all people from Buryatia, a single group of *rashisty* whose thought and behavior could be explained away in categorical terms. To my mind, it is now all the more urgent to understand the reasons behind this state of affairs and the conditions that enable such diversity of positions—from risking one's livelihood in antiwar activism to committing or justifying crimes against humanity—within one society, sometimes even within one household. In this sense, Buryats are not much different from the rest of humankind, but the immanent sociological questions of individual and collective agency, resistance, and the violence of the state now have much higher stakes there.

Buryats are simultaneously perpetrators of the Russian regime, its subjects, and its victims. The region they inhabit was colonized by the Russian Empire in the late seventeenth century, and the centuries under Russian rule have inevitably had a great impact—and a largely detrimental one—on Buryat culture, society, and identity. The war in Ukraine has brought to the fore complex questions of belonging and a reevaluation of the colonization of Buryats, as well as other ethnic minorities in Russia. Buryats have long suffered the consequences of colonization—assimilation policies, decline of native language, second-class citizenship, racist abuse—and in the context of Russia's "Slavic" war, many among them are wondering whether it really is their war to fight. Based on preliminary data, Buryats, as well as some other ethnic minority groups, may have suffered disproportionate losses and disproportionate conscription during the early stages of the full-scale war in Ukraine (Vyushkova and Sherkhonov 2023), raising questions of systemic racism and even suspicions of ethnic cleansing in Russia. As such, it seems pertinent to explore issues of Buryat identity, belonging, and their lifeworlds at this pivotal time.

The current war has brought about a shift in studies of Russia and the post-Soviet region. Many have claimed that Russian studies in particular requires decolonization but also that much of the research on post-Soviet contexts has too often, if sometimes unwittingly, reproduced the Russian-centered perspective, thereby normalizing and legitimizing contemporary Russian imperialism. Scholars from a range of disciplines are reconsidering their approaches and biases based on newfound understandings of violently enduring Russian imperialism. Clearly, research on Russia's ethnic minorities must be reconsidered in light of the war in Ukraine and Russia's resurgent, if never really arrested, imperial project.

I have also had to rethink my research and interpretations considering the war. Anthropologists are all too keen to follow the lead of their interlocutors and rely on local judgments of their situation. This becomes problematic in colonial contexts in illiberal regimes where open public debate on topics of belonging or the expression of grievances toward the dominant group and the reigning regime are disallowed. Under such conditions, identities are layered, individual and collective trauma are rife, belonging is complex, and consciousness of one's culture and history is blurred by the silencing of many voices. Listening to one's interlocutors too closely may unwittingly result in insufficient recognition of the oppressive regime they suffer under yet, at least partly, reproduce. While I did recognize in my previous research the oppressive illiberal context my interlocutors lived in, I now see that it runs far deeper than I had ever thought.

On top of that, both state censorship in Russia and self-censorship have influenced the ways in which I and other scholars of Russia work and the topics we have researched. Based on the experience of my colleagues, as well as my own judgment of the situation, I knew that directly studying political topics could get me in trouble and bring potential risk to my research participants. Avoiding this meant tiptoeing around certain topics or choosing more "ethnographic" themes related to religious practice rather than overtly "political" ones. It is unclear to what extent this was necessary or necessarily the case for all researchers—the Russian state has often worked in unpredictable ways, singling out some cases while letting many others slide by. In my previous publications, I did explore topics relating to the entanglement of religion and politics, Orientalism and racism in Russia, and multiethnic coexistence in Buryatia. However, in retrospect, I also exercised a degree of self-censorship to avoid risks to myself and others and to be able to continue conducting research in the country.

While certain blind spots in my fieldwork and analysis are clearer now, my research topics and findings are as relevant as ever. Issues of religious and ethnic identity, multiethnic coexistence, cultural sovereignty, and group solidarity are all at play as Buryats and other minoritized populations in Russia continue renegotiating their place and their future. Urbanization and the social, economic, and political shifts and ruptures of the last century do not just provide context; they themselves are significant factors shaping ideas and practices of belonging and the ways in which communities respond to new challenges. I hope this book—a story concerning a particular time and place—will one day be read by my friends as well as strangers in a very different Buryatia.

Acronyms and Abbreviations

ASSR	Autonomous Soviet Socialist Republic
BMASSR	Buryat-Mongolian Autonomous Soviet Socialist Republic
BTSR	Buddhist Traditional Sangha of Russia (Rus., Buddiĭskaia traditsionnaia Sangkha Rossii)
Bur.	Buryat
Khambo Lama	Pandito Khambo Lama (Rus., Pandito Khambo-lama; Bur., Bandida Khamba lama)
RUB	Russian ruble
Rus.	Russian
Tib.	Tibetan
USSR	Union of Soviet Socialist Republics

Note on Transliteration, Translation, and Local Language

For the transliteration of Russian words and titles, I use the American Library Association–Library of Congress (ALA-LC) system for Cyrillic, except for terms in the text with established transliteration in English (e.g., Ulan-Ude, Irkutsk Oblast) and names (e.g., Sanya). For Buryat, I also use the same system, with the addition of *ü* for *y*. In cited excerpts, I keep the authors' preferred transliteration.

All translations from original Russian text and speech are mine. I have changed the names of research participants, as well as some inessential details about them, to protect their anonymity, except for the names of public figures.

For Buddhist terms commonly used in English, I use them without translation and use English plural endings (e.g., *datsan(s)*, *khural(s)*). For the sake of consistency and recognizability, I use Russian-language place names and Russian-language location-based *datsan* names.

Introduction

It was October 2022, and I was sitting in a restaurant in Ulaanbaatar, Mongolia, in the mixed company of Buryat Buddhist lamas and laypeople.[1] We were lunching in an unorthodox group, as unusual circumstances had brought us together. The two lamas knew each other from Ulan-Ude, the capital of the Republic of Buryatia, just across the border in the Russian Federation, where they both typically reside. There was nothing typical about October that year. Russia had launched full-scale war on Ukraine over half a year ago, on February 24, 2022. Though Buryatia was more than six thousand kilometers from the combat zone, the war reverberated very much there, and here too at the table we occupied in independent Mongolia.

Within a week of the announcement by the president of Russia, Vladimir Putin, of a partial military draft in late September 2022, it is estimated that almost three hundred thousand Russians fled the country to avoid conscription (Light 2022). Other sources claim seven hundred thousand left within the first two weeks.[2] Among these were many Buryats. According to Mongolian sources, over twenty-two thousand Russian citizens crossed the border to Mongolia in the first weeks following the military call-up.[3] While many left Mongolia shortly after, either traveling on or returning to Russia, Ulaanbaatar suddenly became a vibrant hub of Russian diasporic life, especially for those from Buryatia and surrounding regions in the vicinity of Mongolia. It was now home—at least temporarily—to many Russian citizens of different ethnicities, ages, backgrounds, and diverse socioeconomic standing.

It is perhaps unsurprising that I found myself in all-male company that lunchtime in Ulaanbaatar. While some fled Russia in families, and although some females such as medical professionals were called up to the war, it was predominantly men who were subject to conscription. As we sat around the large table in a Mongolian restaurant, the atmosphere was far from joyous. This turbulent time made our outing less than cheerful, and it provided a kind of intimacy in our group's shared affliction and a mutual understanding that necessitated few words.

My lunch companions were distressed and in a state of deep uncertainty. Three of them were young Buryat laymen who had fled conscription. They had left their families, jobs, homes, and ordinary lives behind and did not know what lay ahead. They had been in such a state for almost a month and were living off either savings or remote jobs based in Russia. For the latter, it was simply a matter of time before their physical absence would be noticed at work, which would likely result in dismissal. They were not sure what to do next or how long they would have to stay abroad. Different options were on the table: everything from staying in Mongolia long-term, to returning to Russia, to illegal migration to the United States or a move to Southeast Asia seemed plausible. One of them planned to study English in Ulaanbaatar; another, to spend all his savings in an unlikely effort to illegally cross the US-Mexico border; and a third, to temporarily move to Thailand and continue working remotely. Some of the laymen were planning to bring over their wives and children to join them once they had figured out the destination and a plan of action. The other two men were lamas. Both were normally based in Buryatia, but they were temporarily in Mongolia, one having accompanied a family member fleeing conscription, the other on a work-related visit. While they intended to return to Buryatia shortly, the peak of the draft period seemed like a good time to be away for a couple of weeks.

It is this time of atrocity and uncertainty that provides the focal lens for this book on Buryat Buddhism and society. Buryats are a Mongol ethnic group who have lived under Russian rule since the late seventeenth century. Today, they constitute around 0.34 percent of the population of Russia, mostly living in the Republic of Buryatia and in the surrounding regions of Irkutsk Oblast and Zabaykalsky Krai. A small minority, in recent years, especially since Russia invaded Ukraine in 2014 and again 2022, Buryats have all too often cropped up in the media and on social media in Russia, Ukraine, and abroad. To many, Buryats have come to symbolize Russian minority militant participation in the war in Ukraine.

Since the 2014 war in eastern Ukraine, Russian as well as foreign media and social media have promoted a sensationalized image of "Putin's combat Buryats" (Rus., *boevye buriaty Putina*). In part, this image drew on Orientalist (and to some extent self-Orientalizing) trope of militant Mongols, going back to Genghis Khan and beyond. But it was expanded with new elements, some staged and some serendipitous. There was an unofficially state-sponsored video by Buryat teenagers preaching the greatness of multiethnic Russia and ridiculing "mistaken Ukrainians" (Rus., *perpeutannykh ukraintsev*) for claiming that Russia was taking part in the war in eastern Ukraine. There was a video of the glamorous Soviet pop music legend turned post-Soviet politician Joseph Kobzon visiting a Buryat tank soldier with heavy battle burns in the hospital in Donetsk, and exclaiming his joy upon meeting a Buryat soldier so far from home in eastern Ukraine.[4] After the Bucha massacre in 2022, when some Ukrainians alleged Asian soldiers participated in the war atrocities, the myth of "Putin's combat Buryats," supposedly the most loyal and militarily capable of all Russian soldiers, revived. While these allegations of heavy Asian Russian presence in Bucha were later rebuked by several investigators (Al Hlou et al. 2022), at this point, Russian state media and some among the Russian opposition, Ukrainian and international sources, were all involved in propagating the racist label.

Buryats were branded, along with Chechens, as the most violent and barbaric of soldiers. Whenever news of atrocities or war crimes committed by Asian soldiers from the Russian army appeared, they were almost inevitably racialized as Buryats. Propounding the nationality of war criminals is a problematic exercise in its own right, but, needless to say, in many cases, the perpetrators transpired to be of a different nationality. These nuanced realities did little to undermine the growing mythos. Even Pope Francis commented that the Buryats, alongside the Chechens, rather than those "of the Russian tradition," were "the cruelest" on the Russian side (*American Magazine* 2022). In contrast, Russian state propaganda continued to promote their vision of multiethnic Russian cohesion. "I am Lak, I am Dagestani, I am Chechen, Ingush, Tatar, Jewish, Mordvin, Ossetian," proclaimed Vladimir Putin after the death of a "heroic" Dagestani soldier in a battle in Ukraine.[5] In his 2023 New Year's address, as in many other public appearances, Putin was sure to have minority soldiers supporting him in the background.

While Buryat representations in the image of the war have been disproportionate, minority soldiers do appear to be overrepresented in the Russian army in the war in Ukraine, especially in the death count. Official data on ethnicity in the Russian army is not available, and the official Russian death count is a notorious underestimation. But data analytics from the Free Buryatia Foundation, a prominent Buryat antiwar movement, have estimated that Buryats are overrepresented in the Russian army by about one and a half to three times compared to the countrywide average, constituting up to 1 percent of the Russian army.[6] Even more strikingly, as of September 2022, Buryats constituted 2.3 percent of the casualties on the Russian side (Vyushkova and Sherkhonov 2023, 132). Based on the Free Buryatia Foundation data, a soldier from Buryatia was more than sixty times more likely to die in this war than one from Moscow in the early stages of the war.[7] Such alleged overrepresentation of Buryat soldiers in the army, especially among the dead, has several contributing factors, although few things can be established with certainty at present. Among the likely reasons are the poor socioeconomic situation in the region, a lack of options for social and economic upward mobility, and the relatively strong presence of military bases in this borderland region. In private conversations and online, some also speculate about heavy minority soldier drafting as part of an unofficial ethnic policy of Russia.

The two Buryat lamas I met with in Ulaanbaatar saw the war as a tragedy for the Buryat people. Lama Bayar felt that what had led Buryats to their current predicament was them being *mankurty*. *Mankurty* is a term commonly used in Russia and other post-Soviet countries for people who come from an ethnic minority background yet are Russified. It comes from a novel by the Kyrgyz author Chingiz Aitmatov, where it refers to prisoners of war who are turned into zombified slaves by wrapping their heads in camel skin and exposing them to the sun. The main character of the novel, a brave nomadic soldier, falls into captivity, is brainwashed, and eventually kills his own mother when she tries to save him. Lama Bayar insisted:

> Buryats don't know much about Buryat culture and history. Many of them don't speak the language. This is all a problem of education. But now Buryats are running at the forefront of the *russkiĭ mir* [Russian world]. What is this *russkiĭ mir* and what do Buryats have to do with it? Buryats are trying to be more Russian than Russians themselves. They want to "protect their motherland" [*zashchishchat' rodinu*]. But what motherland [*chto za rodina*]? What do we have to do with Ukraine, and why should we go there? We have lost our true roots; this is the real tragedy. People like to say that Buddhism has been rebuilt in Buryatia. But nothing has been rebuilt compared to what used to be there. The education, the wisdom, the virtue. People go to a *datsan* now, and they think they are Buddhists.[8] But it shouldn't be that way.

Lama Chimit heavyheartedly added: "It is shameful to be a Buryat today. If you say you're a Buryat anywhere in the world now, you'll be ashamed. And this is fair. We have brought this upon ourselves. Now we will be working to regain our reputation for a very long time. It will take a while before we have something to be proud of again. We will be paying a price for this for a very long time."

The first Buryat lama I met with in Ulaanbaatar, Bayar, was an experienced and highly respected middle-aged Buddhist specialist. Back home he was known for his directness with laypeople and for a deep understanding of Buddhist thought

FIGURE 1. Graffiti in central Ulaanbaatar, October 2022. Photo by author.

and practice. Lama Bayar ran a temple in Ulan-Ude, and while he was strongly opposed to Russia's invasion of Ukraine, he planned to return to his home city. He did somewhat fear conscription but thought that his rather advanced age, health problems, and religious status would help him avoid the draft. Buddhists are not exempt from military service in Russia, but Lama Bayar was sure he could make his case on a religious basis and threaten officials with an international scandal if they arrested him. He was laughing, but despair did not leave his face. Humor was one of the few viable strategies remaining.

Back in Ulan-Ude, laypeople had been consulting Lama Bayar on issues related to the war since February. People began by inquiring about their sons and husbands, friends and relatives, who were professional soldiers (Rus., *kontraktniki*) but had passed out of all communication for a period in February. At that time, news broke of the "special military operation" (Rus., *spetsial'naia voennaia operatsiia*) in Ukraine, as the war is officially called in Russia. It was easy enough to connect the dots, and many were worried about their loved ones. Buddhist rituals were one of the only means available for sending them luck or for divining their possible location, situation, or status. Later, these divinations concerned with conscripts' location and rituals for conjuring luck were complemented by divinatory searches for those who were missing and finally by death rites. In spring 2022, more and more coffins started arriving in Buryatia. People also consulted lamas about whether to join the army as volunteers or, on the other hand, to help them figure out how to talk their relatives out of enlisting. Then, in autumn, the new issue of the military call-up arose. In general, laypeople were looking for advice and a bit of extra luck in dealing with the unusual and volatile circumstances.

Lama Bayar had a clear message to those considering going to Ukraine: Don't. Buddhists, he claimed, should not kill. They should not support a bloody war—especially if they understood karmic laws and rebirth. Killing would bring a great amount of negative karma that would ramify and inevitably manifest in this or future lives in the form of unsatisfactory circumstances and suffering. Furthermore, Lama Bayar explained, the antagonisms of the war against Ukrainians should not make sense to Buddhists, as we can all be reborn in a different part of the world and as members of a different nation. A Buryat might well have been Ukrainian in their previous lives. To Lama Bayar, the most striking and upsetting thing about his consultations with laypeople was the fact that, as far as he could observe, most of them did not doubt the narratives provided by the Russian state. They seemed to uncritically share in the state-sponsored narratives, of the need to "denazify" Ukraine, of the dangers that Ukraine was posing to Russia, and of the nobleness and necessity of the "special military operation." As Russian citizens, many Buryats felt like this was their war to fight to protect their motherland (Rus., *rodina*).

Lama Bayar seemed firm in his antiwar stance, but he did not share it publicly in Russia, only in private conversations and in consultations with laypeople. He regretted that he and those around him were not more outspoken about their antiwar position: "We should have revolted. Instead, we are sitting quietly without doing anything. And I keep thinking about doing something and about what can be done. But I run a temple. I have a responsibility. If I didn't have this responsibility, I would go out there and speak up. But I bear a responsibility towards my laypeople. I must look after my temple." This double bind, caught between submission and resistance, between the pressure of the dominating regime and the protection of the lives and interests of Buryat Buddhists, is a reoccurring theme in this book.

The second lama, Chimit, echoed Lama Bayar. He had an elderly relative whom he was caring for, and this responsibility prevented him from publicly expressing his antiwar stance. Lama Chimit was an established Buddhist specialist whom many laypeople looked to for help. He planned to return to Buryatia shortly. He claimed he did not fear conscription due to his advanced age and poor health. Like Lama Bayar, he was consulted by laypeople about war-related issues and shared his advice with them on how to avoid going to war, as well as his conviction that Buddhists should not support a war, let alone participate in it. He looked for the most appropriate ways to softly communicate this position to the laypeople he spoke with. At the same time, like Lama Bayar, he recognized the entangled predicament his lay clients were in and did his best to support them emotionally and through ritual regardless of their political views or circumstances.

Lama Chimit had long been critical of the official Buddhist leadership in Buryatia: the dominant organization, called the Buddhist Traditional Sangha of Russia (henceforth, the BTSR), and its current leader of three decades, the Khambo Lama Damba Ayusheev.[9] To him, it was unthinkable that a Buddhist leader could be encouraging people to go to war and to engage thereby in killing and destructive activities. He insisted that the Buddhist leadership in Buryatia had long lost their integrity and reputation. The Khambo Lama is widely seen in Russia as the authoritative leader of Buryat Buddhists. However, Lama Chimit contested the legitimacy of this leadership, saying: "He is a bureaucrat [Rus., *chinovnik*]; he is a representative of the government. It is clear that he is doing the wrong thing. This has long been clear, but especially now." Lama Chimit had never supported the BTSR's multiple efforts at social and political engagement, such as sheep-herding schemes and Buryat-language promotion programs. He was also critical of the Khambo Lama's attempts to dissociate Buryat Buddhism from Tibetan Buddhism and his claim to autocephaly, or the independence of Buryat Buddhism from its Tibetan, Mongolian, and other counterparts. After the Khambo Lama's open support for the war, this criticism and disapproval turned into outright animosity.

The reflections and consternations of these two lamas, caught up in a turbulent time, are telling of the broader ambivalences and contradictions that Buryats and Buryat Buddhists are experiencing in the current era. The two lamas are torn between their duty to support the laity and their understanding that many among their lay supporters are in fact fervent proponents of the war or even its soldiers despite the nonviolent teachings of Buddhism. At the same time, the lamas see the long-term, complex histories of the current situation, involving as they do Russian colonization and violence, assimilation policies, collective trauma, successive oppressive political regimes, the detrimental economic situation in the region, and other factors. As part of an intellectual and spiritual elite in Buryat society, a role the Buryat sangha has historically held, the two lamas feel guilt at not having taken the lead in opposing the war.[10] At the same time, this role of lama, and the pastoral and teaching duties attendant to it, appear to prevent them from taking on the outspoken role they themselves expect from virtuous leadership.

It is the complex and ambiguous situation of Buryat Buddhists in contemporary Russia that this book sets out to explore. It will specifically focus on the

Buddhist milieu of Ulan-Ude and will argue that attention to urban Buddhism provides valuable insights on unfolding debates around Buryat and Russia's minority identity, the future of minority groups within broader national and international dynamics, and the continuing role of religion in these contexts. The city provides a particular conditioning form to Buryat Buddhism that, I argue, is not just religiously but also socially and politically consequential. While in the public sphere, synergies between Buryat Buddhist leadership and the Russian state are highly visible, they provide only part of the story. A careful look at the intimate contexts of everyday Buryat religion provides a counterbalance, revealing the complexities and ambiguities of the religious lives of a borderland minority of a vast and powerful state characterized by long-term aggression toward its own citizens and its neighbors. Unwelcome and tragic as it is, the war provides both impetus and structure. It is an analytic impasse that demands that we follow the guidance Lama Chimit provided me with as we parted: There are no simple answers or singular reasons.

Buddhists at War

Buddhist lamas dealing with issues of war and conscription makes for a disturbing sight. Indeed, Buddhist participation in the war has been abundantly exoticized in the media and on the internet. Unlikely images from Ukraine populate the internet, for instance, of a tank with a Buddhist mantra spray-painted on the side, to provide the protection of Ar'iaabaala (Avalokiteshvara), the bodhisattva of compassion. Another series of photographs displayed several lamas, presumably in the war field, consulting with and holding rituals for Russia's Buddhist camouflage-clad soldiers in Ukraine, in a cloud of ritual incense smoke, with Buddhist deities on *thangkas* (Buddhist sacred paintings) looming over them. To many outside observers, such images constitute an inconceivable contrast, given the prominence of nonviolence in Buddhist teachings. Yet participation in war is not new to Buddhists in Russia nor to those outside it. Buryat lamas' involvement in the war adds just another page to the long, complex, and, at times, tragic Buddhist history in the region.

When Russia invaded Ukraine on February 24, 2022, the commonly recognized leader of Buryat Buddhists, Khambo Lama Damba Ayusheev, was silent—at least he provided no official comment or social media posts. For days, the only communication coming from him or his organization, the BTSR, were the daily messages from the Khambo Lama Itigelov. Itigelov was an advanced Buryat Buddhist monk and the leader of Buryat Buddhists in the 1920s. As the story goes, he consciously entered a state between life and death through meditation and was buried. Since his exhumation in 2002, believers consider Itigelov's body to be in a state between life and death. He is located in a special temple in the Ivolginskiĭ datsan, the biggest Buddhist temple complex in Buryatia and the base of the BTSR. Itigelov's guardian lama extracts daily messages from him through meditation. They are then published in Buryat and Russian on social media, together with short interpretations.

Observing the situation from afar, I was hoping, as perhaps others were, to discern cryptic messages encoded in Itigelov's telepathic quotations. Might I be able to find some quiet, just-about-detectable statements against the war hidden in these extracts? Surely the Buddhist institutions of Buryatia, and the undead saint himself, would not support a senseless war being waged in the name of the "Russian world"? My hopes were in vain. Itigelov's message on February 24 was concerned with worshipping a bodhisattva, and the next day the message discussed good deeds in body, speech, and thought. One could certainly not sense from Itigelov's messages that something dramatic had happened in Russia.

A few days later came the official statement of the Khambo Lama Ayusheev: "We are Buddhists and we are supposed to maintain peace, to preserve harmony and calm. However, we live in a unitary Russian state [*v edinnom rossiĭskom gosudarstve*] and we protect the interests of our country, against which a dirty information war has been launched. We support our brothers and sons who are currently in difficult conditions of war. We pray for their wellbeing and their return to their families. We must provide strong and reliable support. We have our guardian deities [*sakhiūusany*] with us, our great Khambo Lamas, and the Buddha is with us!" This statement falls just short of providing passionate support for Russia's invasion of Ukraine. Ayusheev spoke in vague phrases and highlighted the human factor—support for family members fighting in Ukraine. The statement did, however, offer full backing for Russia's aggression and contained no sign, other than the vaguely Buddhist sounding preamble, of resistance or opposition on the part of Buryatia's most influential Buddhist leader. It even went so far as to explicitly assure the reader of the Buddha's support for Russia's war.

A few days later came announcements of a *khural*, a public sutra reading, "for the protection of the lives of our sons—officers and soldiers of the Russian army, for their wellbeing and return home."[11,12] Again, support for soldiers and loved ones is brought to the fore, but there is no indication of an antiwar stance. After a few weeks, reports came out of Buryat lamas visiting Russia's soldiers in Donbas and providing them with "moral and spiritual support."[13] In the local media, a BTSR lama explained: "We all have one homeland: Russia, and there will be no other. And the great tradition of our fathers, grandfathers and great-grandfathers is to bravely protect our land and motherland. Religious specialists are always close to their protectors. All the prayers now concern peace, so that soldiers come home alive."[14] Photographs of the Khambo Lama with Buryat soldiers returning from Ukraine cropped up on the BTSR's social media pages in 2022, expressing appreciation of their deeds. One gruesome shot included seemingly joyous Ayusheev with his junior relative with a scar across his face and an eye missing, presumably from battle injuries.

This is not the first war the Buryat sangha has been involved in. The local *Buriaad Ünėn* ("Buryat truth") newspaper and the BTSR held a social media campaign in 2020 to collect the names of Buryat monks who had fought during the Second World War. They gathered sixty-seven stories at the beginning of this campaign, though likely got more submissions later.[15] These stories included lamas who had suffered from the Stalinist repressions yet went on to fight for the Soviet Union; those who had received various Orders for their military achievements, including the highest award in the USSR, the Hero of the Soviet Union; and those who served from the first days of the war until the last. Among the lama soldiers was Zhambal Dorzho Gomboev, who later became the nineteenth Khambo Lama. Dozens of Buryat lamas and apprentice lamas died or went missing in the war. This heroic sacrifice for the sake of Russia has been much promoted in recent years. Social media posts on Buryat monk warriors are celebrated every year during Victory Day, and their stories are recounted in local museums and the media.[16] While I am not aware of the BTSR promoting stories of lamas going to fight in Ukraine, lay Buddhists have told me of lama soldiers and of lamas encouraging their lay followers to submit to the draft or even voluntarily enlist.

My conversations in Mongolia with laypeople fleeing conscription painted a very different picture. They unequivocally condemned the BTSR and the Khambo Lama for their backing of Russia's invasion. As one layman put it, to his mind, the Buddhist leadership had now passed the point beyond which no redemption was possible. Previously, he claimed, many were critical of their political position and their collaboration with the Russian government. But encouraging military aggression and killing and the loss of Buryat lives in a Slavic war was the final straw. Other interlocutors, too, reflected on the current situation through their previous negative experiences with the BTSR—lamas they knew to be suspiciously rich or those whose behavior they deemed less than holy. The BTSR's official support for the war and those Buryats taking part in it was to my interlocutors the final piece of evidence necessary to prove that they do not truly have the interests of Buryats at heart, or at least do not hold it above their own personal gain.

Buryat Buddhists are not alone in going to war or in supporting one.[17] Zen Buddhist support for Japanese militarism from the Meiji Restoration to the Second World War is well-documented (Victoria 2006). As one Zen monk put it at the time, "[If ordered to] march: tramp, tramp, or shoot: bang, bang. This is the manifestation of the highest Wisdom [of enlightenment]. The unity of Zen and war of which I speak extends to the farthest reaches of the holy war" (Victoria 2006, xiv). In contemporary southern Thailand, "military monks" serve simultaneously as Buddhist monks and soldiers to defend Thai Buddhists in regions fraught with interethnic, interreligious violence (Jerryson 2010a). While not serving as soldiers, Buddhist monks in contemporary Sri Lanka, torn by decades of civil war, are intertwined with the military through serving soldiers and their families, as well as being regularly commissioned by the army (Kent 2010).

While appearing to violate Buddhist lay and monastic precepts, most explicitly the abstention from killing, participation in a war or violent conflict is not incongruent with Buddhism as it is lived and practiced worldwide. As Michael Jerryson puts it (2010b, 3–4), Buddhism, like other religions, is "quintessentially social in nature; and because religious traditions are social, they suffer from the negative elements inherent in the human condition." As such, violence, including warfare, has been "part of the ethical choices of Buddhists as individuals" just as it has been "part of the structural and systematic patterns of political organizations and institutions for many centuries" (7).

Buryat Buddhist involvement in Russia's wars demonstrates the deep historical entanglements and the resulting strong association between the religion and the state. In the previously quoted words of the lamas, Russia is to many Buryat Buddhists "our country," "our motherland," and there is "no other." This support for the empire is already framed as a tradition and an inevitability. At the same time, this very naturalization of the tie between Buddhists and Russia provides strong ground upon which to raise critical questions, as many of my Buryat interlocutors did. "What motherland?" they asked. And what do Buryats have to do with the "Russian world"?

Religion and Diversity in Russia

The Republic of Buryatia is a multiethnic, multireligious region in southeastern Siberia. Since 2018, it has been part of the Far Eastern Federal District. The republic is around the size of Germany, but its population sits just below one million, at 978,588 (Rosstat 2021). Buryats, a Mongol ethnic group, are the titular nation of the republic, but they constitute only 32.5 percent of the population (Rosstat 2021). The majority at 63.9 percent are ethnic Russians. Buryatia is also home to at least 120 other ethnic groups, as indicated in the 2021 census, who together constitute 3.6 percent of the population, diversity being an important point of local pride (see, e.g., Jonutytė 2022; Quijada 2019). Some scholars and ethnic minority activists are concerned with the results of the 2021 census as it

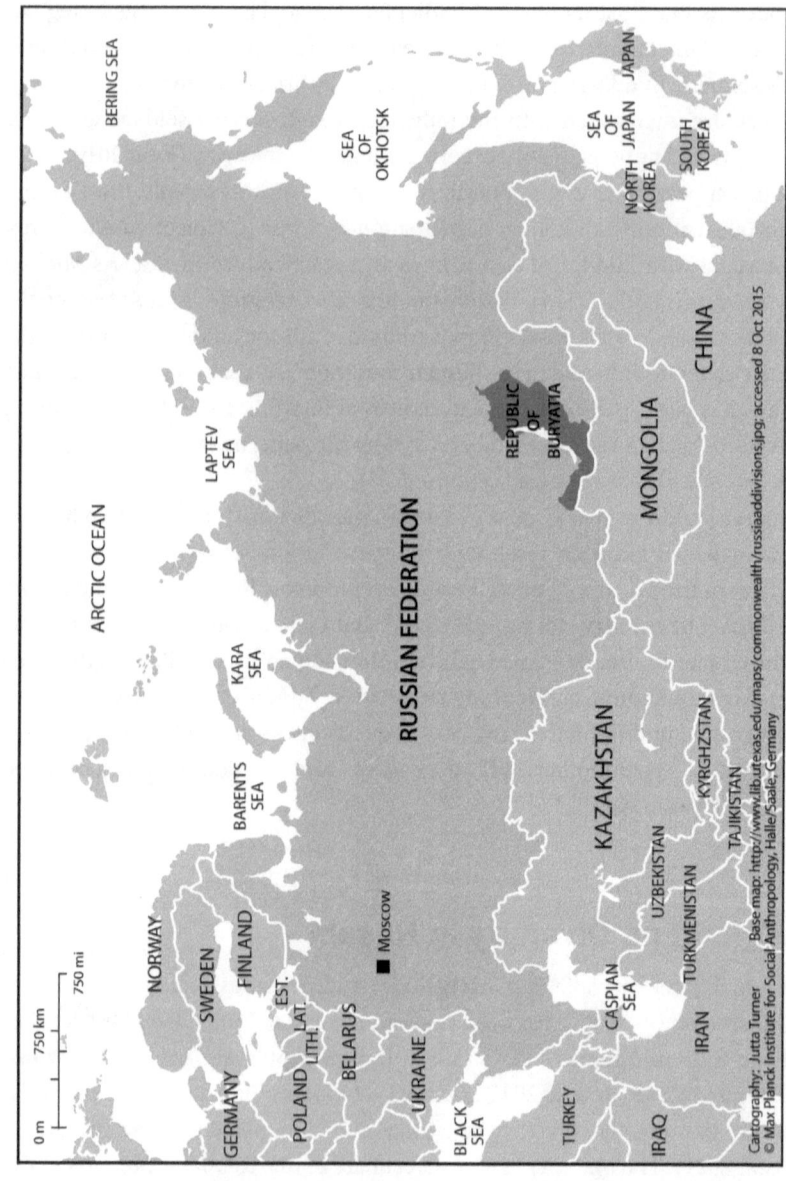

FIGURE 2. The Republic of Buryatia within the Russian Federation. Map by Jutta Turner.

shows significant decline in many ethnic minority populations across Russia and a simultaneous growth of those who refused to provide their ethnic identification.[18] The reasons for this may be growing xenophobia in Russia, but it could also result from reported falsification of the census data (Coalson 2023). Moreover, surveys and polling in illiberal regimes are likely inaccurate due to fear and self-censorship (see, e.g., Yudin 2020).

Previously nomadic herders, Buryats have historically inhabited a much larger area than the current republic. Their lands stretch to both sides of Lake Baikal and far beyond it. There is a historical Buryat minority in what are today the neighboring regions of Irkutsk Oblast (3.6 percent of the population) and Zabaykalsky Krai (7.4 percent). Up until 2008, two autonomous Buryat regions, Ust'-Orda Buryat Autonomous Okrug (39.8 percent Buryats) and Aga Buryat Autonomous Okrug (65.1 percent Buryats), existed as separate administrative bodies, but they were merged with the surrounding Russian regions in a controversial move, arguably intended to undercut minority autonomy (Derrick 2009; Graber and Long 2009). A historical Buryat population also resides in Mongolia (over 45,000) and the north of China (approx. 10,000).

The region inhabited by Buryats was colonized by Russians in the late seventeenth century. Following the formalization of the Sino-Russian border with the Treaty of Kyakhta in 1727, Buryats, like Kalmyks much farther west, emerged as the Mongols of Russia, now living predominantly within the territories of the Russian state. Through various efforts at isolation and Russification, Buryats have become somewhat estranged from Mongols outside of Russia, and their relation to Mongolia remains complex. Some consider Mongolia to be their original homeland, as the only Mongol-majority country, while others look down upon Mongolian ways and prefer to identify with the more "Western" and "European" Russia (see, e.g., Graber 2020, 37; Namsaraeva 2012). Since their political and cultural excision from the greater Mongol ethnic region, Buryats have been a small minority in a vast empire. While the Russian Empire has always been ethnically and religiously diverse, it has been demographically and politically dominated by the Russian Orthodox majority.

Historically, religion constituted an important medium for the management of minority populations in the Russian Empire. Religious institutions, of minority religions in particular, were employed for administrative, diplomatic, managerial, and other tasks of the state (see, e.g., Bernstein 2013; Crews 2006; Tsyrempilov 2013, 2021; Werth 2002). In the late eighteenth century, the institutionalization of minority religions took off, amounting to a "multiconfessional establishment" (Werth 2014, 4). In this establishment, monotheistic religions were more readily recognized as confessions, and their representatives entered a particular, legally defined relation with the state (Tsyrempilov 2021, 23; Werth 2014, 12–29). In

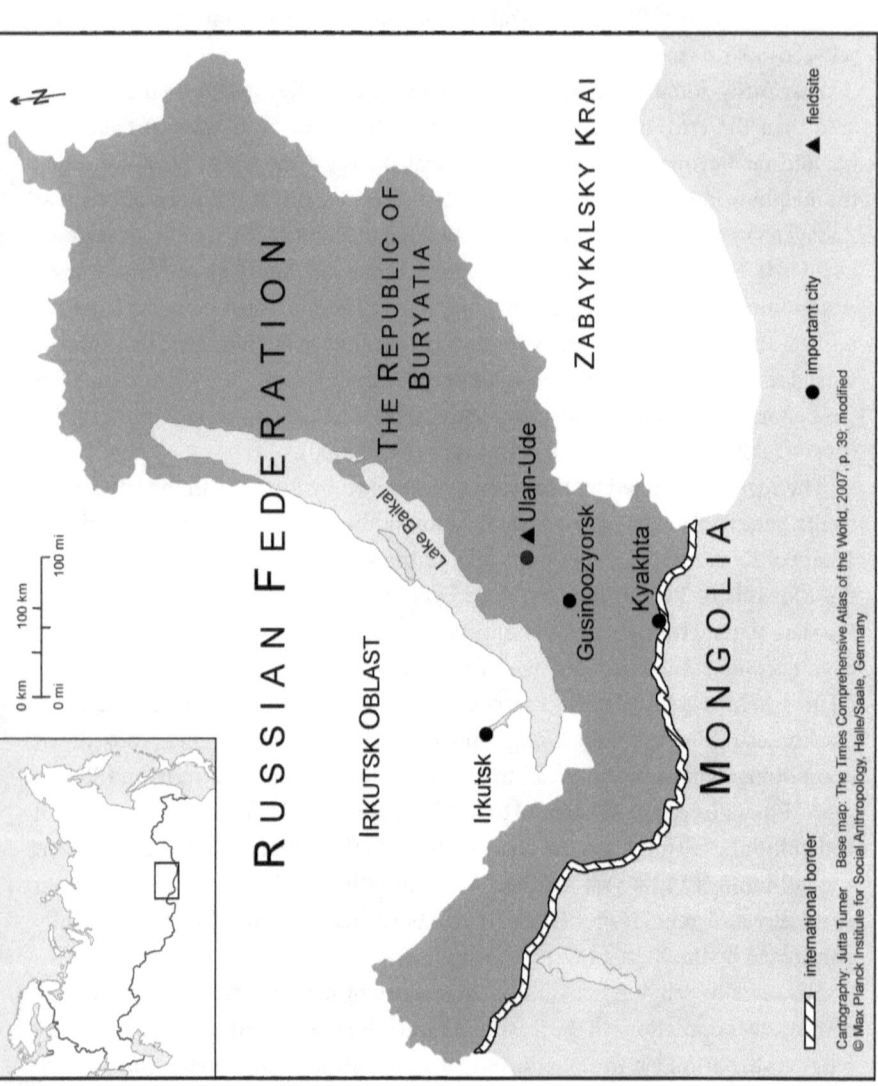

FIGURE 3. The Republic of Buryatia. Map by Jutta Turner.

contrast, the category of "paganism" encompassed all non-Abrahamic religions. This simultaneously meant more freedom for Christian missionaries to convert their followers and less regulation by the state, rendering them "arguably the freest Russian subjects in a religious sense" (Werth 2014, 28).

Religion appeared as one of the foremost factors both in group self-identification and in imperial diversity management. As Paul Werth (2014, 6) puts it, "well into the twentieth century the state's management of the empire's diversity continued to rely substantially on confessional institutions and categories, just as religious modes of self-identification remained central to many of the empire's subjects." He warns that, given the predominance of religious identification as an organizing principle, to speak of a tsarist nationality or ethnicity-based policy would be an ahistorical lens into the lived worlds of Russian imperial subjects and the domestic politics of the time.

In the Buryat case, the long-term association between leading Buddhist clergy and the Russian state is a very prominent feature of the local religious context. Through institutionalizing the Buryat Buddhist sangha and approving of its unitary hierarchy, with an elected post, the Khambo Lama, at its head, the imperial authorities rendered Buddhists "legible" (Scott 1998) and established a lasting relationship that both sides would come to rely on (Tsyrempilov 2013, 2021). For the state, this meant easier minority population management and their use in international diplomacy. For the sangha, it meant securing a strong position in the local religious milieu, in particular through predominance over foreign lamas, shamans, and competing local Buddhist actors.

By the end of the nineteenth century, minority religions had an established, clearly defined relationship with the Russian Empire. Concurrent with this, however, they began to be cast as a threat to the integrity of the empire, since religion was seen as a potential resource for emerging minority national projects. As Werth (2014, 5) puts it, "Increasingly, state officials regarded the activities and outlooks of non-Orthodox clergies as disturbing 'political' manifestations that challenged the autocratic order or the integrity of the empire. . . . A highly contradictory situation thus emerged: While newer conceptions of religious belief implied liberalization of Russia's religious order, the fear of politicized religion suggested precisely the opposite—greater restrictions on the foreign confessions."

The imperial powers nonetheless attempted to move toward the European ideal of allowing "freedom of conscience" with the Toleration Edict of 1905 (Werth 2014, 5). Many among those who had converted, whether under pressure or as strategic choice, decided to return to their previous faith (Schorkowitz 2001a, 220). While in 1917 freedom of confession and conscience was granted by the revolutionary government, antireligious repressions soon began, and the agency of religious minorities within the empire, especially as organized entities, was systematically repressed for much of the Soviet period (Schorkowitz 2001a, 222). The extreme violence of the state in the Soviet period resulted in great losses of people, infrastructure, knowledge, and organizational structures of religious communities.

When religious revivals took off in the post-Soviet period, it was in this historical pattern of fraught, yet close-knit relations between religious institutions and the state. Inevitably, there were shifts and adjustments, but the pre-Soviet past amounted to an immense resource for a population hoping to conjure efficacy, support, and coherence. In some contexts, the socialist-period repressions of religion even became a sign and a symbol of religion's power, significance, and efficacy (Højer 2009; Humphrey and Ujeed 2013). This book therefore understands the deep enmeshment of religion and politics in Russia as having roots in centuries of religion-state relations, although not a direct, linear continuity.

At the same time, the grand field of state-religion relations should not overshadow religious practices and beliefs as they flourish in everyday contexts. Stately narratives of religion may propound alliances with the political regime, mutual reinforcement of legitimation and efficacy, grand histories, and the potential for might. But everyday religion reveals a different side of local life. It points to grievances, uncertainties, and the negotiations of everyday coexistence in a diverse setting. Scholars of religion have therefore drawn attention to "lived religion" (McGuire 2008) and "everyday religion" (Ammerman 2007) as important fields of negotiating spirituality, belonging, sociality, and other elements of religious lives invisible on the grand scale.

A look at "religious intimacies" (Herzfeld 2015), or the ways in which everyday religious diversions from doctrine create meaningful mutuality among practitioners, points to negotiations of agency and representation. Through imperfect religious practice and its sharing within the group, people can create meaningful intergroup connections. At the same time, they negotiate what Buddhism is and what its role is to be in this fast-changing borderland of Russia. It is this "unofficial" side of Buryat Buddhism that I hope to reveal in this text.

Michel de Certeau (1984) has famously explored the dynamics of action in everyday contexts, while being differentially placed in relation to power. He distinguished between "strategies" and "tactics." The former refers to calculations, manipulations, and other ways of acting from the position of power: managing places, actors, and things along the way. The latter pertains to adaptations and manipulations whereby powerless people try to work within the system and make use of it without directly challenging it. Recognizing the contrast between the two modes of acting as shaped by different positions in relation to power is a political concern: It is related to the "battles or games between the strong and the weak, and with the 'actions' which remain possible for the

FIGURE 4. Colored ribbons in the colors of the Russian flag and ceremonial scarves tied to trees in a sacred space on the outskirts of Ulan-Ude, 2015. Photo by author.

latter" (de Certeau 1984, 34). Put differently, the powerful have the luxury of strategies, while the weak must rely on tactics. In broad and coarse terms, lay Buryat Buddhists contend more in the realm of tactics, while the elite Buddhist clergy and institutions, occupying a middle-ground political position, display more facets of strategizing.

Studies of everyday religion highlight mundane religious practices as arenas wherein identity, agency, and community are negotiated and reproduced. For instance, Knut Graw (2012) explores Senegalese and Gambian Islamic divination as an "intentional space" where people articulate their concerns and anxieties and engage with their visions of the future. This divination works to reinforce agency in people's daily lives. He argues that this person-oriented and typically invisible religious practice is a key site of local religious life and juxtaposes it to the more typical approach to religion that focuses on institutions and sociopolitical histories. He argues, "The practices which seem to matter most are often those which are highly personal and thus seem to remain at the margins of public religious life. . . . Approaches focusing too exclusively on religious institutions, their history and their role in society . . . may thus easily overlook what is most relevant for understanding the personal and cultural significance of religious praxis in its respective context" (Graw 2012, 29).

Everyday religion is a site of resistance and alternative sociality. Gareth Fisher (2014) has looked at noninstitutionalized lay Buddhist preaching in Beijing. Preachers and their followers are discontent with the fast-changing economy and society in China and feel left behind. In temple courtyards, these disillusioned laypeople who experience a "moral breakdown" gather to immerse themselves in an alternative religio-ethical milieu, critical of both high-brow monastic Buddhism and aggressive state capitalism, and create novel moral communities. Amira Mittermaier (2014, 2019) has examined Muslim giving practices in Cairo, which provide alternative ways for distribution and subsistence through voluntarily offerings of food and accommodation to the needy. Such giving, Mittermaier argues, foregrounds the "ethics of immediacy," as did the revolutionary Tahrir Square protests. In doing so, these Muslim charitable practices create sociality separate from and critical of the neoliberal Egyptian state that are divorced from bureaucratic and calculating NGOs or major religious organizations. Basic everyday religious practices are a powerful arena for negotiating community, belonging, and resistance.

Michael Herzfeld (2015, 2016) notes that everyday religious beliefs and practices are important sites for forging mutuality. Writing about urban contexts, he argues that mundane religion often involves deviation from the doctrine and betrays institutional normativity. Yet this very transgression, quietly recognized among co-practitioners, creates a bond of "religious intimacy" (Herzfeld 2015). Such "unofficial" affinities in urban space are much less visible than the grand sites of "official" religion, such as majestic temples. They nonetheless are a key component of religious sociality and community in contemporary cities.

It is not the intention of this book to reproduce long critiqued binaries between "great" and "little" tradition (Redfield 1956), between "official" and "popular" religion (e.g., Vrijhof and Waardenburg 1979), or "high" and "low" forms of Buddhism (e.g., Spiro 1982). I do not consider the line between the two to be clear-cut or pronounced. In fact, the two can be intertwined, with official narratives spilling into homely worship or being appropriated by the laity. Prominent religious institutions and their positions on various social and political matters also inevitably trickle down, shaping the forms available for particular actions and the dispositions of those placed lower in the religious hierarchies. Alternatively, popular sentiments and opinions cannot help but inform or even constrain those in positions of religious authority. However, in the Buryat Buddhist case, it is important not to let the official story of the dominating institution and its loyalties to the

Russian state overshadow the substantially different site of mundane religious practices, through which community, a distinctive identity, and a potential for action and resistance are forged.

In this book, I explore diverse everyday religious interactions in Buryat Buddhism. In Buddhist counseling, laypeople express their concerns and grievances and negotiate agency in the often difficult circumstances they face. In turn, lamas share their interpretations and suggested courses of action based on a variety of factors, including their own experience and views. Since these concerns pertain to the lives of the laity, the links between their problems and broader social, political, and economic issues are often clearly made. Through diverse religious giving, Buryat Buddhists practice ethical personhood, despite the fact that this giving is usually far removed from doctrinal ideals. Through religious place making in the city, Buryat Buddhists quietly demand space and visibility. I consider these ethnographic instances to be revealing of the "tactics," in the de Certeau sense, employed by Buddhist laity to negotiate their belonging and cultural sovereignty in the precarious space remaining for ethnic and religious minority tenacity in the Inner Asian borderlands of Russia.

Ethnicity, Religion, and Political Life

The Khambo Lama claims that Buryat Buddhists wholeheartedly support the war, yet laypeople bemoan the dire consequences of the war in Buddhist rituals. Lamas, too, attempt to support laypeople, and some even quietly deter them from going to war. Buryat Buddhist leadership fervently insists on self-sufficiency, yet the Tibetan Dalai Lama remains the main, unquestionable spiritual authority to most Buryat Buddhists. The BTSR proudly promotes the stories of lama soldiers who defended the Soviet Union despite the repressions they themselves had suffered just years prior, yet Buryat Buddhists in Mongolia flee Russia and decry official Buddhist support for the war.

These snippets of the seeming contradictions in contemporary Buryat Buddhism point to the fact that minority religion cannot be interpreted simply as a vessel of Russian imperialism. Instead, I argue, everyday religion is a field wherein Buryat Buddhists negotiate what it means to be a moral person, a Buddhist, and a minority citizen in contemporary Russia. In everyday religious contexts, people deal with uncertainties, express grievances, negotiate everyday ethics, and create formal and informal communities. In this book, I understand such struggles to be politically consequential, as they pertain to the shared social, ethical, and cultural worlds of a minoritized group. Everyday religion in Buryatia is not couched in political terminology recognizable as a form of political action in liberal democracies. However, in the oppressive Russian setting, such social and cultural expressions take on significance as ways to ensure community building, cultural continuity, and a distinctive identity. In a country where the Orthodox Christian "faith in God" (Rus., *vera v Boga*) is inscribed into the constitution, these continuities are increasingly important and difficult to sustain.

Framed differently, Buryat Buddhism, like other religious and cultural practices in the region, is a site of "infrapolitics." Political anthropologist James Scott (1990, 19) coined this term to refer to "low-profile forms of resistance" that may not even be easily recognizable as such, as they "dare not speak in their own name." Infrapolitics is an analytical tool used to go beyond the dichotomy between complete submission and open protest, as the most recognizable forms of political life. It is a more nuanced approach to recognizing the ways in which hegemony shapes subjects while also allowing for agentive interventions. To Scott, infrapolitics is part of the "hidden transcripts" of marginalized groups. He contrasts them with "public transcripts," which are the ways in which the dominant groups represent themselves and reproduce their domination.

Infrapolitics is a concept that renders forms of resistance visible that typically go unseen under other analytical lenses. Scott (1990, 183) notes: "For a social science attuned to the relatively open politics of liberal democracies and to loud, headline-grabbing protests, demonstrations, and rebellions, the circumspect struggle waged daily by subordinate groups is, like infrared rays, beyond the visible end of the spectrum." This oversight is significant, since infrapolitics are prominent among subordinate groups, and their disregard may lead to the conclusion that subordinate groups are altogether apolitical or mere vessels of hegemonic power.

The concept of infrapolitics has been utilized in a broad range of contexts—many of them postcolonial—to unravel the variety of forms of mutuality that underpin political life. In Nigeria, humor appears as a significant infrapolitical field (Obadare 2009). Jokes serve as a way of airing grievances and sharing struggles as well as hopes. In Bangladesh, infrapolitics are present in popular Islam, where a ritual, Mānik Pīr, becomes an arena for displaying discontent about the "material appropriation of labor, production, and property by the dominant classes" (Ahmed 2009, 73). In Hong Kong, a makeshift shrine and ritual activity outside a site where a violently dispersed protest took place serves as an infrapolitical expression, sustaining resistance in only-just visible and indirect ways that manage to avoid repressions (Cheng 2022).

Partha Chatterjee (2004) notes that forms of political participation that operate outside of the narrowly conceived political field, for instance, infrastructural tampering or the perseverance of squatter settlements, are especially important in postcolonial contexts. In these settings, conventional political participation may be inaccessible to large sections of the population, such as Indigenous groups or those unregistered. Chatterjee highlights the administrative sphere, involved with such concerns as land disputes and the provision of basic services, as spaces where political questions of belonging, representation, and contestation are negotiated. Taking Chatterjee's invitation to rethink the locations of the political, Antina von Schnitzler (2013) argues that in postapartheid Soweto, prepaid electricity meters, or more precisely their evasion, have become a political terrain where marginalized citizens make claims toward the state and perform forms of resistance.

In contemporary Russia, venues for direct political participation have long been limited. This is the result of a gradual centralization of power, the elimination of political opposition, and the restriction of public life in the decades of Putin's rule (see, e.g., Dollbaum 2023; Gel'man 2023; Miazhevich 2023). Electoral fraud in Putin's Russia is common; parties are prevented from registering, and candidates are prevented from taking part in the elections. Protests and demonstrations are violently suppressed, and the risks of taking part in them are high. The independent media has gradually come under the purview of the state or been forced to close. Any oppositional voices are quickly silenced, such as the violent assault and later death under suspicious circumstances of the editor of the oppositional news website in Buryatia, Asia-Russia Daily (Balzer 2022, 68), and people going to prison for oppositional social media posts, to name some tragic examples. Since the large-scale war in Ukraine began, the already small space for public political expression has narrowed even further. New draconian legislation was passed. Even calling the "special military operation" in Ukraine a "war" or expressing any criticism toward Russia's actions is punishable as "discreditation of the Russian army" with sentences of up to fifteen years in prison. The few remaining oppositional nongovernmental organizations and actors in Russia, as well as many abroad, have been labeled "foreign agents," and their activities in Russia have been severely restricted as a consequence.

To outside observers, Russian society appears passive and submissive to the illiberal regime (Morris, Semenov, and Smyth 2023, 5; see also Sharafutdinova 2019). Ethnic minorities are also sometimes portrayed as submissive and easily imbued with the motivations and ideologies of the dominating powers. It appears on the surface that Russia's minorities are passionately supportive of Vladimir Putin and his imperial project. Such a vision is strengthened by the often exoticizing media portrayals, which borrow an unexpected image of a contemporary Russian patriot for clickbait. But this reading is complicated by the fact that among marginalized and minoritized groups, public transcripts, in Scott's sense, exist too: "A partly sanitized, ambiguous, and coded version of the public transcript is always present in the public discourse of subordinate groups" (Scott

1990, 19). While the powerful have a vital interest in keeping up appearances, those subordinated often have good reasons to help sustain those appearances (Scott 1990, 70). Still, one should not assume that the hegemonic inscription of the dominant power is accepted plainly and in full. Instead, it is more productive to inquire into "the ways in which subordinate groups may be socialized into accepting the view of their interest from propagated by above" (Scott 1990, 19–20). This is not to say that Russia's minorities are merely pretending to support Russia's politics—many of them certainly do. But it is to say that they live under conditions where there do not seem to be alternatives (outside of violence, imprisonment, and sometimes death), and so this support—however deep or shallow it may be—appears as a necessary precondition for survival under the current repressive regime.

In this context, scholars have argued that genuine political expressions—negotiations of belonging, claims toward representation, expressions of grievances, demands for change—have been active in unconventional, infrapolitical fields (see especially Morris, Semenov, and Smyth 2023). Christian Fröhlich and Kerstin Jacobsson (2019), for instance, describe reappropriations of urban space, such as "free markets" where secondhand goods can be exchanged, or mock protests in city streets, as forms of political expression. In a city whose public space is guarded by illiberal politics and elite interests, citizens retreat to forms of collective action that pass under the radar.

Jeremy Morris, Andrei Semenov, and Regina Smyth (2023) offer an even broader approach to the political field in Russia, relying on the framework of infrapolitics. They foreground persistent social ties as an important element of keeping up shared identities, which they contend are at the core of political life. "Even when identity-based actions are banned," they argue, "such identities are sustained through cultural practices and traditions that are often hidden from plain sight . . . While Russian civil society remains underdeveloped, existing social ties and identities are the building blocks of joint action and organization" (10).[19]

In Russia's ethnic minority republics, the "cultural" field becomes a site for negotiating identities, making claims, and social mobilization (Stewart 2023). Ethnic minorities' national theaters, as well as performances in musical theaters, ethnic festivals, and other formats, constitute a locally meaningful form of collective action. Based on data from Karelia, Tatarstan, and Buryatia, Katie L. Stewart writes, "While public protest is increasingly curtailed, cultural events serve as an alternative means of community gathering and voice" (47). These voices are not necessarily oppositional. In fact, these events also provide a venue for the propagation of government-supported visions of what it means to be a good minority Russian citizen. At the same time, such collective forms of identity and action provide a significant infrapolitical field among ethnic minorities in contemporary Russia.

Guzel Yusupova (2023) argues that minority-language initiatives in recent years also constitute a covert political field. Through Russia's ever more restrictive minority-language policies, minorities, she notes, "have become aware of their group vulnerability in the context of new Russian nation-building processes. Such awareness has led to their self-understanding as a political community, as a united ethnic group, and as a broader group of subordinated ethnic minorities taken together" (64). This social mobilization around minority languages, she highlights, is especially prominent online, as the repressive Russian context provides serious challenges to offline mobilization (Yusupova 2021). Minority languages have become an even more prominent field for negotiating belonging and resistance in the context of the war in Ukraine. Slogans, banners, and social media platforms in minority languages have grown in number and visibility. They have become a way of asserting agency and increasing the visibility of ethnic minority lives and politics (Baranova 2024; Baranova and Darieva 2023). At the same time, representatives of the Russian state also make use of minority languages to disseminate state propaganda, to enlist soldiers, to collect monetary support for the war, and for other causes.

Marjorie Mandelstam Balzer (2022, 129) argues that collective organization among Russia's ethnic minorities in the form of spiritual, cultural, and other activities "need not be secessionist in nature or subversive. Rather, they constitute the very sinew that could help Russia and its citizens" in times of turmoil. She discusses things like cultural festivals, traditional sporting events, and minority-language movements as meaningful contributions to the negotiation of local sovereignty and to claims of belonging, both locally and within the diverse federation. She claims that strivings toward self-determination, cultural revitalization, and spiritual vitality have become intertwined into "a dominant trend in the past thirty years" (Balzer 2022a, 2) among the more populous Siberian peoples, the Sakha, Buryats, and Tuvans.

While this book explores the particular case of an ethnoreligious minority in a borderland region under the conditions of an aggressive state, it also aims to contribute to a better understanding of broader issues of minority agency through religion. Religion has proven to be an important cultural and political resource under colonial regimes (see, e.g., Gombrich and Obeyesekere 1989; Martin 1969; Schober 2010; Subtelny 1989) and a subversive force under hegemonic domination (Contursi 1989; Hale 2008; Mahmood 2005). As issues of decolonization gain more immediate relevance in the region, it is important to recognize the agentive qualities of local sociality and the tenacious upwellings of cultural sovereignty through religious expression. In this regard, urban spaces, and urban religion specifically, form privileged sites for examining the making and remaking of both the subjects and agents of power. I unpack the infrapolitical facets of urban Buryat Buddhism ethnographically through several important aspects of urban religion: Buddhist counseling, religious giving, and religious representation in urban space.

Urban Buddhism: Space for Innovation and Resistance

Urban religion is a term that has often had a bad reputation among Buddhists in Buryatia. In Ulan-Ude, whenever I had to briefly explain my research, I used the shorthand "urban Buddhism" (Rus., *gorodskoĭ buddizm*) to refer to the subject of my study. Locally, many associated the term with the diverse, eclectic religious ideas and practices that populate Ulan-Ude, such as the teachings of nonlocal religious specialists, lay meditation groups, and the social media, especially VKontakte, of Buddhist groups.[20] The term appears to locally imply innovation and divergence from tradition. Once, a laywoman at an urban temple with whom I was queueing to see a lama got visibly upset with me for studying this topic. "Why would you want to show Buryats running around temples not knowing what they are doing?" she asked, confronting me and contrasting the regrettable (to her mind) current situation in the city to both the countryside, where people's faith was supposedly deeper, and to the rich past of Buryat Buddhism. She was not interested in what the ethnographic perspective brings to the table in explorations of Buddhism, taking for granted the inferior nature of urban religious practice. What ultimately convinced her of my serene intentions was her noticing the food donations I had brought to the temple.

Yet my impression of urban Buryat Buddhism did not align with such value-laden distinctions, fairly common among locals. I observed most urban Buddhists to be in fact following the "traditional" Buddhist practices of frequenting temples, consulting lamas, and sponsoring (locally called "ordering"; Rus., *zakazyvat'*) prayers, if somewhat differently from the way these were carried out in rural settings or in pre-Soviet Buryatia. This book focuses on these locally meaningful tensions between urban and rural Buddhism as being consequential for the social, cultural, and political expression of Buryat Buddhists. It will explore urban Buddhism not as a supposed divergence from tradition but as a space for religious, social, cultural, and consequently political experimentation, fostering a sense of mutuality and capacity.

Scholars have long debated the ways in which the urban environment shapes religion. Sociologists of the late nineteenth and early twentieth centuries insisted that urbanization led to the decline in community ties, atomization, and anomie. Georg Simmel (1950 [1903]), often called the "father of urban sociology," envisioned the urbanite as unbound from the tight grip of community and tradition—religion included. In place of these customary ties, an impersonal means comes to mediate all one's relations with the surrounding world: money. Louis Wirth (1938), another early urban sociologist, similarly highlights individualism and superficial relational entanglement as keys to urban life. To him, the city facilitates individual religious association and practice rather than that predetermined by one's kin group, as he saw the case to be in rural settings. Religion thus appears denaturalized in the urban setting.

In related conceptual streams, cities were long associated with rationalization and disenchantment, and urbanization was thought to lead to secularization (see, e.g., Inglis 1963; Wickham 1969). As rational explanations prevailed over magical ones in the city and urban life was guided by efficient bureaucracy rather than stringent custom, it seemed that religion would surely lose its hold. The anthropologist Peter van der Veer (2015, 7) conversely argues that "one of the most tenacious misunderstandings of cities . . . is that they are modern and therefore secular." Rather than seeing cities purely through their materialities and tangible qualities, he insists urban aspirations—of which religion is key element—are a core part of urbanity.

Countless empirical cases demonstrate the continuing prevalence and vibrancy of religion in cities. Further than this, religion has been argued to provide structure and impetus to urban development and could be seen to form the very basis of cities in some cases, such as Ulaanbaatar itself, which formed around a Buddhist monastery (Campi 2006; see also Rüpke 2020). From blossoming Islamic revivals in Middle Eastern cities (Hirschkind 2006; Mahmood 2005), to newfound relevance for Buddhist rituals in urban Thailand (Scott 2009), to booming Christianity in African and Asian cities (Hancock and Srinivas 2008), one cannot deny the continuing relevance and prominence of religion in urban life (see also van der Veer 2015). As a result, recent scholarship is less interested in unveiling a singular model of the interaction between religion and the city and has focused more on exploring the complexity and multiplicity of religious forms in urban life. More than that, religion and the urban can be seen to mutually transform one another, in light of such current social processes as globalization or deterritorialization (Burchardt and Becci 2013, 13).

If there is one aspect of urban life that has received particular interest from scholars of religion, it is diversity. Cities are typically more diverse than nonurban settlements in terms of their social, ethnic, and religious composition. This diversity is often spatially dense: People of different backgrounds live side by side, and they engage with those different from them on a daily basis. Diversity and inequalities are visible. As Saskia Sassen (2007, 123) puts it, cities provide "the terrain on which people from many countries are most likely to meet and a multiplicity of cultures can come together." Ethnic and religious minorities throughout the world make claims to urban citizenship in these diverse settings through place making, ritual, and discursive contributions.

The tight pressed and diverse urban setting facilitates claims to representation and recognition, if not equality. A range of religious and ethnoreligious groups seek to carve out space and acknowledgment in prominent urban settings. This process can be controversial in multiethnic, multireligious settings. Contemporary urbanites often feel conflicted if not outright opposed to novel religious interventions in their cities. This is perhaps best exemplified by the Swiss minaret ban but is also present in other contexts. "The church should know its place," claim "passionate secularists" in St. Petersburg faced with the threat of the Orthodox Church gaining ownership of the city's most famous heritage site, St. Isaac's Cathedral (Kormina 2021). In Europe, it is urban planners who are often left with the task of balancing discreet minority religious inclusion through aesthetic solutions (Gale 2004; Mack 2019). They navigate the difficult terrain between minority rights, majority wishes, and policy, glossing over the tensions as best they can with aesthetic concessions.

Urban diversity appears to destabilize state-religion relations. Peter Jackson (1989) discusses urban Buddhism in Thailand as challenging the established alliance between the Buddhist sangha and the Thai state. It is the diverse and fluid urban context that enables this rift, as competing elite groups struggle for power within the field of the city. Jackson (1989, 9–10) recognizes urban Thai Buddhism as constituted of two distinct strands, one being the state-controlled structure of the Thai sangha, embodying the grand narratives of the synergy between religion and the state. The other is the informal relations, especially those of patronage, between the laity and the sangha, which are more fluid. As Jackson (10) notes:

> Historically, the formal structure of Buddhism has reflected the interests of the politically dominant section of the Thai elite. In contrast, the politically disenfranchised have only been able to express their aspirations and interests through the medium of the unofficial structure of Buddhism by sponsoring monks or movements whose teachings lend support to their own social and political aspirations. As a consequence the unofficial structure of lay-sponsored Buddhist movements bears little relation to the official state-imposed administrative hierarchy of the *sangha*.

To Jackson, it is the urban middle class that is especially influential in this destabilization of state-sangha alliance. Their Buddhism is guided by the choice of which monks and monasteries are to be patronized, and the laity seeks out particular kinds of Buddhism to match their tastes and expectations, which may include devout ascetic monks, reformist movements, or particular kinds of philosophical teachings. As such, the domination of the state-supported sangha is no longer the norm in the urban context, enabling a socioreligious remaking of Thai society.

Marian Burchardt and Irene Becci (2013) draw attention to the heightened presence of globalization, transnational migration, and connectivity as the foremost factors in shaping urban religion. They conceptualize cities as reterritorializing imagined communities, as the nation-state competes with a variety of other levels of association in the city more than elsewhere (15). The city destabilizes the nation-state as the prime layer of identification, with global, regional, and other levels of belonging available as alternatives, including a range of religious affiliations and activities. They note that a prominent field in which these tensions play out is in the politics of place making, "in which multiple and diverse identities of places are negotiated and contested" (17). Similarly, Thomas Blom Hansen (2014) associates urban religion with transnational, "modernist" religious movements and argues that abstracted religion, rather than its local forms, comes to dominate religious life in the city. Hansen (2014, 375) argues, "we are moving from ethnics to ethics: from religious identity articulated through a host of other cultural markers (ethnicity) towards religious identification as a more purified, universalized and ethical set of propositions, and 'values'—the latter being a flexible metaphor for any kind of modern conviction."

Yet urban religions, like cities themselves, are diverse and culturally specific. Generalizable urban characteristics, such as population density and diversity, act as both constraining and enabling factors on religious life, but they do so in locally particular ways. This book therefore explores the urban-rural tension in Buryatia as culturally specific and as relevant in primarily local ways: only partially available to abstracted generalization and theoretical elaboration. More specifically, I argue that the locally controversial urbanization of Buddhism constitutes a focal point in ongoing local negotiations of cultural sovereignty, minority belonging, and relations to power. Despite the dominating narratives of the rural, "traditional" core of Buryat Buddhism and its tight links with the Russian state, creative and often eclectic urban religious practice today complicates the picture, producing not just religiously but socially—and (infra)politically—fertile field. In doing so, urban Buddhist practice invigorates the city, tying it to other powerful socially and religiously meaningful places, practices, and times, be it rural sacred sites, advanced monks from the past, or links with the greater Buddhist world.[21] In the book, I flesh out three socially and politically consequential aspects of religious urbanization in Buryatia: religious diversity in the city, its changing spatiality, and the religio-ethnic representation it entails.

Buryat Buddhism has a particular relationship with the city. Only two historical Buryat Buddhist temples in Russia are urban, and neither is in Buryatia itself. The first urban Buryat Buddhist temple was built in the center of Chita, a Russian-majority city to the east of Buryatia, in Zhukovsky Garden (currently the park of the District House of Officers of the Russian army). It was built for the first Zabaĭkal'skaia agricultural and industrial exhibition in 1899, which was meant to showcase regional achievements in various kinds of production alongside the particularities of the region. Local Buryat Buddhists funded the building of the temple to serve as part of the exhibition, complete with religious objects, adornments, and Buddhist monks. However, despite requests from Buddhists, the governor-general prohibited religious services from taking place in the temple-museum. An Orthodox Christian church stood nearby, and it is unclear whether the self-funded Buddhist temple without ritual function acted as some form of minority claim to representation and substantial presence in a Russian-dominated environment. The museum-temple was short-lived—it burned down in 1914.

Similarly, the second urban Buryat Buddhist temple was built in a Russian-majority setting, although again financed by Buryat Buddhists. The St. Petersburg temple, Datsan Gunzėnchoĭneĭ, was built in 1915. Permission to build it was granted by Tsar Nicholas II in 1909, but construction was stalled for some years by the Russian Orthodox Church protesting the building of a "pagan" church in the imperial capital. While the St. Petersburg datsan was initiated by the prominent Buryat lama Agvan Dorzhiev, both Buryat and Kalmyk lamas were represented in the temple. In contrast to the Chita temple, the St. Petersburg datsan was a fully functioning Buddhist worship site that was also an important Buryat hub in the Russian imperial capital.

Significant developments in Buryat urban Buddhist history did not resume until the post-Soviet period. Urban Buddhist temples started appearing in Ulan-Ude in the 1990s. They were first formed through the appropriation of spaces like offices and gymnasiums: altering their interiors for a quick and cheap conversion into religious spaces, as demand for Buddhist rituals was high and money was scarce. One of the first such Buddhist spaces in the city was a centrally located gymnasium, part of which was temporarily converted into a Buddhist temple. In 1994, a temple complex, Khambyn Khurė datsan, better known locally as Datsan na Verkhneĭ Berëzovke, was established as the urban base of the BTSR. In 2000, Rinpoche Bagsha datsan was opened by a Tibetan lama, Yelo Rinpoche, who is very highly regarded as an incarnate lama and as a celibate and highly educated Tibetan monk. It is served by both Tibetan and Buryat monks, and many locals value it not just for its religious expertise but also for the surrounding greenery, which lends itself to weekend outings, as well as for the lavish and impressive architecture. Many other temples large and small have since mushroomed in Ulan-Ude, remaking its cityscape. Buryat Buddhists have also built temples in other cities outside of Buryatia, and they have long endeavored to conjure state support for a major temple in Moscow—an endeavor that may come to fruition as a result of the extreme loyalty of the BTSR to the Kremlin.

The present book seeks to contribute to the growing literature on urban religion (Burchardt and Becci 2013; Orsi 1999; van der Veer 2015). It demonstrates not only its ornamental or instrumental role but highlights it as a core strand of contemporary life and society. Religion and the city are understood here as being in mutual tension. Religion shapes the city in material and conceptual ways: It transforms the cityscape, imbues the urban environment with new potentialities, and molds the identities and lived experiences of urbanites. At the same time, the city shapes religion through its spatial, economic, and social environment. Despite long decades of the Soviet secular modernity project and the substantial remaking of Buryat society it has entailed, Buddhism today continues to flourish, providing an important part of local visions and pursuits of dignified life and a worthwhile future. In doing so, urban Buddhism is an especially creative and productive field, opening new constellations of vision and

FIGURE 5. An urban Buddhist temple in Ulan-Ude, 2019. Photo by author.

action, alternative to the available powerful grand narratives, be they of secular modernity, Russian hegemony, or traditional patriarchy.

Ulan-Ude: The City

The city that is now known as Ulan-Ude was established as Udinsk in 1666 by Russian Cossacks, who were making their way eastward in Russia's conquest of Siberia. A wooden outpost for tax collection was built in a location previously serving as a nomadic gathering point, on a hill near the intersection of the Selenga and Uda Rivers. Verkhneudinsk, as the town was later renamed, soon lost its significance as a military defense outpost and transformed into a city of commerce in the eighteenth century, due to its location on important transportation and trading routes (Breslavsky 2012a, 25–26; Minert 1983, 23). These included the main trading route with China, the trade from which generated a sizable and regionally significant winter fair in Verkhneudinsk. In the first century of its existence, Verkhneudinsk expanded haphazardly around the main fortress, but toward the end of the eighteenth century, with the development of a significant market area (now Ploshchad' Revoliutsii), the center of the city shifted northward, and the local administration initiated the first city plan, which was organized into the systematic blocks still providing form to the city center to this day (Minert 1983, 49). Up until the end of the nineteenth century, the city continued to expand gradually, its population reaching 8,086 by the first census of the Russian Empire in 1897 (Minert 1983, 11). With the building of the Trans-Siberian Railway at the turn of the century, the population of Verkhneudinsk grew sharply, reaching 20,500 in 1923 (Zhimbiev 2000, 48). Demographically, the city was predominantly Russian, with Buryats comprising less than 1 percent of the urban population in the 1860s (Minert 1983, 10–11).

The Soviet period was in fact the time when the city acquired a more substantial registered Buryat population: from twenty-eight Buryats, or 0.13 percent of the population, just after the establishment of the Buryat-Mongolian Autonomous Soviet Socialist Republic in the 1920s to around 10 percent toward the end of the 1930s (Minert 1983, 87). As Verkhneudinsk became the capital of the newly formed region, many jobs in the city became available to Buryats, in line with the policies of "indigenization" (Rus., *korenizatsiia*), and Buryat urban migration increased. Moreover, the Buryat population of Ulan-Ude increased in the 1930s due to its administrative expansion through the incorporation of several surrounding Buryat settlements into the city (Zhimbiev 2000, 110). As Balzhan Zhimbiev (2000, 47) argues, the first significant step in the transition of Verkhneudinsk from being a Russian trading city into a city in and of Buryatia came in 1934 when it was renamed Ulan-Ude, *ulaan* meaning "red" (i.e., communist) in the Buryat language. This was part of a larger project of nation-building for ethnic minorities in the Soviet Union: an accordingly named territory for each titular nationality (in this case, the *Buryat-Mongolian* Autonomous Soviet Socialist Republic) and hence the use of the Buryat language for the name of the city.[22]

The city continued to expand throughout the twentieth century, reaching 361,700 inhabitants by the demise of the Soviet Union in 1991.[23] Urban migration progressed in the 1970s and '80s with the spread of internal passports in the countryside, which increased the mobility of rural inhabitants, combined with the abolition of strict regulations against moving from villages to cities (Zhimbiev 2000, 111). As the city expanded, new urbanites belonged primarily to one of two groups: either ethnic Russians and others from regions further west or ethnic Buryats from the surrounding countryside. While many Buryats took up white-collar jobs in Ulan-Ude, incoming Russians mostly worked in the new factories in and around the city. On the whole, urban migration and urbanization were some of the defining social phenomena in Buryatia in the twentieth century: The population of Ulan-Ude increased by a factor of more than seventeen in the years of the Soviet Union. Furthermore, the proportion of the total urban population in Buryatia, which includes several smaller towns, rose from 9.2 percent in 1923 to 60.4 percent in 1991.[24] While in administrative terms there are three more cities (Rus., *gorod*) in Buryatia, they are considerably smaller, and Ulan-Ude is held by locals to be the only real city in the republic. It is indeed more often locally called "the city" (Rus., *gorod*; Bur., *khoto*; colloquial Bur., *goorod*) in Buryatia than "Ulan-Ude." The process of urban migration has continued in the post-Soviet period, with the urban population reaching 436,138 in 2021 (Rosstat 2021).

Many of the key processes in Buryatia in the twentieth century—mass migration to Ulan-Ude from the Russian west, urban migration within Buryatia, centralization of the economy in the Soviet Union, expanding industrialization—resulted in not just a changing demography of the republic but also a significant shift in urban-rural relations. As Zhimbiev (2000, 6) argues, Verkhneudinsk as a trading town crucially depended on the surrounding "feeder" rural areas both for subsistence and for bringing in business. The socioeconomic shifts in the first half of the twentieth century, however, "disabled key elements of the well-being of rural communities, such as traditions of land use, and the socioeconomic relations that previously were cornerstones of their relations with the trading town . . . Rural areas came to be envisaged as totally dependent on the departmental city" (6). In turn, the city itself came to be largely dependent on central subsidies from Moscow, thus undermining the mutual dependence of Ulan-Ude and the surrounding countryside and decreasing contacts between urban and rural dwellers. By the 1930s, the city had become a significant source of supplies, including food, to rural areas, reversing the previous order (50). While this was again temporarily reversed in the later Soviet period due to various shortages in the city, overall, tremendous changes in a short period in Buryatia, as in many other parts of the Soviet Union, resulted in acute social and cultural differences—and at times tensions—between urban and rural inhabitants.

Much of the urban-rural divide also cleaved along ethnic lines: As most newcomers to the city up until the 1960s were ethnic Russians, Ulan-Ude was primarily a "Russian" city in terms of both the majority demographically and the way it was experienced by locals. Buryat newcomers in the 1960s and 1970s, as many of my Buryat interlocutors recounted, were moving into an environment that they felt to be hostile and antagonistic. Due to the occupational differences between Buryats and Russians, the two ethnic groups were also somewhat divided as to the areas of the city they resided in, for instance, with more Russians around factories (see also Humphrey 1983, 33).

Regional ties, which have been crucial in Buryat migration to the city, manifest themselves in Ulan-Ude up to this day in a number of different ways. They have a role in petty crime networks but also in networks of material and moral support, for instance, in helping to find a job in the city (Manzanova 2007; cf. informal *blat* relations in Ledeneva 1998). As I discuss later in the book, they are relevant in religious life, too, as some laypeople prefer lamas from the same region of origin, and some Buddhist temples are founded by networks of outmigrants from the same region (Rus., *zemliāchestvo*). These networks can be official and structured through nonprofit organizations or simply loose social ties with people from the same village living now in the city.

In Buryatia today, the vision of progress, prosperity, and modernity as necessarily urban remains deeply ingrained in the worldview of many, dating as it does to the Soviet period. Urbanization was a cornerstone of the Soviet linear narrative of progress, and cities were focal points of Soviet secular modernity, where human command over nature was most evident. This was especially palpable in places like Buryatia, where "traditional" rural lifestyle contrasted sharply with urban life and where Indigenous citizens bore the brunt of the Soviet modernizing project (see, e.g., Alexander and Buchli 2007; Batomunkuev 2003; Humphrey 2007). At the fall of the Soviet Union, much of the infrastructure and wealth of cities in the region crumbled, yet the status and prestige of urban living remained unwavering, manifesting in continuing urban migration and the aspirations of many.

Contemporary Ulan-Ude is a city marked by social and economic inequalities and an urban environment that is difficult to navigate. It is one of five cities with the lowest quality of life in Russia, and Buryatia is among the bottom five regions in the same parameter.[25] It is also a region with one of the highest crime rates in the country, with only two others surpassing it.[26] Socioeconomic affliction is spatialized in the city, with many poverty-stricken areas considered unsafe by locals. *Nakhalovki*, as squatter settlements are locally called, are widespread in Ulan-Ude and appear to be a persistent phenomenon as newcomers move to the city in search of unlikely opportunities (Breslavsky 2014; Karbainov 2007). As illegal settlements, these areas are typically without running water, efficient waste management, and other public infrastructure. Despite the multiple grave problems that Ulan-Ude faces, the city is deeply loved and cared for by many of its inhabitants.

The tenacious prestige of urban life is often coupled with a perception of the countryside as declining and inevitably mired in poverty and alcoholism. At the same time, images of idyllic rural settings and the Buryat steppe are drawn on in constructions of Buryat identity and aesthetics, as is often the case with national identities (see, e.g., Williams 1975). The current urban-rural hierarchy contrasts with the pre-Soviet social structure wherein affluence, education, and advancement up the social ladder were all very much attainable in the countryside and often tied to Buddhist monasteries. However, as becomes clear further on, this valorization of the city is slowly changing, and the countryside is regaining some prestige and status. This is partly due to the efforts of Buddhist actors and institutions, as well as to a renewed interest in Buryat culture and language. At the same time, Buryats are "taming the city," and the urban environment is also becoming a "Buryat" and a "Buddhist" place (Jonutytė 2022, 2024; see also Breslavsky 2012b).

Methods

This book is based on thirteen months of ethnographic fieldwork in Buryatia, primarily in the capital city of Ulan-Ude (August 2015–August 2016, October 2019), as well as two two-week stints of fieldwork in Ulaanbaatar, Mongolia (October 2022, July 2023). The bulk of fieldwork was conducted in Russian, which is the dominant language of the urban public sphere. In the city, Buryat often serves more as an intimate language to use with family or close friends—and even then, only among a minority of Buryats. My effort to learn the Buryat language was taken by most as a sign of respect, and many locals contrasted my attempts with the lack of interest of many Buryats who do not learn "their" own language. While Buryat language and cultural activists do discuss the political and structural hurdles that have resulted in a sharp decline in Buryat-language knowledge, on the everyday level it is often considered to be an issue of individual responsibility and a moral failure of the younger generation.

A 2010 census of Buryatia indicates that 43.6 percent of Buryats know the Buryat language and as little as 0.4 percent of Russians (Dyrkheeva 2015, 165).[27]

The figures are even lower in the capital city: only 2.4 percent of respondents in a sociolinguistic survey in Ulan-Ude reported using the Buryat language in work or at school (Khilkhanova 2007, 81). The Buddhist setting is somewhat of an exception to this. The BTSR has made a significant effort to popularize the Buryat language and to boost its prestige with such projects as schoolchildren's contests and a Buryat-language radio station. This stance of the dominant Buddhist organization toward the Buryat language, as well as the fact that most lamas come from a rural background, where it is much more widely spoken, have resulted in Buddhist temples being some of the only urban settings where the Buryat language is fairly prominent. Many interlocutors, especially of the younger generation, admitted that this sometimes made them feel uneasy and embarrassed in temples, since the youth and those who grew up in the city usually have limited or next to no knowledge of Buryat.

During my time in Buryatia, my day-to-day activities consisted of participant observation in urban Buddhist settings. This included visiting temples with interlocutors and on my own, participating in daily public religious services (Bur. and local Rus., khural), as well as special one-off rituals, and chatting with people while spending time in and around temples. I attended Buddhist lectures and teachings that took place regularly or on a one-off basis in various religious and secular venues. These were organized by either the lamas or their close followers and consisted of either reading and interpreting Buddhist texts or a discourse on a selected topic, invariably followed by lay questions. Ethnographically, these lectures were an interesting forum for observing emerging religious normativity and heightened lay concern with correct Buddhist practice. At the same time, such lectures were sites where religious imperfections were recognized and shared in striving toward being a better Buddhist.

I also spent time at one of the international lay Buddhist dharma centers in Ulan-Ude, participating in their weekly gatherings for meditation, teachings, socializing, planning, and managing the regular activities of the center, as well as attending special events and visits of Russian or foreign teachers. Several Ulan-Ude dharma centers are representative of a "modernist" kind of Buddhism, where lay meditation and an extensive knowledge of Buddhist texts and practices are key, as is the belief in the compatibility of Buddhism with science and modern life (McMahan 2008). At the same time, more conventional Buddhist beliefs and practices were also firmly present there, such as beliefs and rituals concerned with nonhuman actors or the practice of unconditionally following a guru. As I later argue, the "modernist" and "traditional" Buddhist strands are often intertwined, and as in neighboring Ulaanbaatar, "most lay people have an awareness of Buddhist concepts that is characterized by heterodoxy and eclecticism" (Abrahms-Kavunenko 2012, 295). In emic categories, however, the focus of this book is on what is locally known as "traditional" (Rus., *traditsionnyĭ*), if urban, Buddhism rather than its "modernist" strands.

Another component of my fieldwork involved sitting in on consultations with lamas (Rus., *priëm u lamy*) that take place in temples, offices outside of temples, or sometimes at lamas' or laypeople's homes. Such consultations are the focus of chapter 4. They are occasions when laypeople talk to a lama about any kind of concern or problem they are facing. Consultations often include a divination, an astrological prognosis, or a ritual. My account of the subject is based on more than twenty occasions when I either accompanied my interlocutors to see a lama or observed a session while sitting in a lama's office with everyone's consent. Such consultations are typically a private matter, and I am deeply grateful to the lamas and laypeople who allowed me to observe them. In addition, I gathered several dozen detailed accounts of Buddhist counseling sessions from both laypeople and lamas in interviews and conversations. While invisible in academic and popular accounts of Buddhism in the region, such Buddhist consultations are a key site where religious subjectivities and agencies are molded and religious intimacy is forged.

I conducted semiformal interviews with lamas and laypeople, as well as other actors relevant to the religious revival, such as shamans and people in the tourism industry. I met most of my interview partners through referrals from friends, acquaintances, and university contacts or through Buddhist activities and engaged a broad range of people in terms of age, background, and kind of Buddhist practice. I also approached lamas randomly in temple settings and asked to interview them. Such approaches were sometimes met with suspicion, but since lamas typically spend the better part of their day in interactions with laity resolving their concerns, most of them did not refuse to answer some questions posed by another interested person. Buddhists typically understand the path to enlightenment as being very diverse and individualized, so even a scholarly interest in Buryat Buddhism fit naturally into the consultation format.

In addition, I made trips to the countryside as well as several pilgrimages. The visits to rural temples were mostly to accompany my interlocutors, but I also made several such trips on my own to interview lamas there and learn more about rural Buddhism. This provided a valuable context and contrast for the main—urban—site of my research. In addition, I took part in six pilgrimages to rural temples and sacred sites, where I was able to engage in participant observation, talk to fellow pilgrims, and learn more about the history and contemporary sacred geographies of Buryat Buddhism. I also took part in four excursions in and around Ulan-Ude, which inevitably included important religious sites such as Ivolginskiĭ and Rinpoche Bagsha datsans. They provided an additional perspective on more formal and deliberate kinds of local self-representation. I also familiarized myself with other local religions by talking to, befriending, and interviewing their lay and clergy members and by participating in events and rituals. Moreover, I took part in nonreligious events related to local matters, Buryat culture, and language. All of these provided me with valuable experience and knowledge of the lively ongoing cultural revival and the role of religion in it.

In Ulaanbaatar, I conducted participant observation with recent arrivals from Buryatia, fleeing military conscription since September 21, 2022. This mostly included informal socializing, as well as accompanying my interlocutors to settings relevant to the newcomers, such as mobile operator and money exchange offices and informational centers. I conducted twenty-four semiformal interviews with conscription-age men from Buryatia in addition to participant observation in informal settings. Additionally, I complemented fieldwork in Buryatia and Mongolia with online research.

A prominent anxiety among my informants was their insecurity in talking about Buddhism. Laypeople who did not feel expert enough to talk about Buddhism directed me to lamas. However, most lamas also felt that their knowledge was insufficient, calling themselves "simple" (Rus., *prostoĭ*) or "common" (Rus., *rîadovoĭ*) Buddhists or explaining that they only address straightforward, mundane requests of the laity and are not experts in Buddhism. These Buddhist uncertainties are a reoccurring theme in this book. Both laypeople and lamas were usually reassured by my clarification that I was indeed looking for everyday, ordinary perspectives on Buddhism. However—perhaps due to the local conceptions of sociology, ethnology, and journalism to which locals compared my research since the discipline of social (cultural) anthropology is not familiar in Russia—some were still apprehensive that scholars and others might compare such practices in an unfavorable way to "true" Buddhism, writing of them as parochial, exotic peculiarities. Moreover, center-periphery relations and power inequalities have long been an issue in ethnological research in and beyond Russia, so some of my interlocutors were understandably cautious to open up to a researcher from outside.

My fieldwork was somewhat complicated by the political tensions between Russia and Europe, caused primarily by Russia's annexation of Crimea, the military conflict in Ukraine since 2014, and further exacerbated by the full-scale invasion since 2022. During this time, it was abundantly clear that Russia had grown increasingly aggressive toward neighboring states and its own citizens and that Russian nationalist, racist, and xenophobic tendencies were very prominent in the country. Ethnographic fieldwork in this context was precarious, but understanding the predicament of minoritized populations appeared important. The effectiveness of Russian propaganda via the media and other means was observable in everyday life. In 2014, political and economic sanctions that were enforced by Russia itself, such as the ban on the import of some foreign goods and medicine, were interpreted by many in Russia as instead being imposed by Europe, thus further strengthening the antipathy. Some, although few, locals felt passionately moved by the antagonizing and vilifying portrayals of Europe and especially the Baltic countries in media and politics and even openly expressed their animosity.

Cold War–like suspicion of spying was omnipresent during fieldwork in Russia, although it did help that I was researching Buddhism—a topic that was not considered overly political. Most people, however, stuck to the oft-repeated phrase in Russia that politics should not affect interpersonal relationships. My being Lithuanian often worked to my advantage as I was usually recognized through a shared Soviet background, and some interlocutors were curious to compare Lithuania and Buryatia.[28] These comparative conversations were especially prominent in the Ulaanbaatar fieldwork, as many Buryats were interested in and could speak openly about a potential future independent Buryatia. In both Russia and Mongolia, my knowledge of the Buryat language, religion, and culture was positively appraised, usually cutting through the above-mentioned suspicions and obstacles.

Outline

This book on urban Buryat Buddhism in the post-Soviet period and its social, cultural, and political significance in Russia's Inner Asian borderlands consists of five core chapters. In chapter 1, I explore what it means to be a Buryat, both historically and today, through the lens of colonialism and minoritization in the Russian Empire, the Soviet Union, and in post-Soviet Russia. I also delve into the position of ethnic minorities in Russia following the invasion of Ukraine, as issues of xenophobia and minority marginalization have become increasingly important. I then move on to exploring Buryat Buddhist entanglements with the Russian state in chapter 2. Institutionalization and isolation have been central to imperial minority religious policies, and this relationship appears to revive in the post-Soviet period. Chapter 3 dives into the vivid field of urban Buddhism in Buryatia, characterized by diversity, eclecticism, and experimentation. Yet "traditional" Buddhism remains important in the city too, both as a relation with the past and as an ideal to strive toward. This chapter will contrast the grand narratives of Buryat Buddhism in the previous chapter with everyday religion in the city. Chapter 4 delves deeper into such everyday religious settings, exploring Buddhist counseling in Ulan-Ude as a site where laypeople relate their everyday struggles to Buddhism and seek to reinforce their agency through divination, conversation, and ritual. In chapter 5, Buddhist giving comes to the fore as another local practice of "religious intimacy" (Herzfeld 2015, 2016) that diverges from doctrine yet plays a key role in local ethical and social lives.

1

BURYATS IN RUSSIA
From "Aliens" to Model Soviets to Complex Modern Identities

The multifaceted identity of many Buryats today is rooted in the complex history of the region, and understanding it requires a historical excursion into the shifting forms of political organization and contexts of belonging over recent centuries. Pastoral nomadic Mongol tribes and smaller Indigenous groups populated the lands surrounding Lake Baikal in southeast Siberia. Russian Cossacks started colonizing the region in the seventeenth century, and the Sino-Russian frontier was fixed with the Kyakhta Treaty in 1727. This meant that Buryats were now separated by a border from other Mongols, save for Kalmyks, a Mongol group that migrated far west to the Volga region and were in the Russian Empire, too. In this empire, Buryats, as other minorities, were *inorodtsy* (Rus., aliens; lit., of a different birth), *inovertsy* (of a different religion), and *inozemtsy* (of a different land) and defined by the extractive relationship as *īasachnye narody* (peoples who paid the tribute). They were defined and engaged with through categories of difference from the dominant Russian Orthodox group. The following centuries under Russian rule, including forms of governing, multiethnic and multireligious setting, and minoritization in a Russian-dominated empire, were factors in the formation of a distinct and complex Buryat identity.

The process of Siberian colonization is usually referred to as a "voluntary accession" (Rus., *dobrovol'noe prisoedinenie*) or a term synonymous to it in official Russian discourse. However, many historians' accounts stress its coercive and violent character (Chimitdorzhiev 2001; Forsyth 1992, 89; Khamutaev 2011; Sablin 2017, 403). In fact, the first documented direct contact between Russians and Buryats came in battles in 1628 and 1629 (Forsyth 1992, 89). Over the seventeenth century and increasingly thereafter, Buryats entered political and economic relations with the Russian powers. They, like other subjects of the empire, were forced to pay tribute to the rulers. This took the form of a yearly payment, mostly in fur. Conflicts over tribute extraction were present, but Buryats were able to continue, in part, their ways of life. The tsarist authorities largely supported and reinforced existing social hierarchies in Buryat society, according certain official rights, such as administering the law and settling disputes, to the traditional ruling class (Bur., *noën*) (Chakars 2014, 28). By and large, Buryats maintained their nomadic herding lifestyle and continued to govern themselves in groups led by *taishaa* tribal leaders and *zaĭsan* clan leaders. This system was gradually tightened and bureaucratized, especially through the Speranskiy reforms of the early nineteenth century.

While the term *inorodtsy* came into usage in the seventeenth century, it became institutionalized as a legal category in 1822, signifying a particular kind of governance of ethnic minorities (Khodarkovsky 1997, 15). Inorodtsy were split into three categories—settled, nomadic, and wandering—their rights and obligations to the state depending on the category (Slocum 1998). Buryats fell into the middle group, and as such they were granted some means of self-governance. They were to hold twelve steppe dumas, autonomous administrative organs that consisted of elected chiefs, functioning as an intermediary between Russian officials and local subjects (Atwood 2004, 64). Yet being classified as nomadic inorodtsy provided Buryats, like other colonized peoples, with a "distinctly second-class status" in the empire (Slocum 1998, 181; see also Kappeler 2001, 169), with no provisions for them to become full citizens (Slezkine 1994b, 85). As John Slocum (1998, 174) notes, "If, in its original juridical sense, the term referred to the not-yet-assimilated peoples of Russia's Asian borderlands, by the early twentieth century the term carried the connotation of the non-assimilable peoples of all the borderlands."

The position of Buryats in their own lands started shifting radically in the late nineteenth and early twentieth centuries, as the central government introduced new policies to facilitate mass settlement of the Siberian lands. The Trans-Siberian Railway, constructed at the end of the century, contributed greatly to the process. New land ownership laws and a new administrative system were introduced, which disrupted Buryat ways of life and caused concern among them (Bazarov 2011, 251–52; Chakars 2014, 37–40). While there were 200,000 settlers in Siberia in 1700, between 1898 and 1908 alone, four million settlers moved to Siberia (Chakars 2014, 37). All commonly owned land was seized and redistributed in the form of individual, privately owned plots to Indigenous people as well as settlers (Chakars 2014, 38). This was incongruent with the Buryat nomadic way of life.

Not only were Russians populating the Buryat lands in great numbers; Orthodox Christian missionary activities constituted a significant presence of influential Others in the region. Orthodoxy arrived to the areas around Lake Baikal with Cossacks, but priests were few, and initially there was little effort to convert the local population. This is because only non-Orthodox people were to pay tribute, so more Christians meant less income for the metropolis (Murray 2012, 27). The mission ebbed and flowed in the following centuries, first gradually growing and amounting to mass conversions in the early eighteenth century, only to be curbed by imperial regulations toward the end of the century (Khodarkovsky 2001). The mid-nineteenth century marked renewed interest in missionary activity, in the name of assimilating minorities (Murray 2012, 30). In 1865, the Orthodox mission was "officially declared a part of government policy" (Schorkowitz 2001a, 211), resulting in the extensive, state-sponsored growth of conversions among all layers of Buryat society. Some Buryats were forced to convert, and some accepted baptism only for the material benefits offered by conversion (Schorkowitz 2001a, 212–13). Many Buryats thus returned to Buddhism and shamanism after the release of the Toleration Edict of 1905, which allowed subjects of the Russian Empire to profess any or no religion and to convert from Orthodox Christianity to other religions, which was previously illegal (Schorkowitz 2001a, 214–15).

In light of these profound social, economic, and demographic changes, as well as a wide range of social and political ideas at the time, alternative political movements emerged in the early twentieth century. As Robert Rupen (1956, 385) argues, "Buriat 'nationalism' was born of a strong reaction against Russian expansion into Buriat territory, a development which reached a critical point around 1900." Buryat intellectuals such as Tsyben Zhamtsarano, Mikhail Bogdanov, and El'bekdorji Rinchino led some of the various research initiatives and the promotion of Buryat culture and language, as well as political movements. Up until the Russian Revolution, they did not advocate separatism but promoted "incipient nationalism," seeking full rights in the Russian Empire instead (Rupen 1956, 385). After the February Revolution, they organized All-Buryat Congresses in 1917 to formulate the demands and needs of Buryats in whatever the empire was to become (Sablin 2016). Ideas and strategies for improving Buryat society were discussed and planned for. Some of these early twentieth-century Buryat intellectuals were also part of a pan-Mongolist movement, which celebrated the cultural similarities among various Mongol groups separated by borders, facilitated exchange between then, and even hoped to unite different Mongol groups into one political body. These efforts, however, were subsequently undermined in the turmoil of the civil war and its Bolshevik-led conclusion.

Exemplary Soviets

The early twentieth century was a tumultuous time in the region. There were multiple waves of Buryat southward migration to China and Mongolia fleeing various threats, including the First World War conscription, the Bolshevik Revolution, collectivization, and the Stalinist repressions in the 1930s. As a consequence, Buryats today are divided by the borders of three nation-states: Russia, Mongolia, and China (see, e.g., Baldano, Dyatlov, and Kirichenko 2020; Namsaraeva 2012; Nowicka and Zhanaev 2017). In Russia, the immanent tension between assimilation and reifying difference remained imprinted in the governance of minorities in the Soviet period.

"Indigenization" (Rus., *korenizatsiia*) was an ethnic minority policy of the early Soviet Union in the 1920s and 1930s, simultaneously shaping administrative, political, economic, cultural, and other fields. It provided, as Yuri Slezkine (1994a, 313) argued, "the most extravagant celebration of ethnic diversity that any state had ever witnessed." At its core was the attempt to guide rising nationalist and decolonial sentiments toward a novel imperial structure. The Soviets achieved this through "systematically promoting the national consciousness of its ethnic minorities and establishing for them many of the characteristic institutional forms of the nation-state" (Martin 2001, 1). On the one hand, indigenization was intended to work toward abolishing tsarist Russification of the non-Russian populations of the Soviet Union. On the other, the goal was to embed all nationalities deeper into the Soviet structures through policies of affirmative action.

An important aspect of the indigenization policy was territorial administration. Larger ethnic groups concentrated in a confined region were granted the status of an Autonomous Soviet Socialist Republic (ASSR) within the Russian Soviet Federative Socialist Republic. This meant that Buryats were a titular nation within Buryat-Mongolian ASSR (BMASSR), Bashkirs within Bashkir ASSR, and so on. At that time, however, Buryats were already a minority in the region: while BMASSR encompassed 91 percent of the Buryat population in the country, Buryats comprised only 43.8 percent of the population in the republic (Chakars 2014, 53).

"We are going to help you develop your Buriat, Votiak, etc. language and culture, because this is the way you will join the universal culture [*obshchechelovecheskaia kul'tura*], revolution and communism sooner," proclaimed an early

Soviet official (quoted in Slezkine 1994a, 420). Local languages were standardized and promoted in public life. Media and publishing in local languages burgeoned. Local cultural expressions were formalized and supported, so that each nationality had to have its own folk ensembles, national costumes, painters, sculptors and writers in the national form, and other isomorphic cultural outputs. Affirmative action ensured a rising number of Indigenous administrators, educators, artists, and other white-collar workers. Over the years, Soviet nationalities policies amounted to a "spectacularly successful attempt at a state-sponsored conflation of language, 'culture,' territory and quota-fed bureaucracy" (Slezkine 1994a, 414).

Under Stalin in the 1930s, much of the indigenization advancements among the numerically smaller peoples like the Evenki and the Chukchi were revoked, and nationalities policies lost their revolutionary spirit.[1] Instead, the larger ethnonational groups (Rus., *natsional'nosti*) who had their own titular republics, among them the Buryats, were further encouraged to build their own distinct national cultures and were supported in doing so, which resulted in a "curiously solemn parade of old-fashioned romantic nationalisms" (Slezkine 1994a, 446). These cultures were understood in an objectified, professionalized sense, and by the end of the 1930s, republics of major nationalities of the Soviet Union had their own theaters, operas, national academies, classic writers, and the like.

As such, they shaped the ways in which Buryats, like other nationalities, have come to self-identify and what they consider as important elements of their culture and heritage. Importantly, however, these developments should not be seen as a one-way process of political centers molding their subjects. As newly trained Buryats came to dominate white-collar jobs in educational, cultural, and administrative institutions and the media, they were not merely filling the slots created by these new policies. Instead, many were actively utilizing the Soviet system and ascending the social and political ladder at exceptional rates, emerging as a "Soviet success story" and a "model minority" (Chakars 2014). While this came at the steep price of the decline of much of traditional culture and their own language (especially in the later Soviet period), Chakars suggests that Soviet Buryat history cannot be seen as one of either resistance or oppression. Instead, it involves a balancing act in everyday lives of combining advancement in the modernist state and their own culture, resulting in complex and often hybrid identities. Buryat navigation of this period serves as an example of the complex negotiation of minority position in an empire. Some made use of the new opportunities to improve their positions, whether believing in the Soviet project or making compromises out of necessity. Others saw their lives and livelihoods shattered by the rapid changes, typically enforced in a top-down manner, despite early efforts at indigenization. To return to the conceptual terms suggested earlier, it was tactics rather than strategies that were available to most minority subjects of a vast empire.

While some of the Soviet economic and social policies provided opportunities for certain citizens at times, others destroyed livelihoods and took lives. In the mid-1920s, around 90 percent of Buryats were nomadic and seminomadic, so attempts at forced sedentarization and collectivization were extremely harrowing (Forsyth 1992, 332). They were met with resistance, the mass slaughtering of animals, and other forms of resistance, which was violently repressed. By 1937, around 92 percent of all Buryat households were settled and collectivized (Forsyth 1992, 333).

The late 1920s and 1930s were tragic decades in that many fell victim to Stalin's dekulakization, or the campaign against prosperous peasants, as well as the elimination of religious specialists and other newfound enemies. Since research of the period in Russia is restricted, only limited data are available. Even so, and even if official statistics are trusted, over seven thousand people in Buryatia were convicted and sent to labor camps or executed between 1926 and 1938, and thousands more were arrested (Chakars 2014, 75). While the extent of the purges is well known in Buryatia, and many Buryats lost relatives to them, this remains largely unspoken of today, and the figure of Stalin remains ambiguous or even positively appraised. This, as Caroline Humphrey (2002, 32) argues, is because of the "fractality" of Soviet power: Buryats were both the ruling and the ruled, the perpetrators and the victims, and "the communist subject cannot see himself as essentially different from the leader and cannot escape the quandary of responsibility." Moreover, the political climate in Russia today remains one where public discussion of Soviet atrocities is subdued and penalized.

Buryat political geography shifted in important ways in the early Soviet period, as Stalin's administration grew wary of the potential dangers of the politico-territorial unity of the Buryats, as well as their association with the wider Mongol world. Thus, in 1937, BMASSR territory was cut by 40 percent by separating Ust'-Orda Buryat Autonomous Okrug in the West and Aga Buryat Autonomous Okrug in the East, which diminished the representation of Buryats in the republic to 21.3 percent (Chakars 2014, 77). Moreover, the word *Mongolian* was removed from the name of the region. As an additional effort to shape Buryats into loyal Russian-Soviet subjects who were, importantly, distinct from Mongolians across the border, Buryat language policies were altered in the following years. Not only was the script for the Buryat language changed from classical Mongolian to Cyrillic, but the literary Buryat standard was shifted from the Selenga dialect, which is close to Khalkha Mongolian, to the Khori dialect, which is more distinct from it.[2] This contributed further to the crystallization of a distinct Buryat identity that was for political purposes increasingly removed from the (pan-)Mongol one.

Following Stalin's rule, the late Soviet period was seemingly quieter, but vast change continued in society. Education levels increased, as did urbanization. The agenda of Soviet modernization gradually and deeply took root in the region. The early nationalities policies not only largely stopped being enforced by the late 1930s; there was also a turn toward increasing domination of the Russian language and culture; many among the repressed were so-called bourgeois nationalists and others. The prestige of a modern urban lifestyle was growing, and diversions from the vision of Russian-dominated Soviet modernity were not tolerated.

A significant wave of change came in the late 1980s with perestroika (reconstruction), the political and economic restructuring of market reforms, and glasnost (openness), the policy to increase the transparency of state operations. These reforms were introduced by the new party leader Mikhail Gorbachev. They aimed at restructuring the Soviet political and economic system to end stagnation and conjure more citizen support. Like elsewhere in the Soviet Union, in Buryatia, the late 1980s were a time of reform. In many regions, these reforms also meant more space for open discussions of the darker sides of Soviet history and calls for cultural and religious resurgence (see, e.g., Balzer 2000; Hamayon 1998). Buryatia partook in the waves of cultural and national revivals of the time, but here, the movement "was not extremely radical" (Chakars 2014, 228), stopping short of ethnic violence or powerful separatist movements. Buryats expressed their grievances about the cultural, linguistic, and human loss caused by Soviet policies and actively participated in the cultural and religious revival. The Buryat national movement formed, formulating demands to the Soviet state related to reinstating the historical Buryat territories and reviving Buryat traditions, both issues stemming in large part from the Soviet period. While the cultural demands were initially met at least in part, the political ones were not, and they continued to be raised over the coming years (Chakars 2014, 249–50). As the Soviet Union dissolved, 85 percent of votes in Buryatia were cast in the referendum in favor of the preservation of the USSR (Chakars 2014, 256).

This brief survey of Buryat history in Russia points to the complex predicament of a minoritized population in an empire. In the face of ample limitations and the outright violence of the state, Buryats employed a variety of approaches. Some sought to collaborate with the dominant powers and actively partake in new political regimes. Many took advantage of educational and professional opportunities. Others employed various forms of resistance, fled their homeland in search a haven, or strove toward a different future through alternative political movements. Above all, people sought to preserve themselves and their livelihoods under unpredictable and often hostile political, social, and economic conditions.

Buryats and Russia

"I am a Buryat, but I also consider Russia as my homeland. This culture of Russia, ethnic Russian culture is close to me, so to speak [*Mne blizka, poluchaetsia, vot eta rossiĭskaia kul'tura, russkaia kul'tura*]," Chingis told me in Ulaanbaatar in October 2022, having recently fled the military draft in Russia. "I don't think there is a man up there in the Kremlin who is sitting there and trying to come up with a plan on how to annihilate Buryats or something like that." He chuckled at some of the vocal outrage that the seemingly disproportionate conscription of ethnic minorities in the war had caused in the media and social media and among activists. Later in the interview, however, as we were discussing his fleeing Russia in light of the military draft, his tone shifted. He had experienced great stress during a sleepless night on September 21, when the military call-up started in Buryatia. Buryat activists on social media had called it "St. Bartholomew's Night" (Rus., *Varfolomeevskaia Noch'*) due to its scale and intensity, after a prominent sixteenth-century nighttime massacre of Protestants in Paris. In Buryatia, officers were waking people up at night, delivering draft notices in the wee hours to sleepy, unsuspecting draftees or their relatives. Chingis, a Buryat man in his mid-twenties, was awoken by the noise of conscription rounds in his village, gathered what was going on, and fled his house for his aunt's house nearby. Because he was not registered in that house, the officers would not look for him there, and she would help him hide. After days of hiding in her house—he even drew the curtains so that no one could see him from outside—he saw he could not remain in Buryatia safely and decided to flee for Mongolia.

After our interview, Chingis reflected that our conversation had been a good chance for him to gather his thoughts and vocalize some of the conflicts he had been harboring. His relation to Russia was indeed one such point of contradiction. On the one hand, being a Russian citizen was an important part of his identity. He had a Russian passport, spoke the Russian language from an early age, had completed Russian education, and shared many cultural references with other citizens his age. Having spent a few weeks in Mongolia, he was highly aware of his Russianness, as Mongolians sometimes look down upon Buryats for having lost a significant part of their Mongol heritage and having been Russified (see Bulag 1998; Namsaraeva 2012, 161). To some Khalkha Mongolians, Buryats from Russia are simply "Russians" (Mon., *oros khun*), a word that, depending on the context, may carry degrading connotations, especially when aimed at a Buryat. On the other hand, Chingis did not feel fully accepted into Russian society either. Although he was reluctant to see an intentional act of discrimination in Russia's policies and attitudes toward Buryatia, such as "a man up there in the Kremlin" wishing to harm Buryats, his own recent experience begged to differ. He saw men just like him—his neighbors, acquaintances, classmates—being shoved into three buses from his village on that night. Most of them would be sent to the front lines in Ukraine with little preparation and insufficient gear. This contrasted sharply with other regions of Russia, especially big cities in the West, where mobilization was hardly noticeable at the time.[3] "Maybe there is that evil man in the Kremlin after all?" Chingis nervously said with a chuckle toward the end of our conversation.

"I am Kalmyk, but today we are all Russians" (Rus., "Ya Kalmyk, no segodnia my vse russkie"), proclaimed a billboard on the streets of Elista, the capital city of Kalmykia, in spring 2022. Kalmykia, like Buryatia, is a republic within the Russian Federation with a titular ethnic minority group. On the billboard, the flag of Kalmykia—a white lotus flower on blue and yellow, symbolizing purity, friendship, and peace—is enveloped by the flag of Russia. Apart from the above statement, there is also the hashtag #ZaМир, literally "for peace," but the Latin Z, which has become the symbol of the Russian army in Ukraine, substitutes the Cyrillic equivalent in the Russian phrase. The peace here thus stands for Russian rule over Ukraine. The billboard is an attempt to solidify popular support for the war, foregrounding the complexity of identities that are representative of many ethnic minority citizens of Russia. The poster portrays such enmeshment as positive and hopes to conjure the heartfelt sense of sharing a specifically Russian type of belonging despite the hardships it may bring. At the same time, the poster represents a state-sponsored discursive shift, blending civic and ethnic belonging and assimilating ethnic minorities into the dominant group.

Russia is a multiethnic federation. It is home to around 190 ethnic groups, and at least 17 percent of its population are not ethnic Russians. The origins of much of this diversity lie in colonization and imperial governance, as discussed earlier. But the post-Soviet Russian state has continued to grapple with the immanent tension between assimilation and reifying difference. Since the early 2000s, however, the scales seem to have significantly tipped in the direction of assimilation. Scholars observe a shift away from multiethnic inclusivity toward an ethnic-Russian focus (Rus., *russkost'*) in Russia's ethnic policies in recent years. Ethnic (Rus., *russkiĭ*) and civic (Rus., *rossiĭanin*) Russian belonging are increasingly conflated in official discourse and everyday use. As Helge Blakkisrud (2016, 250) puts it, "to maximise its room for manoeuvre, the Kremlin has been deliberately blurring the borders of the Russian ethnic 'self,' making it possible to reinterpret this 'self' as something more narrow but also broader than the body of citizens of the Russian Federation. Internally, such an identity holds the potential to encompass most of the population."

As the Soviet Union was dissolved, fifteen republics declared independence, among them the Baltic and the Southern Caucasian states. The Autonomous

Soviet Socialist Republics that were part of the Russian Soviet Federative Socialist Republic remained in the Russian Federation. The Russian president Boris Yeltsin famously announced that regions within the federation can "take as much sovereignty as they can swallow." This was hardly the case in practice. In 1992, eighty-six out of the eighty-eight subjects of Russia bilaterally signed the Treaty of Federation outlining the relations between the central government and the various subjects: republics, krais, oblasts, and others. Two regions, Chechnya and Tatarstan, refused to sign the treaty. Tatarstan eventually signed a bilateral treaty with Russia in 1994, which granted it a special status within the federation, with additional local authority, such as control over its resources. In 2017, the treaty expired, and Moscow refused to renew it, "sen[ding] chills down the spines of many citizens of the 'non-Russian republics,' as indeed it was meant to do" (Balzer 2022, 165). In Chechnya, struggles for independence led to two destructive wars between 1994 and 2000, with continued insurgency. Since then, Chechnya boasts a de facto, if not de jure, special status in the Russian Federation, in return for loyalty and stifled separatist movements (Russell 2011).

In the early post-Soviet years, the Buryat national movement of the late 1980s, now comprising different organizations, did not consolidate into a major political force in the region (Chakars 2020; Khamutaev 2005). Some argue that this was because voters considered their members too far removed from concerns with the harsh socioeconomic situation in Buryatia at the time (Chakars 2014, 257). Politically active intellectuals were few, and they failed at organizing themselves and increasing their visibility. Finally, through selectively supporting the Buryat national movement's cultural activities, government officials were able to take credit for many of their achievements (Chakars 2014, 257–58).

Small-scale oppositional politics and activism continued in Buryatia in the later post-Soviet years. This included ecological activism, protests, and campaigns against unfavorable policies and appointments from Moscow and the local government (Balzer 2022, 67–79). Since the late 2010s, the biggest public outrage was brought on by the arrest of a Sakha shaman, Alexander Gabyshev, who was trekking around eight thousand kilometers from Yakutsk to Moscow to, in his words, "exorcise the devil out of the Kremlin" but was arrested along the way and forcibly taken to a psychiatric hospital (Jonutytė 2020a; Balzer 2023). Discontent over Gabyshev's arrest added to local grievances concerning the allegedly rigged mayoral elections in Ulan-Ude and led to protests that included thousands of participants and the violent interventions of riot police. The shaman's case was also close to the hearts of many in Buryatia because of the high authority of shamans in the region and the relevance of many of his grievances about social and economic inequalities in the country. Gabyshev's story thus resonated very differently in Buryatia than it did in Russia's western parts, where, unlike in Buryatia, many oppositional commentators on the internet supported his trek not because of his shamanic background but in spite of it, claiming support to the Siberian's vision while employing racist and exclusionary language to do so (Jonutytė 2020a).

The experience of many members of minoritized ethnic populations in contemporary Russia may be similar in many ways. But their history within the empire has resulted in distinctions and hierarchies among the different groups. An important boundary has typically been drawn in Russia between "Indigenous groups" (Rus., *korennye narody*) and larger ethnic groups (Rus., *natsional'nosti*). The former currently comprise forty groups, legally defined as the "Indigenous small-numbered peoples of the North, Siberia, and the Far East" (Rus., *korennye malochislennye narody Severa, Sibiri i Dal'nego Vostoka*), with fewer than fifty thousand members per group. The larger ethnicities could also be considered Indigenous in international discourse in terms of their autochthony and other characteristics, but they do not typically self-identify as such. This is largely because of the ways in which ethnic groups have historically been ranked in Russia, particularly in the Soviet period outlined earlier, and because of concomitant popular connotations and social hierarchies. To many Buryats, being called "Indigenous" would imply being not yet modern and carry negative overtones of a lack of cultivation and progress (see also Graber 2020, 30–36). Only recently have such popular assumptions been discussed more broadly and challenged more prominently, especially among ethnic minority activists. As ethnic antiwar activism is gaining weight, and as minority diasporas from Russia are expanding across the world, the concept of indigeneity is being reevaluated by many Buryats and others. They are considering their predicament, history, and rights in relation to other Indigenous groups worldwide and exploring the potentialities of Indigenous identity. At this time of crisis, new alliances among the different minoritized populations are cropping up, if mostly online and abroad.

Minorities Since 2000: A Diverse Federation or a Security Threat?

Vladimir Putin, a KGB intelligence officer and a St. Petersburg bureaucrat, was lifted to presidency of the Russian Federation on New Year's Eve 2000. He has remained in power ever since and is currently (in 2025) serving his fifth presidential term, with an intermission of premiership in 2008–12. Constitutional changes in 2020 enabled Putin to reset the count of his presidential terms back to zero, potentially allowing him to remain in power until at least 2036.[4] Throughout his rule, concern over large-scale electoral fraud has been rife (Gel'man

2023). After witnessing nearly a quarter century of his rule, one can speak of distinct characteristics of Putin's vision of federalism and minority policy, with homogenization, Russification, and centralization at its core (Prina 2015, 3–5).

Many politically engaged citizens in Buryatia, as well as outside observers, highlight Putin's policy of "merging" (Rus., *ukrupnenie*) as an important turning point in political life in the region. Officially, the merging of some of the smaller federal subjects with the larger ones aimed at simplifying governance and combating some of the socioeconomic inequalities in the country by merging poorer regions with wealthier ones (Derrick 2009, 317–18). However, scholars argue that "a rationale based on ethnicity, not primarily on socioeconomic concerns, underpins the policy" (Derrick 2009, 320). All five federal subject mergers conducted between 2005 and 2008 joined ethnic minority subjects to larger Russian-majority regions. Two of the five were Buryat regions: Ust'-Orda Autonomous Okrug was joined with Irkutsk Oblast, and Aga Buryat Autonomous Okrug was joined with Chita Oblast (subsequently renamed Zabaykalsky Krai). Having previously constituted a large part of the autonomous okrug population—that is, having had more substantial minority self-governance—Buryats are now a small minority in the Russian-dominated oblasts. With the merger, they lost their power over budget allocations and local dumas and no longer had their own representatives in the Russian federal duma.

The mergers were conducted after referenda, but observers note ample fraud in them (Graber and Long 2009). In Buryatia, the referenda led to the emergence of a local activist movement, intended to inform the population of the two autonomous okrugs on the details of the mergers and their potential dire consequences for the residents, as well as facilitate public discussions on them. However, activists were not allowed to register an NGO promoting a critical view of the merger, despite forty-two organizations being registered in its support (Graber and Long 2009, 149). The media in both regions was filled with state-sponsored pro-merger campaigns, while oppositional voices were silenced. Observers were barred from entering polling stations. The referenda were passed in both cases with well over 90 percent of the votes for in the autonomous okrugs and high voter turnout (Graber and Long 2009, 150). Both during fieldwork in Buryatia and up to this day, many Buryats speak about the merging of the Buryat autonomous okrugs as indicative of their decline in political and economic autonomy and a significant step toward the Russification of the Buryat regions.

Sometimes talk crops up of merging the ethnic republics themselves with Russian-dominated regions (Derrick 2009, 322), and at least some of my Buryat interlocutors considered this an entirely realistic next step in undermining ethnic minority autonomy. Some of the other aspects of declining republic autonomy are the renaming of the "president of the republic" (Rus., *prezident respubliki*) as the "head of the republic" (Rus., *glava respubliki*), as well as the suspension of the elections for this post (direct elections were nullified between 2002 and 2017). Putin has overseen an "overhaul of Russia's federal system" (Sharafutdinova 2013, 358), with a significant decline in regional power and increasing centralization through a "vertical of power."

Importantly, these shifts have taken place under a repressive illiberal regime, where the public and informational spheres are extremely curtailed. In Russia, there are continuous reports of rigged elections both on the federal and regional levels. Oppositional parties and candidates are barred from taking part in elections (Gel'man 2023), exemplified in Buryatia by the Ulan-Ude mayoral elections in 2019. While Igor Shutenkov, the candidate backed by Putin's United Russia party, which dominates Russian politics, officially won the election, many considered the actual winner to have been Vyacheslav Markhaev, a prominent, well-liked Buryat candidate of the Communist Party in the region. Oppositional media has gradually been eliminated over the last two decades, and only state-supported narratives make it to the news on both national and local levels.[5] Many oppositional politicians and intellectuals have had to flee Russia to seek political refuge, including academics and cultural, political, and language activists (Balzer 2022, 68). Putin's Russia has been defined as an "electoral authoritarian regime" (Gel'man 2023, 25).

One of the main spheres quoted by representatives of ethnic minorities as a clear indication of the central government's undermining of minority rights is the language policy of Putin's Russia. In the 2002 All-Russian Census, 72 percent of all Buryats reported some knowledge of the Buryat language. By the 2010 census, the number fell to 45 percent (Graber 2017, 155). A 2007 law took away the 15 percent of teaching time dedicated to the "national-regional component" of the curriculum, which had been used for teaching minority languages (Prina 2015, 127–28). Legislation in 2012 further diminished minority-language teaching: it was now to be provided "within the opportunities offered by the education system" and its teaching "should not be to the detriment of the teaching and learning of the state language of the Russian Federation" (Prina 2015, 128). Since 2017, minority languages have become an optional subject, and their teaching must be limited to a maximum of two hours a week (Yusupova 2021, 1). This led to the dismissal of many language teachers, as well as to protests across Russia's ethnic republics (Yusupova 2021). In 2019, an Udmurt language rights activist, Albert Razin, committed self-immolation in front of a government building in Izhevsk, Udmurtia, to protest Russia's minority-language policy as well as the Russification of the Udmurt people.

Federica Prina (2018) identifies a contradiction in Russia's ethnic policies since the early 2000s. She argues that while the Russian state has sought to place ethnic policies almost exclusively within the cultural sphere, minority institutions are an integral part of Russia's sociopolitical order. They are co-opted to support Russia's metanarratives of interethnic tolerance and mold a form of minority belonging that fits into national unity, conforming to the needs of the political center. Ethnic diversity is treated as a security threat in Russia (Prina 2021). The federal government ensures both a discursive and legislative grip on its minority republics by casting their attempts at autonomy as separatism and religious extremism (Oliker 2018). At the same time, minority groups make claims to their rights through cultural forms because other venues for political expression remain extremely limited (Prina 2018; Stewart 2023; Yusupova 2021). It is precisely in light of an illiberal, repressive Russian public sphere that the religious and cultural practices explored in this book take place.

The "Denazification" of Russia

A Buryat friend shared a traumatic, racist episode on a bus in Moscow, when a group of youngsters yelled at her: "*Ni hao!* [Chinese for 'hello'] Go home!" By that time, she had lived and studied in Moscow for several years and had nothing to do with China. Another friend recalled how on a several-day trip to an academic conference in Moscow, he was stopped and searched on two different occasions on the metro. An acquaintance, a Buryat teacher in her thirties, was beaten up on the St. Petersburg metro while other passengers looked on. After this assault, she decided to move back to Buryatia. Yet another interlocutor made the decision to move abroad after having been severely beaten by a far-right group's members in Moscow in the 2010s.[6]

These are just some of the countless examples of racism from my field notes, and many more remain unshared. In the late 1990s and early 2000s, a powerful far-right anti-immigration movement emerged in Russia, especially in the large cities in its western parts. Racist attacks against Asians, people from the Caucasus, and others became prevalent. It was not uncommon for such attacks to result in deaths. According to one source, 86 people were killed and 599 were wounded in racist attacks in Russia in 2007, 87 killed and 378 wounded in 2008 (data from the SOVA research center, cited in Humphrey 2011, 1). These are likely to be underestimations. The situation caused outrage and lively discussions among minority representatives online that provided a platform for negotiating—and questioning—their sense of belonging (Humphrey 2011).

In the 2010s, the Russian government cracked down on racist crime, and there was a significant decrease in reported racist attacks (Balmforth 2016). However, many ethnic minority representatives consider these efforts insufficient because racism remains rife both in everyday and systemic forms and because a powerful undercurrent of Russian far-right actors and sentiment remain and have even been strengthened in Russian society. It has been argued that Russia remains "the most violent country in the former Soviet Union for ethnic and racial minorities" (Arnold 2015, 243). Racist violence is high, with skinhead and other far-right groups continuously concerned with a steep demographic decline among Russians, which some of them refer to as a "genocide" (Arnold 2015, 243; Oushakine 2009). While the SOVA Center for Information and Analysis reports a threefold fall in hate-motivated crime in Russia in 2022, this is likely the result of significant outward migration from Russia by many in the vulnerable groups, as well as by the likely underreporting of hate crimes in contemporary Russia and the fact that some of the right-wing radicals are reportedly fighting on the Russian side in Ukraine.[7]

Early in my fieldwork, I was surprised by how many of my friends and colleagues in Buryatia had lived away from Buryatia, studying or working, mostly in Moscow, St. Petersburg, and Irkutsk, but eventually returned to Buryatia. I took this to be a proof of their love and commitment to their region and a wish to contribute to its better future by bringing their knowledge and experience home. This was certainly true, but I left out one important factor—perhaps as a result of my overidentification with the situation and my own privilege. That missing factor was racism: everyday racism in the form of offhand remarks and suspicious looks, as well as the threat of physical assault. Another factor is the systemic racism that Russia's ethnic minorities, as well as immigrant residents, face at work and outside (Arnold 2015; Kuznetsova and Round 2019; Zakharov 2015). In Russian-dominated cities, it is very common to only rent flats to Russians, Slavs, or "a Slavic family" and to directly indicate this in ads. Even within the military, ethnic minorities appear to be significantly underrepresented in the top ranks (Vyushkova and Sherkhonov 2023, 134).

All this sheds light on the recent calls of Russia's ethnic minorities to "denazify" Russia. One of the official pretexts for Russia's invasion of Ukraine is the alleged need to denazify it to help the oppressed Russian population there, especially in the eastern parts of the country, the self-proclaimed Donetsk and Luhansk People's Republics. In his speech announcing the large-scale "special military operation" in Ukraine, Vladimir Putin claimed that a "genocide" was being carried out by the Kyivan government, requiring a "demilitarization and denazification" of the country. In Russian official communication and mainstream media, discussions of Ukrainian nationalism, "fascism," far-right movements, and discrimination against ethnic Russians have been a staple in recent years. Such claims have been met with outrage among some representatives of ethnic minorities in Russia.

In spring 2022, ethnic minority activists initiated a flashmob where they invited people to share their experiences of racism in the country. Thousands of entries were submitted, with 1,500 sent in within just the first several days.[8] The Free Buryatia Foundation, Russia's first and most prominent ethnic antiwar initiative, called 2023 the "year of the decolonization of Russia," gathering minority representatives from all across Russia in a shared campaign.[9] Activists of Buryat, Tatar, Yukagir, Chechen, and many other backgrounds expressed shared grievances with Russia, united in their antiwar stance, and called for the decolonization of the country. As one activist in the video put it, "Russia's aggression against Ukraine contributed to a spiritual awakening of national identity among our peoples. Many national movements have appeared, people stop being silent, stop being afraid, we have been oppressed for too long."

Indeed, the war in Ukraine has served as a catalyst for discussions about the state of ethnic minorities in Russia and the future of federalism (see also Dolyaev and Dugar-DePonte 2023; Khovalyg 2023; Yangulbaev 2023). In the same video, activists spoke of the need to reconsider the legacy of the Stalinist period and its residual collective trauma; the importance of restoring "intellectual sovereignty" and greater political, cultural, and economic autonomy; and the violent and uneven military draft of September 2022, which amounted to an "ethnocide." These are just a few of the many grievances expressed in this video and many other communications of Russia's ethnic minorities today. The war in Ukraine thus brought together a wide range of issues relevant to Russia's minority populations. Decades and centuries of grievances coincide with substantial losses of minority soldiers in the war, as well as the multiple effects of war in the region, such as limited mobility, increased prices, the reverberations of the sanctions, and others.

While the effects of the war on Russia's minority populations have been grim and the discontent among them is seemingly high, oppositional organizations, such as the Free Buryatia Foundation or the League of Free Nations, hardly represent all Buryats or other groups. The organizations do not have a chance to do so, having been outlawed in Russia. The core activist group is based abroad, although with some anonymous volunteers in Russia, at least until late 2022. Based on conversations with locals and those who recently left the country, it appears that many in Buryatia are aware of the activities of these groups but consider their activists too far removed from life in the region. In Ulaanbaatar, I heard much criticism toward some of the Buryat oppositional organizations as not just alienated from the current realities of Buryatia but also as too obviously siding with the Ukrainians, inefficient, and focused on their individual gains from activism rather than the greater cause. At the same time, it was clear to me that the work done by the ethnic antiwar movements was effective, as their data analysis results on the disproportionate losses and disproportionate drafting of ethnic minorities or their insights on decolonization were well known among those who had just left Buryatia. Despite abundant criticism of some aspects of these organizations, their work in raising the awareness of minority issues in relation to the war was bearing fruit, as concepts such as decolonization and ethnocide were becoming widespread amid varying stances toward them.

In May 2023, even Putin felt the need to address the issue of decolonization in Russia, stating that Russia's "opponents . . . are provoking the 'national communities,' supposedly establishing different kinds of sociopolitical organizations in the name of Russian peoples, while actually representing only themselves and provocateurs such as themselves, brazenly announcing the need for the so-called decolonization of Russia."[10] He claimed it was the Western countries' attempt to drive a wedge in the interethnic relations of Russia's citizens, attempting to incorporate these regions into their sphere of influence. All this, according to Putin, was an expression of the West's own racism and neocolonialism. At the same time, however, his statements clearly demonstrate the new relevance and visibility of minority issues in contemporary Russia.

"Our National Thing": Ethnicity and Religion in Post-Soviet Buryat Buddhism

In Russia, ethnicity is often understood and experienced as being closely linked with religion. Buryat Buddhism is no exception to this. On a very early Friday morning in the first weeks of fieldwork in summer 2015, I was making my way to the transport stop where shuttle buses leave to Ivolginskiĭ datsan, the largest Buddhist temple complex of Buryatia. I was excited and curious to finally see the body of Khambo Lama Itigelov—the telepathically communicating monk from the introduction and a very important object of worship in Buryatia.

The incorruptible body (Rus., *netlennoe telo*) of Khambo Lama Itigelov is a major phenomenon and event in Buryatia today. Dashi-Dorzho Itigelov was the Khambo Lama, or the head of Buddhists in Buryatia, in the early twentieth century and a very advanced tantric practitioner, as well as an expert in Buddhist philosophy and medicine. As the story goes, in 1927, just before the violent Stalinist repressions took off, Itigelov sat down in lotus position and asked his disciples to chant a sutra that is usually chanted after someone has died. Since the disciples were reluctant, Itigelov started chanting it himself, and as others joined in, he reportedly went into deep meditation (or, as some claim, nirvana) and apparently stopped breathing. He had left instructions to his disciples to bury him and then to unearth his body thirty years later. Lamas reportedly did so twice during the Soviet period and were astonished to find that his body had not decayed, but they conducted the appropriate rituals and buried him again each time fearing the attention of the Soviet powers. In 2002, he was finally exhumed and examined by forensic experts who ostensibly could not establish whether he was alive or dead, claiming that he was in a state between life and death unknown to science.[11]

Since then, many want to see the miraculous monk, suspended between life and death, who, according to some, possesses magical qualities in healing and conjuring luck. He is displayed to the public eight times a year during Buddhist festivals, one of which is specifically dedicated to him. These days are announced in advance for the year, in accordance with the lunar calendar, and are marked by two *khural* services: one in the morning and one in the afternoon, usually lasting several hours each. Itigelov is then displayed in the main temple until the evening. On all other days of the year, he remains in a separate house of worship called the Palace of Itigelov (Rus., Dvorets Khambo-lamy Itigelova) built especially for him. The BTSR stresses that Itigelov is a sacred treasure and the temple is therefore closed to tourists and only open to pilgrims or those who have a pressing need to see him. In fact, however, an unofficial ticket system existed in the mid-2010s, where one could buy a ticket, the purchase expressed as a wish to "worship" Itigelov and the money given as a donation rather than payment.[12]

It is usually an inconvenient journey of over an hour to travel the thirty kilometers: first waiting for a *marshrutka* to fill up and often overfill so that some passengers stand, advancing slowly through the Ulan-Ude traffic, transferring to another *marshrutka* and waiting for it in turn to fill up, then finishing the last five kilometers bouncing in an old shuttle bus on bumpy roads. It was a special day though—a Day of Worship of the Incorruptible Body of Khambo Lama Itigelov (Rus., Den' pokloneniia netlennomu telu Khambo-lamy Itigelova)—and shuttle buses filled up quickly and headed directly to Ivolginskiĭ datsan, even as early as six o'clock in the morning, which was a pleasant surprise. When I arrived at the datsan, at around seven o'clock, it was already buzzing with people circumambulating the grounds, leaving coins and sweets in front of sacred objects, spinning prayer wheels, prostrating themselves, buying ceremonial scarves (Bur., *khadag*) and souvenirs, drinking tea and snacking in the cafeteria, and simply waiting around. The event was supposed to start two hours later with a morning khural, and people were already queueing outside the main temple.

The crowd was forming by the packed temple, with front seats reserved for the main sponsors of the BTSR. While waiting outside listening to the prayers via loudspeaker, I took the opportunity to chat with an elderly woman queueing next to me, who worked as a teacher in a local school. She told me that teachers and students in Ivolga, a town nearby, got a day off to attend the festival: a clear manifestation of the influence of the BTSR on the regional level. Attendance of boys born in 2003—just after the unearthing of Itigelov—was especially encouraged. They were to receive a special blessing from Itigelov and thereby acquire exceptional power and success.[13] These boys were later expected to take part in the traditional Buryat wrestling tournament (Bur., *bükhe barildaan*).

When the khural ended, well into the morning, it was announced that the crowd should now disperse to make way for Itigelov, who would be carried to the stadium across from the temple. After people reluctantly made their way to the stadium and policemen jostled the elderly women from the front row, Itigelov was carried across on a concealed throne, accompanied by festively dressed lamas and magnificent ceremonial music. Khambo Lama Ayusheev then gave a speech in a mixture of Russian and Buryat, and the boys born in 2003 were lined up in front of Itigelov's covered throne and told to prostrate themselves, which they did awkwardly to loud dramatic music, while being admonished by the Khambo Lama. They then came up to the throne one by one and received blessings from Itigelov, who sat patiently underneath a barely lifted drape on his throne. Afterward, Itigelov was ceremoniously carried back to the temple, and many queued again to worship him there. In the stadium, a festive event started up, complete with traditional sports, music, speeches, and exchanges of gifts.

FIGURE 6. The day of worshipping Itigelov, Ivolginskiĭ datsan, Ivolga, 2015. Photo by author.

Around lunchtime, a sports tournament of the "three masculine games" (Bur., *eryn gurban naadan*) began in the stadium and in a field nearby. The three games are Buryat traditional wrestling, archery, and horse racing, the latter staged less often due to the organizational difficulties involved. The three masculine games have historically been tied to Buddhist monasteries, taking place during *oboo* rituals and other big festivals, such as the Maidari celebration (Krist 2004, 107).[14] During the Soviet period, these sports were secularized, and competitions would take place during a festival of traditional sports in the summer called Surkharban. These competitions were held away from Buddhist monasteries, and competitors would represent their work collectives rather than village or patrilineal kin group as had previously been the case (Humphrey 1983, 380–82).

Since ascending to power two decades ago, the current Khambo Lama Ayusheev—previously a teacher of physical education—has had reviving the Buddhist element of these games and bringing them back to Buddhist temples as an important goal. The intention is not only to desecularize them and hence revive the previous custom but also to attract more people to attend Buddhist festivals and reintegrate Buddhism into the lives of the laity. Even when these games are organized in a secular setting, such as during the Day of the City (Rus., Den' Goroda) festival, lamas are now typically present as referees or helpers. This results in a double process: it both desecularizes Buryat traditional sports and contributes to the popularization of Buddhism. An excerpt from my interview with Khambo Lama Ayusheev sheds light on the connection between the games and Buddhism:

> THE KHAMBO LAMA: In all contests of Buryat traditional wrestling, a lama has to be in charge. [He may be] bad, stupid, but [there should be] a lama. And intelligentsia should sit over there [pointing at my smartly dressed Buryat colleague in glasses, sitting in the corner of the room]. Without a right to say anything. That lama can be eating dumplings [*buuzy*], he can be napping, but he is a lama. He can understand nothing in wrestling, nothing at all, but he is the main man there. He collects money and distributes it [to the winners]. And officials [*chinovniki*] stand nearby and contribute money so that the lama gives them away.
>
> KRISTINA: So a lama should always lead these competitions?
>
> THE KHAMBO LAMA: Yes, yes, yes. This is because it is ours, it is our national thing [*eto nasha natsional'naia veshch'*].

Here, Buryat traditions such as traditional Buryat wrestling are deemed inseparable from Buddhism by the Khambo Lama, as they are by many lamas and laypeople alike. This is openly criticized by some local Buddhists, especially urban middle-class intellectuals, who, sometimes unaware of the pre-Soviet link of the traditional sports and Buddhism, speak disapprovingly of Ayusheev as a physical education teacher who is more interested in sports than Buddhism. A friend, Zhambal, an urban intellectual and an occasional critic of the Buddhist leadership, buried his face in his hands when I told him that I saw the Khambo Lama leading the traditional wrestling tournament during the All-Buryat Altargana Festival: "The leader is just like the people [Rus., *Kakoĭ narod, takoĭ i vozhd'*]... Plebeians!" Zhambal was very disappointed that lamas these days, as he said, "waste their time" on such things as sport instead of studying Buddhist texts or advancing in their Buddhist practice.

This, however, is only one perspective. Ayusheev's patronage of the traditional sports is indeed a Buddhist endeavor, albeit based on a different idea of Buddhism than that of urban intellectuals. The Khambo Lama sees traditional sports as an essentially religious activity: "When we organize wrestling tournaments, we offer our gratefulness to bodhisattvas, and wrestlers are the connection with our protector Ochirvani, who gives us strong sons and guards us from harm" (Ayusheev in Makhachkeev 2013, 43).[15] Wrestling, as Ayusheev sees it, is not just a tradition and is not so much only a game or physical activity to improve one's fitness as it is a spiritual pursuit and a ritual offering to deities. To be more precise, the different aspects of this action are inseparable: It is at once ritual and entertainment, a marker of religious and ethnic identity, and seemingly secular but actually religious.

As the Day of Itigelov's Worship wore on, I noticed fewer and fewer Russians around. Khambo Lama Itigelov himself is a major object of worship, not just to Buryats but also to many others in Buryatia, as well as to non-Buryat Buddhists from elsewhere. Itigelov's showings are also well attended by Mongolians, who combine this pilgrimage with a shopping trip to Ulan-Ude and visits to relatives. In the case of this day of worshipping Itigelov, the Russian visitors attended the khural and worshipped Itigelov in large numbers, but barely any Russians remained for the events held outside the main temple itself: the traditional sports competition and a Buryat music concert afterward. This is because while Buryat identity is often understood by locals as inextricably linked to Buddhism, Buddhism is not exclusively linked to Buryat ethnicity, as many Russians also frequent Buddhist temples and events. Therefore, Russians were interested in the festival only insofar as Itigelov himself was concerned: attending the khural and worshipping his body. Buryats and Mongolians, on the other hand, considered it to be a religious, cultural, and ethnic event, all these components being intimately bound together. As is clear later in the book, in Buryatia, Buddhism is a resource for all to tap into, but the local narratives of diverse inclusion do not always correspond to the lived realities of Buryat minoritization.

2

BURYAT BUDDHISM
Politics and Identity of a Minority Religion in Russia

The synergy of religious and state matters, as exemplified by the Buddhist Traditional Sangha of Russia's (BTSR) support for the war, is in no way a new phenomenon. In popular imagery, Buddhism is often perceived as being removed from its social and political setting. Buddhist practitioners are expected to inhabit remote monasteries on hilltops and to meditate in solitary caves. The sight of a monk clad in burgundy robes in a lively urban center catches the eye of many observers, especially those unfamiliar with Buddhism as it is lived and practiced in contemporary Asia. But this is a selective, partial idea of what religion is or should be. Solitary and meditative practices are indeed an important part of Buddhism, and social and political matters are considered aspects of samsara, the endless cycle of mundane life that one should aspire to escape from to enlightenment. Yet social and political engagement is an essential part of life and, by extension, of religious life. Far from shying away from worldly issues, Buddhist professionals often spend a significant part of their time and energy immersing themselves in them, especially through providing guidance, divination, and ritual help to laypeople.

The idea of Buddhist social and political aloofness is also rooted in academic contexts. For instance, the religious scholar Joseph Kitigawa has argued that "Buddhism never offered anything that could be called a social or political philosophy.... Social transformation can take place as a side effect of the religious transformation of individuals who constitute a social group" (quoted in Whalen-Bridge and Kitiarsa 2013, 1). Some scholars argue that social and political engagement by Buddhists is the result of Western influence. In their interpretation, its followers were "occupied in the ritual observance" before the activist input of "twentieth-century Caucasian readers" (Queen 1996, 31).

However, there is no shortage of Buddhist social and political involvement across time and space. The *chakravartin* is an important Buddhist concept, referring to a righteous leader who protects and fosters religion. The epitome of this is the emperor of the Maurya Empire in the third century BC, Ashoka, who patronized Buddhism and greatly contributed to its spread across the continent. In contemporary contexts, too, religion and statehood may go hand in hand, like in Thailand, where the sangha is directly regulated by the state (Keyes 1987), or postsocialist Mongolia, where Buddhism is reconceptualized as "national heritage" (Sneath 2014). A whole strand of Buddhism—socially engaged Buddhism—takes social engagement to be the core of religious practice (Fuller 2021; King 2009; Queen 1996), while in other cases, political resistance is built on a Buddhist basis, as in monastic protests against the military regime in Myanmar (Gravers 2012). As Paul Fuller (2021, 13–14) puts it,

> Our idea that Buddhism is not engaged and that there is a historically pure form of Buddhism that had no social message and no cultural contact could well be due to the legacy of the Western encounter with Buddhism in the eighteenth and nineteenth centuries. In this encounter, Buddhism was often contrasted with other religions and made distinct from them by stressing those aspects of Buddhism which are ascetic and removed from society. It was clear . . . that this caricature of Buddhism would have suited Western colonial powers, as a passive Buddhist population made the job of exploiting Asian populations much easier.

In the Buryat Buddhist case, the entanglement of religion and Russian political life is indeed a powerful thread running through its history. An ethnic and religious minority in a diverse empire, Buryat Buddhists have had few means to effectively resist dominating powers, but they have also made use of this relationship. Today, in the context of war, lamas of the BTSR talk of their duty to the Russian state and the inevitability of supporting it. Above all, this emerges out of the long-term patterns of the relationship between Buryat Buddhists and the Russian state, which can be summarized as *containment, centralization,* and *collaboration.* These themes run through Buryat Buddhist history since its significant presence in the region, and they are especially visible today.

In fact, religion emerges as one of the main venues for expressing and enacting minority loyalty to the Russian state. Historically, one prominent moment when such an alliance was enacted occurred when the tsar was recognized as an incarnation of a Buddhist deity, White Tara, in 1764. Scholars argue that this act incorporated Buryat Buddhists into the empire while simultaneously incorporating Russia into the Buddhist world, thereby pursuing mutual agency (Bernstein 2013; Tsyrempilov 2013, 2021). This sacralization of the tsar was dutifully remembered in the post-Soviet period, as Buryat Buddhist leaders hoped to reinforce their synergy with the political powers. The Russian president thus became an incarnation of White Tara (Tsyrempilov 2021, 1). While the idea of a contemporary leader of a secular, non-Buddhist-majority state being a Buddhist deity may seem peculiar, this is just one instance in a long history of ethnic and religious minorities engaging in a give-and-take with the state in order to survive and secure the small degree of cultural sovereignty that they can. In this sense, the current apotheosis is hardly different from Buryat Buddhists in the 1920s claiming that Lenin may have been a Buddha (Snelling 1993, 205) or writing speeches of adoration to Stalin in the 1940s (Tsyrempilov 2009, 105). Buddhists are not unique in this pursuit. In the post-Soviet period, dominant shamanic organizations have also demonstrated continuing loyalty through, for instance, mass camel sacrifice for the benefit of the Russian "state, our people, the peoples inhabiting our vast country" (The Moscow Times 2019) or through providing local shamanic resistance to the Sakha shaman Alexander Gabyshev's protest trek (Balzer 2023, 35; Jonutytė 2020a, 6).

Between Submission and Subversion in the Russian Empire

Buryat Buddhist synergy with the Russian state is an important lens through which the history of Buryat Buddhism is often framed. Records of Russian officials mention the presence of Buddhism in Buryat territories as early as the mid-seventeenth century (Galdanova et al. 1983, 12–13). At that time, Buddhist temples were nomadic, and lamas first appeared in entourage to the princes of the Selenga and Khori Buryats, who adopted the practice from Mongolian khans (Tsyrempilov 2013, 41). The institutionalization of Buryat Buddhism started in 1727, after the Sino-Russian frontier was finalized with the Treaty of Kyakhta, which led to a strictly enforced border and limits on migration. This was important because up to that time the clergy had come from across the frontier, and there were many exchanges across borders throughout the Tibeto-Mongolian Buddhist world.

The following year, an edict was issued that defined relations between Buryat Buddhists and the Russian Empire. Three points formed its core: the isolation of Buryat Buddhists from institutions in the neighboring Qing Empire, the reduction of the financial burden that new lamas brought upon the local population, and the centralization of leadership over Buryat Buddhists (Tsyrempilov 2013,

45–48). In 1741, imperial authorities approved one hundred fifty staff (Rus., *shtatnye*) lamas. The empire granted tax exemptions and designated a head lama (Tsyrempilov 2013, 57).[1] The edict also established that any contact between staff lamas and Buddhists outside the Russian Empire was punishable by death (Tsyrempilov 2013, 62). Buryat Buddhists thus entered into a relationship with the imperial authorities, which, as Dittmar Schorkowitz (2001a, 203) argues, was instrumental to the consolidation of Buddhism in the region in the following century.

The recognition of Buddhism as one of the official religions of the Russian Empire and the establishment of its centralized hierarchy with the Khambo Lama as leader is often held up as one of the key events in Buryat Buddhist history. In 1764, Empress Catherine the Great acknowledged a Buryat lama educated in Tibet, Damba-Darzha Zayaev, as "the main Pandito Khambo Lama of all Buddhists that reside to the South of Lake Baikal" (Galdanova et al. 1983, 24).[2] The Khambo Lama is an elected position of Buddhist leadership in Buryatia, as opposed to the comparable institutions of religious and administrative authority of the Dalai Lama in Tibet and the Jebdzundamba in Mongolia, which are passed on through reincarnation.

The institution of the Khambo Lama ensured a constant and direct link between Buryat Buddhists and the imperial (and later Soviet and federal) government. As Nikolay Tsyrempilov (2013, 235) argues, the centralization of the Buddhist administration in Buryatia has been the result of mutual interaction between local Buddhists and imperial authorities. Imperial officials saw the need to centralize religious institutions, closely supervise them, and often restrict their activities. Their interest in managing Buddhists was also driven by international politics. Like other non-Orthodox minorities, Buddhists were used by the empire for diplomatic purposes (Tsyrempilov 2021, 25). By the end of the nineteenth century, the Russian Empire made use of Buryat Buddhist ties to exert its influence in Asia when it employed them as pilgrims-cum-spies in Tibet (Bernstein 2009). Furthermore, a Buryat lama, Agvan Dorzhiev, was a political adviser to the Thirteenth Dalai Lama and a crucial diplomat in negotiations to provide Russian patronage to Tibet (Snelling 1993). In the Russian Empire, religious minorities were also delegated to mediate between the authorities and laypeople, for instance, by promoting certain policies or campaigns, such as spreading agriculture, combating epidemics, or assisting the military at the front (Tsyrempilov 2021, 27). In the Soviet period, too, Buryat Buddhists were used to exert influence and spread revolutionary propaganda in Mongolia and other Asian countries, as well as to provide an impression that religious freedom prevailed in the Soviet Union (Bräker 1983; Sinytsin 2013).

On their part, Buddhists were forthcoming in their cooperation with the imperial authorities since they "saw such a role of the state as natural and necessary" and "looked for firm ground in their relationship to the ruling powers" (Tsyrempilov 2013, 55). Moreover, they showed interest in centralization to protect their domination in the local religious market, where there were also wandering and foreign lamas, as well as shamans (Tsyrempilov 2013, 233). Buddhists were supported in their attempts to convert shamanists, since shamanism was seen by the authorities as more difficult to control (Gerasimova 1957, 32). In other words, the political and administrative formation of the Buryat sangha was not a one-way process of submission to the power of the ruling authorities but a series of negotiations where both sides and the multiple actors within them had differing and changing interests. However, the limits on the agency of the Buryat sangha should also be clear: They were a minority dealing with the powers of a vast empire and were only reckoned with as the imperial authorities saw fit.

Within these constraints, however, both the imperial strategies and the ways in which Buryat Buddhists accommodated them were changeable. There was diversity in the approaches that different groups within the Buddhist sangha and laity took in dealing with state powers. Some sought close contact with the state, working to extract benefit from it; some even vied for influence—at one point, there were two competing centralized Buddhist administrations in the region (Tsyrempilov 2013, 84). Others, like the unregistered steppe lamas, fled state oversight while continuing to pursue a Buddhist path and often taking part in the life of monasteries (Kuvaev 2020). Laypeople, too, navigated these constellations of power and religion, at times employing Buddhism for various social and political projects (Tsyrempilov 2015; Zhanaev 2021, 9).

Much of this was also true for other minority religions in the empire. As Robert Crews (2006, 10) puts it, "Religion came to depend on the institutions of this state, just as the empire rested upon confessional foundations." Buddhists constituted less than 0.5 percent of the Russian Empire population in the 1897 census (Werth 2014, 4). They were a tiny minority within a massive and diverse empire. The largest religious minority was Muslims, who constituted 15 percent of the total population in the early twentieth century (Crews 2006, 1). A monotheistic religion, Islam was deemed a "developed" faith and therefore more permissible than many others, but it was nonetheless subject to extensive repressive policies (Crews 2006). Like Buddhism, it had not previously had a unified religious hierarchy but was "confessionalised" in the imperial period (Crews 2006, 8). By the mid-nineteenth century, as Paul Werth (2014, 47) puts it, "the majority of Russian subjects were under the authority of religious bodies that had been created or legitimized by state power and were regulated by imperial statute." Religious and spiritual communities like shamanists, whose religious behavior was considered "pagan idol worship," fared worse. Due to their fluidity, lack of institutionalization, and illegibility to the ruling powers, their conversion to Orthodoxy was supported by the state (Tsyrempilov 2021, 23).

Soviet Buddhism

This disparity of power between a minority religious group and empire becomes especially evident in the Soviet period, which was marked by tragic losses of human lives as well as the dismantling of religious infrastructures. Buddhism continued to spread in the early years of Soviet rule. In 1923, the so-called golden age of Buryat Buddhism, there were 9,134 lamas in Buryatia and forty-four monasteries (Sinitsyn 2013, 37). Soon afterward, attacks on the Buddhist church began. By 1937, there remained only 900 lamas and fifteen monasteries (Sinitsyn 2013, 103). By 1940, there were none (Sinitsyn 2013, 108). This was the result of an active and aggressive antireligious campaign, which involved propaganda via various means (media, public meetings, etc.), alongside the demolition of monasteries and violent repressive actions against lamas, many of whom retreated to lay life or were executed or sent to forced labor camps or prisons. While initially the Bolsheviks were relatively sympathetic to Buddhism as a religion of an oppressed minority group, by the mid-1920s, a large antireligious campaign was underway, aiming to remove religion from public life, education, and eventually to eradicate it completely (Amogolonova 2018, 244–46).

Although Buddhists were not able to stop the campaign, many did resist it. Prominent monks like Agvan Dorzhiev, who had considerable connections in the government, wrote letters of complaint to the authorities, as did laypeople (Sinitsyn 2013, 94; Snelling 1993, 218–20). Lamas encouraged the laity to protest the closing of monasteries and designated their own candidates at local elections (Sinitsyn 2013, 105). They also engaged in small acts of resistance, such as burning crops and killing livestock, and stored weapons in monasteries (Sinitsyn 2013, 94). Moreover, there were ritual forms of resistance. Laypeople and lamas threw pyramids of dough and paper (Bur., *sor*), which symbolize the destruction of the enemies of faith, in the direction of a nearby Soviet office (Humphrey 1983, 421) and held other rituals against enemies of Buddhism (Sinytsin 2013, 47, 103). Some interpreted the coming of Soviet power as a sign of a fast-approaching Shambhala war—a holy war against forces hostile to the faith—and built stupas, conducted rituals, and spread rumors (Humphrey 1983, 418; Sinytsin 2013, 57).

Instead of resisting, others chose survival through displays of loyalty and submission. As Darima Amogolonova (2018, 247) puts it: "The Soviet authorities sought to present the Buddhist clergy as a class enemy comparable to other counter-revolutionary elements, such as the kulaks (wealthy peasants) or the remnants of the nobility. To protect themselves against such accusations, many lamas went out of their way to proclaim their identification with the Soviet project, a move they viewed as a continuation of the imperial tradition of loyalty." Amogolonova (2018, 247) notes that it was especially the more conservative monks who made use of the submissive "Soviet language" to simultaneously ensure their good standing with the new powers and eliminate the Buddhist reform movement that was gaining momentum among the Buryat sangha at the time.

Toward the end of the Second World War, antireligious policies softened. One of the most widespread explanations for this claims the Soviet intention was to lift the spirit and bolster patriotism during a devastating war (Chumachenko 2002, 7). Some suggest Stalin's personal affection for Orthodox Christianity was a factor (Chumachenko 2002, 7) or that religious organizations were potential tools for foreign policy (Bräker 1983, 43). Others argue that at the core of the new policies was an attempt to gain control over religious activities in the USSR—contained, officially sanctioned religious activity being easier to supervise than uncontrolled grassroots pursuits (Sinitsyn 2013, 136). In 1948, a new temple complex, Ivolginskiĭ datsan, was opened, and the historical Aginskiĭ datsan was reopened after a temporary closure. From that time, Ivolginskiĭ datsan became widely recognized as the center of Buddhism in Buryatia, if not the whole of Russia. It was strategically placed just outside the capital city—close enough to be tightly controlled but not in Ulan-Ude itself to prevent it from being too prominent (Hürelbaatar 2007, 138). The number of lamas was very limited, and their activities were closely regulated. The two open datsans were difficult to access, and few laypeople frequented them, aware of the trouble it might cause for them with the authorities, who kept a close watch on comings and goings.

Along with opening two showcase temples, state authorities also established the Central Spiritual Board of Buddhists of the USSR.[3] Among its main functions was to represent Buddhists of the USSR in international Buddhist gatherings and thereby demonstrate that religion was supposedly freely practiced there. In some ways, it replicated the pre-Soviet Buryat Buddhist hierarchy and was led by an elected Khambo Lama. The five Soviet Khambo Lamas who held the title after 1946 had all suffered under Stalinist repressions either in prison, in exile, or in gulag labor camps before taking on the role. They also engaged in periods of secular labor and military service before taking on the leadership of the board.

Despite the devastating religious repressions of the Stalinist period, many in the Soviet Union continued to practice religion. Tamara Dragadze (1993) refers to the "domestication" of religion in this period, its removal from the public sphere while it continued to be practiced in private settings. Valeria Gazizova (2022) considers

Kalmyk Buddhism to have functioned "underground" in the Soviet period in several ways. It went underground in terms of functioning secretly but also in the literal sense of many religious objects being hidden in the ground only to reemerge at a later time (see also Bernstein 2013, 89–124, for similar practices in Buryatia). According to Gazizova, it was in this "underground" religious practice that women emerged as the leading carriers of the Kalmyk Buddhist tradition, contrasting with the previously male-dominated nature of the religious sphere. Since former male monks continued to be surveilled by the KGB, it was safer for women to carry forward Kalmyk religious traditions and conduct rituals (Gazizova 2022, 28).[4] In Buryatia, people continued to conduct essential Buddhist and shamanic rituals, like clan offerings to spirits (Bur., *taĭlgan*) and group offerings to local master spirits (Bur., *oboo*), throughout the Soviet period, in private and actively veiled from the eye of the authorities (Humphrey 1983, 373). Shamanic practice continued as well, and despite the severe repressions against shamans, there appeared to be more shamans in the Soviet period than lamas even in areas where Buddhism had previously dominated (Humphrey 1983, 415). Shamans emerged as true bricoleurs, adapting to the new circumstances and incorporating the Soviet realities into their practice (Humphrey 1983, 410–18).

Based on fieldwork in Buryatia in the 1960s and 1970s, Caroline Humphrey (1983, 420–432) reported continuing Buddhist practice in the region during the Soviet period. If at a limited capacity, the two monasteries operated, subsisting on lay donations. In the countryside, it was mostly laypeople or officially disrobed lamas who conducted the necessary rituals, albeit on a much smaller scale than in the prewar period. In Ivolginskiĭ datsan, laypeople gathered nightly for secret group prayers, starting in 1947 (Zhambalova 2011, 89). It was during the Soviet period that a new genre of ritual, *sangaril*, developed in Buryatia, where laypeople would gather, typically at night, to collectively read prayers previously read only by lamas (Zhambalova 2011, 89). This practice developed due to the restrictions on public religious practice, and local lamas claim that such lay gatherings to read prayers had not existed in Buryatia before the 1940s. These kinds of gatherings continue up to this day in some villages in the region (Zhambalova 2014, 122).

Inevitably though, and despite partial continuities, the Soviet repressions had a devastating effect on local religious life. While this period is often discursively cut from Buryat religious timelines (Bernstein 2013, 93; Jonutytė 2024, 913), its impact on contemporary religious life in the region is substantial. Saskia Abrahms-Kavunenko (2015) has highlighted religious innovation and creativity as essential to resurging religion in postsocialist Mongolia. Lars Højer (2009) has noted the valorization of religion in the postsocialist setting, where attempts at its repression now appear to point to its inherent potency. Justine Buck Quijada (2012) has argued that post-Soviet religion in Buryatia continues to be marked by the Soviet legacy, where religion and science entered a mutually constitutive tension. While the Soviet atheist-modernist regime juxtaposed science as the "correct" counterweight to religion, such a disposition now largely coexists with the renewed presence of religion. Sonja Luehrmann (2005) writes about a "recycling" of skills and spaces occurring in the post-Soviet period, where, for instance, Soviet cinemas become churches, and teachers of atheism become those of religion. Post-Soviet religion in the region reemerges in not just a changed time but also a vastly different spatial setting, which it adapts to while also altering it (Jonutytė 2024).

Post-Soviet Buryat Buddhism: Multiplicity and Containment

There have been vigorous debates on the *post-Soviet* label in recent years. Ever since the start of full-scale war in Ukraine, if not earlier, the *post-Soviet* label has in the eyes of many become politically problematic. In 2023, the Lithuanian foreign minister famously announced that Lithuania—and presumably many other regions that were in the USSR—are "not post-soviet [*sic*], we're never-soviet."[5] While a polemical statement, it is hardly a new suggestion that the post-Soviet region has been too readily interpreted through the lens of the dominant power regime, that is, the imperial (Russian) lens. During a time of large-scale war in the region, the issue of an appropriate analytical lens has become especially pertinent.

Of course, *post-Soviet* and its sister term *postsocialist* are not just part of political vocabulary. The terms have been amply debated in academic circles both for their ideological and analytical merits. Anthropologists, sociologists, and other scholars have argued against the continued use of the label *postsocialism*, as it lacks analytical value and has contributed little to social theory (e.g., Hann 2006, 5; Hann, Humphrey, and Verdery 2002; Stenning and Hörschelmann 2008; Suchland 2011). Martin Müller (2019) has summed up the critiques of the term in five main areas: it refers to a vanishing object of research, overemphasizes rupture, is too territorially bounded, risks orientalism, and constrains the political potentialities of the region. Critiques from native scholars have also been prominent, highlighting both the unproductiveness of the term and the ways in which native scholars have been excluded from its academic production (Červinková 2012; Tlostanova 2017). Yet some researchers nonetheless claim that insights can be gained from thinking about postsocialist contexts comparatively, especially through the postcolonial lens (Chari and Verdery 2009; Spivak et al. 2006), while others argue for the continued use of the term, if in more refined and intentional ways (Ringel 2022).

In religious life in Buryatia, the post-Soviet condition remains distinctly relevant both emically and etically because of the ways in which it shapes the current religious milieu and the relations of current practitioners to their ancestors and their "traditional" religious practices. On the one hand, religious practices are themselves a way to relate to the past and one's ancestors (Buyandelger 2013; Quijada 2019). This is especially the case in local shamanism, where the layperson can communicate with their ancestors through rituals and thereby carry their presence into the current time. Manduhai Buyandelger (2013) has argued that among Buryats in Mongolia in the early postsocialist period, the many socioeconomic struggles were seen as stemming from a troubled relationship with the past. They interpreted "misfortune as the result of the forgetting of the past that is rooted in the contexts of oppression and resistance, and in tragic events associated with a loss of ancestral lands, displacement, and violence by more powerful states and empires" (Buyandelger 2013, 29). Shamanic rituals provided a powerful way of remembering, reconnecting with the past, and, through this, mending one's potential future. In addition, kin connections in the present could find themselves strengthened by ancestral engagements (Abrahms-Kavunenko 2016).

Buddhism also provides a powerful connection with the past of the region. Through the monk Itigelov's incorruptible body and other sacred sites and objects, Buryat Buddhists claim religious, cultural, and institutional continuity (Bernstein 2013; Quijada 2019). Justine Buck Quijada (2019) argues that Buddhist rituals in Buryatia provide a meaningful and productive way of engaging with the past. She claims that Buddhism provides a distinct "historical genre" in the region, legitimating and reinforcing the current Buryat Buddhist leadership.

Buryat Buddhists are aware of, and sometimes comment on, the Soviet period and its effect on local religion, even if this effect is sometimes brushed off as simply an intermission in the inevitable domination of Buddhism (Bernstein 2013, 93; Jonutytė 2024, 7–8). In some cases, the post-Soviet condition also becomes an emic category, with laypeople and lamas commenting on, for instance, the lack of local Buddhist expertise or the overreliance on religious authorities as outcomes of the Soviet period.

However, the post-Soviet condition is also relevant in terms of the innovation and eclecticism present in local religious life. Johan Elverskog (2006) argues that there is not one but two Buddhisms in postsocialist Mongolia: one ethnic and one transnational. While the first relies on ethnic belonging and the Mongolian Buddhist tradition, the second is based in internationally active, often lay, groups. Interestingly, the two Buddhisms in Mongolia appeared to Elverskog (2006, 41) to be "working hand in hand to achieve the same end," that is, the establishing of a distinctly local and novel national Buddhist tradition. Tara Sinclair makes a distinction, in post-Soviet Kalmykia, between "revival" Buddhism among those who see themselves as continuing the pre-Soviet "traditional" religious practice and "reform" Buddhism among followers of Tibetan émigré lamas who seek to "purify" local religion. Saskia Abrahms-Kavunenko (2012, 2015) highlights eclecticism in Ulaanbaatar, where openness and improvisation form a crucial part of postsocialist Mongolian Buddhism, noting also a creative tension between its "cultural" and "reform" strands. The, if only partial and dynamically navigated, temporal gap of the socialist period appears to be crucial in shaping contemporary religion in the region.

At the same time, it is not just the temporal framework that is significant in contemporary Buryat Buddhism. Elsewhere, I have argued (Jonutytė 2024) that the post-Soviet resurgence of religion is not a temporal matter of revival after a period of lapse but a spatiotemporal concern. Buddhism has not simply returned, but in returning, it has encountered a different spatial milieu heavily shaped by the socialist period. Post-Soviet Buddhists are reckoning with this new spatial setting, which Buddhism is both being shaped by and is itself shaping in turn. Perhaps the best example of this is the urban context itself. Verkhneudinsk was a relatively small and almost exclusively Russian colonial town up until the 1920s. Over the Soviet period, it grew into the midsized city of Ulan-Ude, with a substantial Buryat presence. As Buddhism revived in Buryatia from the 1990s, it did so not only after a temporal "break" but also in a completely novel urban setting that it seeks to remake.

In the post-Soviet period, the centralized Buddhist organization remained, now under the name of the Central Spiritual Board of Buddhists.[6] The younger generation of lamas trained in socialist Ulaanbaatar took over. In 1995, a young lama, Damba Ayusheev, was elected to lead the board and became the Twenty-Fourth Khambo Lama. He is still in power today, having reorganized the structure of the sangha to form the BTSR in 1997. Several organizations subsequently split from it over various disagreements. The situation today is not unlike that in pre-Soviet Buryatia, where there was the dominant Buddhist administrative hierarchy with the Khambo Lama at its top and a plurality of lamas and practices of other Buddhist schools. Both then and now, there are monastery-based and individually functioning lamas, conservatives and reformers, temples related to the leading administration and those that operate outside of this institutional structure.

The BTSR has been in a peculiar situation since the 1990s: It is one among many organizations, it stems from a Soviet institutional structure, but it is also effectively a descendant of the pre-1930s Buddhist administration. By the early 2000s, its leader, Khambo Lama Ayusheev, was still in a precarious position despite having rebuilt several temple complexes and made significant efforts to centralize and reform Buddhist institutions. At the time, many critics drew attention to the insufficient education and inappropriate behavior of lamas across Buryatia. Due to the lack of lamas and insufficient local expertise to train them, some apprentices only completed a very short course of study before taking up work in the new temples, and understandably they were sometimes found lacking in both competence and discipline. Another point of critique was—and still is—the fact that local lamas are typically not monastic: not celibate, living outside of datsans, and upholding few vows. This situation was critiqued by the Dalai Lama himself, and while some condemn this as a lesser form of Buddhism, others see it as a local tradition. To establish authority and reinforce the legitimacy of its leadership, the BTSR, with Ayusheev at its fore, took a number of measures. The early ones followed the unearthing of Itigelov—the revered lama between life and death—in 2002.

Itigelov is a major figure in the Buddhist revival in Buryatia. This revival had been gathering force since the late 1980s but escalated significantly following Itigelov's unearthing. I met many Buddhists in Buryatia who told me that Itigelov strengthened their faith and motivated them to visit temples more often and be more pious. I also heard from many non-Buddhists that Itigelov provided an inspiration for them, fulfilled their wishes, or helped them with a blessing or a piece of advice.[7] Anya Bernstein (2013, 89–124) suggests that Itigelov's body should be understood as a hidden treasure (Tib., *terma*) in the Tibetan Buddhist context. These are signs and objects, specifically left by advanced practitioners and deities to be unearthed at an auspicious (purposely chosen) time in the future and intended to deliver a timely teaching or provide necessary aid. Both laypeople and lamas often say that Itigelov "returned" exactly when he knew he was needed and that he is delivering a message. Many regret, however, that at this point no one has the means to decode his teaching and hope it will not go to waste because of that. This assumed intentionality and hidden wisdom augment the weight of the BTSR, who are the guardians and managers of Itigelov.

Not only did Itigelov attract many new local believers and reinforce the faith and practice of old ones; he also put Buryatia on the map for many spiritual seekers and curiosity lovers both in Russia and abroad. His story spread widely in the Russian and foreign media.[8] Numerous political leaders of Russia visited and worshipped Itigelov, among them, Vladimir Putin, Dmitrii Medvedev, and the chief of privatization in Russia, Anatoly Chubais. International Buddhist authorities have also paid their respects to Itigelov, including one of the two claimants to the title of Karmapa (leader of the Kagyu school of Tibetan Buddhism), the Buddhist scholar Robert Thurman, and the leader of one of the biggest lay Buddhist organizations in Europe, Diamond Way Buddhism, Ole Nydahl. A splendid new temple was built specifically for Itigelov, theological conferences are organized regularly in his honor, and an NGO was founded to represent him. Itigelov sends daily messages via his guardian lama at the temple, and they are posted on the internet.[9] Itigelov's fame and influence remain considerable more than twenty years after his unearthing.

"Buddhism is *sviatynia* [Rus., sacredness].... If there is *sviatynia*, there will be Buddhism," Khambo Lama Ayusheev repeatedly stressed in my interview with him. Ayusheev's focus on *sviatyni* is indeed firmly grounded in important strands of the Buddhist tradition. Together with several other prominent sacred objects and sites, Itigelov is at the forefront of the Buryat Buddhist revival today, as envisioned by BTSR.[10] Yet this vision meets some resistance among Buryat Buddhists. It is not just the invention of tradition (Hobsbawm 1983) that is controversial to them but also the commercialization of Itigelov and Buddhism more generally, as well as the tension between different approaches to Buddhism in Buryatia: tradition and ritual versus Buddhist modernism and knowledge.

"Self-Sufficient" Buddhism?

The consolidation of Buddhist authority and legitimacy within the BTSR occurs in the context of a contemporary Russia wherein an important political trend has been deliberate isolation from most foreign actors and institutions. The close monitoring and limitation of ties with religious actors outside of Russia have been key in Russia's dealing with Buddhism since its early days in the region, likely due in part to its predominant presence in borderland areas. However, foreign connections have been an especially pertinent issue across Russia since the early 2000s, when Putin came to power. Russia's foreign policy orientation has been increasingly isolationist, and the West—and by extension foreign countries in general—have been reinterpreted as enemies and threats (Richters 2013, 13).

In 2009, President Medvedev famously expressed this isolationist sentiment. He highlighted that, despite the economic crisis, "our country is strong and powerful.... We will endure all these difficulties. We also have our own resources to support the traditional confessions in Russia . . . so we do not need any foreign aid at all[;] we will deal with all problems ourselves."[11] Today, foreign citizens cannot establish religious organizations in Russia, and they cannot organize teachings or distribute literature and other religious materials unless they are formally invited to do so by an existing Russian religious organization. This is an important constraint as Vajrayana Buddhism (tantric Buddhism, including, most famously, Tibetan Buddhism) is a transnational affair, and migrating lamas have played a significant role in the consolidation of Buddhism in the Baikal region from its early days (Bernstein 2013; Dugarova 2023; Garri 2014; Tsyrempilov 2012).

There are several controversial issues in Buryat Buddhism concerning this "foreign aid." First, the BTSR refrains from inviting the Fourteenth Dalai Lama to Russia, recognizing that the Russian government is wary of the impact this might have on relations with China. The Dalai Lama has not visited Russia since 1992, excepting a one-day unofficial visit to Kalmykia in 2004 (Holland 2014). Second, the BTSR is widely criticized for its repeated denial of the Tibetan and Mongolian origins of Buryat Buddhism and its cosmopolitan features. Ayusheev's position is that Buryats "took Buddhism themselves" through the lama Damba-Darzha Zayaev rather than received it as a transmission from Tibet via Mongolia, which is the widely accepted historical account (Bernstein 2013). Zayaev did indeed study in Tibet, subsequently returning to the Russian Empire to become the First Khambo Lama in 1764. However, Buddhism was already widespread in the region at the time, advancing from Mongolia with Tibetan and Mongolian lamas. It is not so much the facts that Ayusheev debates here but their interpretation and the construction of a purposeful narrative. His version of the history of Buryat Buddhism stresses the active "taking" rather than a passive and submissive "being given," thus downplaying foreign influences and ties with the Buddhist world and highlighting the will and might of the Buryat people. Simultaneously, however, this stance facilitates self-isolation from the wider Buddhist world.

The debate over "foreign aid" in religious matters sometimes takes the form of discussion concerning the role of Tibetan lamas in Buryatia (see, e.g., Bernstein 2013; Garri 2014). There were around two dozen Tibetan émigré lamas in Buryatia in the 2010s, and more also paid short visits to give teachings or rituals. Many laypeople value Tibetan lamas for "purifying" Buryat Buddhism and perceive them as more "authentic": not only are many of them celibate, but they have received a highly valued education in Tibetan monasteries. However, their presence conflicts with the ideology of self-sufficiency and autocephaly keenly professed by the BTSR. In 2015, a prominent Tibetan lama, Shiwalha Rinpoche, was expelled from Russia for offering teachings on Tibetan Buddhism (Bigg and Kizirov 2015).

Some criticize Tibetans for being foreign, "not ours" (Rus., *ne nashy*), and out of touch with Buryat traditions.[12] Anya Bernstein (2013, 83–6) describes an *oboo* ritual during a particularly dry summer month that was supposed to bring rain but was unsuccessful. While the "pro-Tibetan" side blamed the failure on the alcohol and meat offerings made by Buryat lamas (impure offerings in Tibetans' opinion), the "anti-Tibetan" side complained that Tibetan lamas were unskillful in taming local spirits. However, while some feel strongly about the issue, most are not particularly selective about the nationality of lamas.[13] As one lama put it, "This is all samsara," explaining that nationality should be irrelevant in the Buddhist world and that the Khambo Lama is too involved in politics.[14] At the same time, some of my interlocutors pointed to Kalmykia, a Buddhist region that has tighter links to Tibetan Buddhist institutions, as a better example for reviving post-Soviet Buddhism.

Bernstein (2013) discusses these negotiations over "self-sufficiency," autocephaly, and the purity of Buryat Buddhism in light of the concept of cultural sovereignty. On the one hand, Buryats have over centuries been minoritized and marginalized in Russia, treated as a small peripheral group. Yet on the other hand, they have also had a complex and marginalizing relationship with their co-ethnics in Mongolia (see also Bulag 1998) and coreligionists in the Tibetan Buddhist world. To them, Buryats are not only Russified but also a peripheral, northernmost region with late and "incomplete" religious transmission. As Bernstein (2013, 9–10) puts it,

> Many in the Tibetan exile community consider Buryats' current attempts to revive their Buddhist traditions to be of dubious authenticity and in need of Tibetan "missionaries" to help them with this task. In this context, a major arena where assertions of cultural sovereignty take place today is the contemporary practice of Buryat Buddhism, which many local leaders consider the most important cultural currency. Thus, what is at stake in such regionally particular religious domains is not only Buryats' relationship with the Russian federal government and the phenomenon of the so-called regional sovereignty . . ., but also the issue of cultural recognition within the larger Mongol-Tibetan world.

Khambo Lama Ayusheev is often criticized by some Buryat Buddhists, in particular urban intellectuals, as being boorish, unsophisticated, and overly submissive to Moscow's whims. Since the Dalai Lama remains a high—even the highest—moral authority to many Buryat Buddhists, and Tibetan lamas are much esteemed in the region, this blunt denial of Tibetan links confuses and angers many Buddhists. Yet, as Lila Abu-Lughod (1990) has argued, resistance to one power structure inevitably results in submission to another. In her own work, she argues that Bedouin women who resist patriarchy through creative consumption submit to capitalist domination and gendered hierarchies of the Egyptian society within which Bedouins are marginalized. She suggests that resistance should therefore not be romanticized, but it should be treated as a "diagnostic of power" (Abu-Lughod 1990, 42). After all, as Foucault (1978, 95–96, quoted in Abu-Lughod 1990, 42) has suggested, "Where there is power, there is resistance, and yet, or rather consequently, this resistance is never in a position of exteriority in relation to power." Here, too, the Buryat Buddhist leadership appears to be in a double bind between the Russian state and other powerful fields that, at least partly, minoritize and marginalize them, namely, the Mongolian and the Tibetan Buddhist worlds.

Buddhism and Political Life in Post-Soviet Buryatia

In 2022, those entering Ivolginskiĭ datsan, the oft-claimed center of Buddhism in Buryatia, and even Russia, are met with a large photograph of Vladimir Putin. In it, he proudly walks alongside the Khambo Lama Damba Ayusheev during his visit to the temple complex in 2013. The side of the path is lined with respectfully bowing lamas, each holding a blue ceremonial *khadag* scarf, which symbolizes the eternal blue sky, as well as harmony, tranquility, and loyalty. The poster reads: "Vladimir Putin helped establish 'social flocks' in Buryatia and helps their development. The Buddhist Traditional Sangha of Russia received 33 million roubles for the construction of a wool processing plant and its equipment. It was granted by the decision of the President of Russia V. V. Putin on the 14th of November 2019, from the Reserve Fund of the President of the Russian Federation."[15]

In 2015, I attended a public ritual in one of the rural districts of Buryatia, dedicated to a prominent local historical lama. In his introductory address before the ritual began, the Khambo Lama recounted a story about a road to a nearby temple that was recently renovated. Vladimir Putin had visited Buryatia and included some temples in his visit. The driver and a lama in charge of the itinerary were discussing the best route, and the lama told the driver: "We are not going to take this road with the president." Putin, Ayusheev stressed, being a wise leader and a good manager (Rus., *khoroshyĭ khoziaĭstvennik*), asked: "Why will you not take this road with the president?" Ayusheev smiled and repeated this point several times, highlighting the attention to detail that makes Putin a good manager and, by extension, a good president. Others would have missed this small detail during the excursion, but he did not, demonstrating true skill and genuine interest in local life. It was Vladimir Putin, Ayusheev stressed, who gave money for the renovation of this road to the temple. As we drove on "Putin's road" to the temple later that day with a pilgrim bus, the story circulated among the Buddhist passengers. Giggles mixed with comments of admiration and gratefulness as we swiftly approached the temple on the smooth road across the expansive steppe.

In these ways and others, the president of Russia populates Buryat Buddhist religious worlds. His person crops up regularly in various announcements at temples of the BTSR. President's felicitations to Ayusheev on his birthday or to

Buddhists more broadly on Buddhist holidays are printed out and hung in the Ivolginskiĭ datsan precincts and shared on social media. Locals also report having seen the president's portrait in temples. In 2009, the BTSR announced that the president was an incarnation of White Tara and organized a worship ceremony for him, although they eventually had to cancel it to avoid putting the president in an awkward position (Tsyrempilov 2021, 1).

During my fieldwork, a public service timetable of one of Buryatia's datsans emerged online. Sagaan Dara Ėkhė, a khural dedicated to White Tara, was to take place in December. In brackets, an explanation was given: "for the well-being of V. V. Putin, for professional growth, success at work, civil servants." The post was quite controversial, with commentators debating the appropriateness of praying for the president's well-being. As one put it: "I think that praying for the leader of a country . . . is a must. Why? So that he lead the country in a wise and capable way. And each one who curses and criticizes, is harming us, Russian citizens [*rossiĭanam*]." Others were more critical: "Complete sucking up [*otsos polneĭshyĭ*] . . . ah, well, *khamba* [Khambo Lama]." "Did they go completely crazy? You should maybe organize a prayer so that they stole more without consequences and courts!" Still other commentators considered this to be selling out: "Ayusheev came up with a new branch of Buddhism to suck money out from idiots [*novuĭu vetvu buddizma po otsosu deneg u lokhov*]. . . . Without money don't go to a datsan, you won't improve your karma!"

Putin regularly appears in the BTSR's social media pages, and Buryat lamas participate regularly in state-sponsored activities, such as meetings of the Religious Council, of which the BTSR is part, or its charitable activities. The Khambo Lama is a regular guest at the Kremlin's major events, in particular the annual president's address and the Victory Day parade on May 9. In May 2023, Ayusheev received Russia's Order of Honour directly from Vladimir Putin in a ceremony at the Kremlin. It was granted for "active social engagement activity, directed towards the strengthening of the friendship between peoples and interconfessional understanding."[16] The mutual benefit of this relationship appears prominent here, as during his acceptance speech for the award, Ayusheev asked Putin to approve the building of a Buddhist temple in Moscow.

This direct endorsement of the dominant political powers appears to be an extension of historical cooperation between Buryat Buddhists and the state. Buryat lamas themselves have used the language of indebtedness and duty to talk about this relationship. Ayusheev has referred to Buryat participation in the war in Ukraine as a "sacred debt" to Russia.[17] In the same speech when he received the award, Ayusheev claimed: "260 years we live together in joy, we develop our religion, enrich our people, our Buddhists. We deserved to build a temple in Moscow like we have in St. Petersburg. I hope for your patronage, as it will be symbolic for us. We, Buddhists, have proven our loyalty, our devotion, especially now, during the special military operation, where our soldiers-Buddhists are fighting with dignity, showing heroism and courage."[18] A Buryat Buddhist laywoman with a son and grandson at war seconded him: "Let them fight, they are fulfilling their duty.... Who will defend the Motherland?!"[19]

Yet the current moment also opens space for voices of criticism and disillusionment. Critiques of the close links between the BTSR and the Russian regime have long been present. In 2016, outrage broke out on social media because of a blurry photograph of a batch of Putin statuettes in bronze, allegedly manufactured in the souvenir workshop of Ivolginskiĭ datsan. Many social media users critically commented on the new heights of entanglement between Buddhism and the Kremlin—that Putin statuettes could be made at a datsan. Discussions of the statuette production also unleashed more general expressions of discontent with the Buddhist leadership: "Don't go to Ivolgniskiĭ datsan.... They have not been Buddhists there for a long time." "The Khambo Lama is a physical education teacher, who cannot read, write, or speak in Sanskrit, Tibetan, or Pali. And this is our 'everything'! How low has our 'Buryat' Buddhism degraded in the BTSR version. This is horrible!" Yet others criticized Ayusheev's hypocrisy, his foul language and behavior, or his business-mindedness.

In conversations with Buryats who had fled Russia for Ulaanbaatar, the depth of laypeople's disappointment in Buryat Buddhist leaders was evident. Buryat Buddhist layman Zhargal explained that he previously had mixed opinions toward the Khambo Lama: "Yes, he was doing a lot of weird stuff, befriending Putin, always going to Moscow, and all that. But he was also doing things locally; he seemed to have our interests at heart." After Ayusheev announced his support for the war, Zhargal was angry: "He is sending Buryats to die. And for what?! He is actually encouraging violence and death, and Buryatia will long suffer the consequences of this. This is treason. He is a traitor of the Buryat people." Another layman, Sanya, who had already been critical of Ayusheev said that this was "the ultimate drop that overfilled the glass." Sanya had hoped, despite his misgivings about him, that the Khambo Lama would have stayed silent—even this would have demonstrated sufficient resistance under the extreme pressure he must have been exposed to. To Sanya, Ayusheev's open support of the war proved that he was neither a real Buddhist nor a loyal Buryat but valued his own position above all else. My interlocutors contrasted Ayusheev to the leader of Kalmyk Buddhists at the time, Telo Tulku Rinpoche, who fled Russia in light of the full-scale invasion of Ukraine and was the first religious leader of Russia to speak out against the war in October 2022. A few months later, he was recognized in Russia as a "foreign agent" and stepped down from the official leadership of Kalmyk Buddhists. While this was a brave and moral deed, as many reflected, a public statement against the war also stripped him of his position of leadership and with it power in Russia and was thus also a controversial move.

Anthropologist Catherine Wanner (2018) has argued that the ambient presence of religion in postsocialist Eurasia has lent a strong moral authority to religious leaders. In contrast to political or economic actors, religious ones are deemed to be more virtuous and trustworthy. Together with the ambient presence of religion—or its spread, often unrecognized—in the public sphere in the region, this moral authority is especially potent in shaping people's views and behaviors. She argues: "At this critical juncture, when norms of gender, ethnicity, regionalism and language politics are being redefined, the ambient presence of religiosity makes political initiatives and political protest expressed in a religious idiom particularly effective. Religion has become a resource used to provide the moral justification for proposed norms of behavior and to legitimate the legal regulations and coercive mechanisms to enforce them" (Wanner 2018, 88).

The synergies between Buryat Buddhism and the Russian state described in this chapter are centuries in the making. They define the limits of engagement of the Buryat sangha and dictate its political positioning. They shape and are shaped by the strategies employed by Buryat Buddhist elites, such as centralization, and struggles for influence. Yet the Buryat sangha represents only a tiny religious minority in a large and diverse state, dominated by another ethnic and religious group. This synergy should not be seen as an exhaustive definition of Buryat Buddhism or of the whole of the sangha. Beyond official representations and stances lie everyday religion and its multiple participants, both professional and lay. They are also part of this religious ambience, and they partake in Wanner's "resource" of religion, directing it toward different social and political goals. Within these everyday practices, multiple tactics become visible, such as small acts of resistance to new political regimes or female leadership in "domesticated" religious forms. While the state-religion relationship affects these practices in very direct ways, it does not completely fill all the space of religious belief, expression, and agency in the region. It is this everyday religion in Ulan-Ude that is the focus of the next chapters.

3

URBAN BUDDHISM IN BURYATIA
Continuing Expansion Encounters
Fragile Diversity

The contemporary Buryat urban Buddhist milieu constitutes an important shift from its "traditional" rural setting. In this chapter, I delve into this contrast both descriptively, exploring what it consists of, and analytically, teasing out the broader implications of this shift. In what follows, I highlight three core elements of this rural-to-urban religious transformation, outlining the ways in which they challenge and reconfigure the local field of power and infrapolitics: changing religious topographies, diversity, and representation. The discussion in this chapter provides some background and the conceptual basis for an exploration of urban Buryat Buddhism, while in the two chapters that follow from it, I delve into the ethnographic detail of two important urban Buddhist practices: lay-lama interactions and acts of giving.

Rural Buddhism in Buryatia

Historically, monasteries in Buryatia—just like the Buryats themselves—were predominantly rural, although often small settlements would form around a monastery, some of which survive to this day while others have dissolved. This is also the case elsewhere in Asia, where many cities, such as Ulaanbaatar, have formed around Buddhist monasteries (Campi 2006). In Buryatia until the second half of the eighteenth century, Buddhist temples and the clans supporting them were nomadic and based in felt yurts rather than fixed buildings (Galdanova et al. 1983). Gradually, under the influence of the Russian administration, parish territories were established. In monasteries, there were staff lamas (Rus., *shtatnye*) who resided in monastery compounds and were supported by them, as well as unregistered, or steppe, lamas who were often related to the monastery but were not supported by it and resided outside of it, often with a family. This territorial parish system has in some ways been revived in the post-Soviet period by the Buddhist Traditional Sangha of Russia (BTSR), which has facilitated the rebuilding of most of the pre-1930s datsans. In addition, it and other organizations have built new temples both in the countryside and in the city.

Buryat Buddhism, as well as Buryat identity more broadly, is strongly associated with the rural milieu. Historical mobile Buddhist temples eventually settled to became focal points in the nomadic steppe, there serving as spiritual and "intellectual, social, cultural and medicinal centers for the population" (Sinitsyn 2013, 30–31). Through ritual and other means, these monasteries upheld relations with the surrounding landscape and its deities, which was seen to ensure people's well-being.

Concerns with taming, controlling, and harnessing the power of local spirits, deities, and other invisible nonhuman actors are commonplace in Buryat Buddhism. As in the Tibetan religious context (Mills 2003; Mumford 1989), in Buryatia, an

FIGURE 7. A rural Buddhist temple complex, Atsagatskiĭ datsan. The village of Atsagat is seen in the distance, 2015. Photo by author.

important source of religious authority, be it Buddhist or shamanic, stems from successful chthonic management. Relevant nonhuman beings are of multiple kinds, both threatening and benevolent. The knowledge of and concern with them varies greatly among Buryats today. Some, especially those who have strong links with the countryside, distinguish between several kinds of invisible nonhumans who require consideration and ritual care. Others simply have a vague idea that some invisible actors exist out there, without knowledge of the kinds of beings and their powers. While some regard these entities with utmost seriousness and caution, others talk of them in the tone of ghost stories that rely for their effect on mystery, humor, and only a hint of belief.[1]

The nonhumans that Buddhist lamas attempt to manage do not exist in an entirely separate realm and have direct effects on everyday life. They help people to attain various desired outcomes, such as healing, finding a partner, avoiding misfortunes, or making good business decisions. Conversely, if abandoned or angered, they may bring about problems and misfortunes, suck on one's life energies (Rus., *zhiznenye sily*), cause one's soul to leave the body (Rus., *dusha uletela*), and bring bad luck. In neighboring Mongolia, unruly and capricious spirits that were largely abandoned in the socialist period are seen by some as being at the root of the changeable fortunes since the 1990s. Attempts to bring them under control and resolve the social, economic, and other problems attendant to their neglect have contributed to the booming resurgence of shamanic (Buyandelger 2013; Pedersen 2011) and Buddhist rituals (Abrahms-Kavunenko 2018; Højer 2009).

Driving or walking outside of the city, one often carries coins, grain, or cigarettes to leave as offerings and thereby assure the mercy or favor of local spirits. *Oboo* and other rituals are held for the purpose of honoring and giving offerings to local spirits. People are often wary of taking unknown roads or simply walking around too much in the countryside, being concerned to avoid contact with local spirits—stories of lucky or tragic encounters with them abound. In the city, such concerns are less pertinent. Some believe that nature spirits still reside on some hills, river islands, creeks, and other landscape features in Ulan-Ude. These, however, are few, and they are not very well known. As local Buddhists told me, most spirits and deities of the landscape left the city a long time ago as the urban environment is ill-suited to their peaceful existence. Still, locals may avoid walking around hills and other patches of untamed nature in and around the city. Moreover, cemeteries are seen as especially dangerous as they overflow with untamed and lost spirits that can attach to a passerby and feed off their life energy, which may result in illness and misfortune.[2] Spirits of people who died an untimely death are understood to remain attached to their previous place of residence or that of their loved ones, thereby causing danger and sometimes harm.

While avoidance is one of the foremost strategies for dealing with these nonhuman actors, Buddhist and shamanic rituals are widely employed upon suspicion of spirit-inflicted adversities or to prevent them.

In contrast to rural datsans, the relationship between most urban temples and the surrounding landscape and its beings is not as pronounced, and they focus instead on more generic Vajrayana Buddhist khurals, such as those dedicated to the Buddha of medicine and healing (Ėkhė Otosho), the boddhisattva who protects and brings wealth (Namsaraĭ), or on the reading of the Golden Light Sutra that brings clarity and helps close a cycle of misfortunes (Altan Gėrėl). During these public services, lamas read out selected sutras to summon particular deities. While each of the khurals is different, the rituals typically involve purification of space and participants, offerings, conjuring protection and luck, and accruing merit to the participants, among other things. Only in some cases, for instance, in *zemliachestvo* temples related to a particular Buryat rural region, may an urban temple organize rituals such as oboo in the countryside.

Marian Burchardt and Irene Becci (2013) highlight that religious urbanization results in changing "topographies of faith." As religion takes spatial forms, particular characteristics of urban space, such as diversity, mobility, and density, reconfigure religious practices, beliefs, and institutions, resulting in new forms of religious spatialization. This might mean new religious sites, shifting hierarchies, novel translocal religious connections, and many other forms of religious change. With rapid urbanization in Suzhou, China, for instance, divine territoriality has been reconfigured, as local temples have been hemmed in due to the fast pace of urbanization (Goosseart 2015). These temples had been territorial and housed distinctly local deities integrated into the broader locality-based spiritual bureaucracy; they ruled over a certain area and protected its inhabitants, who paid taxes to this divine administration. As the city expands and villages are transformed into urban districts, such territorial temples close, and their deities are moved into bigger aggregate temples, which essentially become "divine housing estates" (Goosseart 2015, 53), thus largely shedding their relationship with the surrounding territories and their inhabitants. Another example of shifting topographies of faith may be found in postsocialist Bucharest; the largest Eastern Orthodox cathedral in the world to date was built to resacralize the city and recenter the national church, thereby reinscribing the sacred topographies of the region (Tateo 2020).

In a similar way, in post-Soviet Buryatia, the urbanization of Buddhism can also be understood as a shift in local religious topographies. New significant urban religious centers have emerged, while key rural monasteries of the past now struggle to attract lay interest and donations. Particular relations with the landscape lose relevance in the city, where the environment is largely taken to be neutral with concern to nonhuman life and religious significance. At the same time, novel and newly relevant religious practices emerge. One ethnographic episode exemplifies this especially well.

I was driving back to the city one evening with a retired Buryat engineer, Andrei, after a day trip to a remote temple. A devout Buddhist, Andrei was glad to use his professional expertise in helping rebuild several temples in Buryatia. Andrei's father was a pious Buddhist; in fact, he had lived in a monastery as a teenager and trained to become a monk before being disrobed and forced to lead a lay life by Soviet authorities in the 1930s. Coming from a religious background, Andrei wanted to contribute to the Buddhist revival. He used his skills as a distinguished (Rus., *zasluzhennyĭ*) Soviet engineer to do so, taking part in the rebuilding of temples and stupas.[3] As we entered the outskirts of the city from the hilly southern side, Andrei pointed to hilltop stupas he had built. When I asked him why those spots were chosen, he told me to simply look around as the landscape spoke for itself: hills, the river, woods, rocks, a cemetery nearby. This spot had been teeming with local spirits and other unruly nonhumans, and stupas and other Buddhist architecture and rituals tame such beings and, by extension, such places. What about the city itself? I wondered. Do these beings live there as well? Andrei was entertained by my question, and smirked with enjoyment at his own joking reply: "In the city, *chinovniki* [Rus., officials, bureaucrats] are the only dangerous spirits!"

The ways in which Buddhism helps to deal with daily struggles like the "spirit attacks" of urban officials is the focus of the next chapter. Below, however, I explore the ways in which urban Buddhism continues to draw from the efficacy and authority of its rural counterpart. The relationship between the two remains somewhat tense, and shifts in Buryat religious topographies and practices are not neutral, instead carrying the weight of moral, political, and broader cultural valuations.

Rural-Urban Tensions in Local Buddhism

Rural datsans in Buryatia today differ in size and prominence. Some struggle to survive with only a couple of lamas, while others count over a dozen. Lamas usually reside outside of the datsan compounds with their families and take turns staying in and maintaining the temples. Inhabitants of nearby villages, as well as urbanites visiting their home districts, form the core lay community of rural datsans. Some also attract outside visitors, as pilgrimage sites or prominent historical compounds. The abbot (Bur. and local Rus., *shiëëtë*; Rus., *nastoĭatel'*) is in charge of organizing and fundraising for the day-to-day running of his datsan, as well as bigger festivals and rituals a few times a year. Rural datsans rely heavily on the local lay community, although the arrangements vary. Several big rural datsans also have a small temple or lama office in a nearby town, where one lama on rotation consults clients and runs private rituals. He may give part of the income earned to his datsan, which, as I was told, constitutes a noteworthy income.

Despite the prominence of Buddhism in Ulan-Ude, its urbanization is an issue of local controversy. There is a general opinion in Buryatia that running a rural datsan is more demanding than running an urban one. Villagers are typically cash-poor and cannot contribute large donations. Rural lamas mentioned that they often have to encourage laypeople to donate. The Siberian climate is extremely harsh, and there is usually no central heating, running water, or sewerage system in villages. Under these conditions, a lot of work is needed just to keep the datsan running. Lamas have to get up early to fetch wood and heat the temple before the morning service, sometimes shoveling snow out of the way first to get to the temple. In addition, datsans are often remote and sometimes without telephone signal. Rural lamas often have to cover long distances to visit their lay parish, and since the reward for that is a donation, they can never be sure if it will even cover transport costs. Donations are occasionally made in kind. As a rural lama told me, lamas are constantly scrutinized by the watchful eye of the villagers, and word spreads quickly. Just one occasion of inappropriate behavior, such as heavy drinking, can ruin a reputation, depriving the lama of their main source of income. In contrast, urban lamas, when in casual wear, are not under the magnifying glass of a close-knit community. The fact that there are few opportunities for entertainment is itself often mentioned as an additional difficulty when living in the countryside as a lama.

Rural lamas proudly point out that it is a tradition in Buryatia to serve in one's "native" (Rus., *rodnoĭ*) datsan (i.e., in one's home district). In post-Soviet times, this usually means studying in one of the two Buddhist institutes in Russia (or sometimes Mongolia or India) and then returning to one's home datsan. However, more and more lamas are deciding to move to Ulan-Ude or to cities outside of Buryatia instead. Rural datsans nowadays struggle to sustain a viable number of lamas. One of the biggest datsans in pre-Soviet Buryatia, with over seven hundred lamas two centuries ago, could barely count five in the 2010s—none of whom resided there permanently. Another dominant monastery of pre-Soviet Buryatia, Baldan Breibun, also known as TSongol'skiĭ datsan, previously a significant center of Buddhism in the region with almost three hundred staff lamas and possibly as many unregistered ones, had around twelve lamas in the early 2000s, only some of whom resided there.[4] This still made it one of the strongest datsans in the region at that time (Batomunkuev et al. 2004).

The abbot of a small rural datsan, Lama Ayur, told me about his efforts to retain lamas at his datsan. He had given interest-free loans to young lamas to keep them from moving to the city, helped them start a sheep herd, transferred some of his own clients to them, and even provided some with bonuses in cash from his own pocket. This abbot was especially disadvantaged, as his datsan is located about ten kilometers down a dirt road from the nearest village, with no public transportation. This makes it difficult to access physically and renders it unattractive to young lamas. To remain a relevant part of local life, Lama Ayur has had to turn to creative means, extending well beyond the strictly religious realm. In fact, I first met him in Ulan-Ude, where he was running errands for the benefit of his local villagers. He was trying to find a physical education teacher to work in their area—the position had been vacant for a while. That, however, was only one of many things he had done for his community, including teaching agricultural techniques, providing seed potatoes, and helping locals navigate bureaucratic matters. The young lama had hoped to spread Buddhist teachings when he was initially selected to be the abbot of a newly rebuilt temple in his home district. He was expecting a spiritually rich life in a datsan, filled with religious teaching and an intensive individual practice. However, much of his time now is taken up by caring for the laity in other spheres of their lives. While initially he found this frustrating, he now sees such practical help as being necessary to sustain the Buddhist community.

Khambo Lama Ayusheev is a firm critic of urban Buddhism in Buryatia. To him, Buddhism, like the Buryats, is and should be traditionally rural, and so genuine, virtuous, and advanced lamas are only found in the countryside. The Khambo Lama himself clearly expressed this stance in my interview with him:

> KHAMBO LAMA: There are lamas who moved to the city of Ulan-Ude, yes? What kind of lamas went there? Those who could not live in their own datsan. What is this? Refugees, emigrants, what do you call them? What we had before, at all times in the development of Buddhism, which is three hundred years now, we had two types of lamas: staff [Rus., *shtatnye*] and steppe [Rus., *stepnye*]. Now staff lamas are those who sit in datsans, and steppe lamas are those who are in cities. That is why we don't respect them at all!
>
> KRISTINA: But steppe lamas can be, so to speak, advanced?
>
> KHAMBO LAMA: Of course not [waves his hand in dismissal, annoyed]! He ran away from his datsan after all! He could not bear it, we can say. Imagine a policeman, traffic police [Rus., *militsioner, GAIshnik*], yes, he worked, he stopped cars, and then he was dismissed from the police, yes? He will no longer stop cars!
>
> KRISTINA: Aha, yes.
>
> KHAMBO LAMA: Because the same policemen will put him to prison! And us here, we cannot punish anyone, he sat in a datsan and read

prayers, and now he reads prayers in the city. And so, Kristina, when you talk about this . . . You need to begin with this: always, at all times, before us and after us there is a concept: staff and steppe lamas. At present steppe lamas are called urban lamas [Rus., *gorodskie*]. So these people, who left their datsans for some sort of violations, for some sort of transgressions, their pride did not let them do what? Sit in the datsan and act by the rules. And considering the fact that datsans are based in rural settings, far away from people, there is no flow of people, not enough money, only a person who has a certain faith can tolerate these deprivations. A person who is weak in his spirit, a person who is greedy for money, where do they go?

KRISTINA: To the city?

KHAMBO LAMA: To the city. And you are writing... about them! [Laughs.]

The Khambo Lama went on to explain that the BTSR has one datsan in Ulan-Ude, Datsan na Verkhneĭ Berëzovke, but this is only because the project was started before his tenure and was blessed by the Dalai Lama, so he—and the BTSR that he runs—had to keep it to prevent unsanctioned urban lamas from taking it over. As Ayusheev claimed, he now allows only deserving lamas who have served a long time in a rural datsan to "retire" to the Ulan-Ude datsan, along with some young lamas who have returned from studying in India but do not want to move back to their native datsan.

The rural abbot from earlier, Lama Ayur, told me that when a lama decided to leave his datsan, he spread rumors about the departing lama to harm his reputation. Surprised to hear this, I double-checked to see if I had understood him correctly. Lama Ayur lowered his head bashfully and explained that he understands that this lama did it because the life of a rural lama is difficult and he had to support his family. But, he explained, he does his best to support them in the village, and if that does not work, the lama is a traitor. He does not respect his motherland and his native datsan, and a damaged reputation is what he deserves for that.

Remaining in one's village as a lama is perceived as both loyal and virtuous. Rural lamas are respected for their endurance of the financial and physical difficulties of a harsh rural life and for the assumed spiritual depth and purity that enables them to do so. They are seen as guardians and preservers of Buryat traditions who bravely bear their difficulties and prioritize the needs of their lay community and of the Buryats as a whole above their own comfort. Anya Bernstein (2013, 145–52) argues that a strong, stoical, and, importantly, male body is seen in Buryatia as an ideal "body for the dharma." I would add "rural" to this description. In contrast, urban lamas are often defined as weak and cowardly, and their migration to the city is often referred to as having "run away" (Rus., *ubezhali*), implying a rash and timorous action.

While a significant portion of urban lamas share Ayusheev's vision of virtuous and traditional rural Buddhism, it is not attainable to all be it for financial, logistical, or other reasons. A lama from a small urban temple serves as a good example. A skinny but athletic young man with cropped haired, a slightly distrustful expression, and a pair of trainers sticking out from underneath his maroon robe shared his professional biography with me. He had decided to become a lama following advice from his uncle, the head lama of a small temple, and so studied for several years in Ivolginskiĭ datsan. Unhappy and bored, he moved to St. Petersburg, where he then stayed for several years as a lama apprentice. Annoyed with, as he put it, the funny looks that he got for being an Asian in St. Petersburg, he moved back to Ulan-Ude, soon married, and has since worked in his uncle's temple. The young lama contended that it would indeed be great to live in a rural datsan and have time and peace for personal practice there. However, he reported, he will only be able to do that, if ever, when he becomes old and doesn't have to provide for his family anymore. For now, he has a demanding wife and a small child to come home to every day.

When temples and lamas move to an urban setting, it is not just their location that changes. Since datsans are seen by many to be not just religious institutions but also part and parcel of Buryat culture and traditions, and since these are predominantly associated with the countryside, the rise of urban temples and lamas since the 1990s has posed a challenge to the more conservative layers of Buryat Buddhism and inspired debates about the worthiness of urban lamas and institutions. Some religious actors in the city have attempted to tap into the authority of rural Buddhism. At the same time, there are also voices, especially from the urban laity and urban intelligentsia, that disagree with the reading of Buryat Buddhism as essentially rural, as I detail later. The different stances in the economy of virtue of urban Buddhism point not just to differing imaginaries of and for Buryat Buddhists but also to a complex moral economy of knowledge, ritual, wealth, and authority.

Rural Buddhism as Urban Resource

Despite the changing "topographies of faith" in Buryatia, the rural setting remains an important source of inspiration, authority, and efficacy. Because of this, much of urban Buddhism implicitly or explicitly draws from the rural roots of Buryat Buddhism to conjure power and legitimacy in the urban context. Perhaps the clearest example of this is *zemliachestvo* temples in the city. A zemliachestvo is a formal or informal network of people who come from the same district in the Buryat region. There are several temples in Ulan-Ude that are mainly funded and supported by such regional networks. These temples were established and are sustained by a core group of people from the same district of Buryatia (Rus., zemliaki), and many laypeople who attend these temples also come from the corresponding region, although they are typically open to outsiders, too. The abbot of a zemliachestvo temple is usually from the same region, and so are some but not all of the lamas who work there.

Even in temples that are not related to a particular regional network, it is quite common among laypeople to seek out a lama that is their *zemliak*. My interlocutor Gerelma from Kizhinga District invited me to join her for a consultation with a lama at the Datsan na Verkhneĭ Berëzovke. This is Gerelma's datsan of choice because it was the first one that she visited when she moved to Ulan-Ude some fifteen years ago. A newcomer to the city, she went to the biggest datsan and randomly went into one of the houses to see a lama. She liked him, and he also happened to be her *zemliak*, so she has continued to mostly turn to him for rituals and consultations. When she cannot find him at his usual desk, Gerelma also has two other lamas that she consults.

During our temple visit, Gerelma wanted to enliven a Buddhist icon, a *thangka*, she had bought, through a consecration ritual. As we walked around the temple, the first two lamas of her choice were not there. Gerelma decided to go to the third one, whom she had visited in the past but did not know so well. He was nonetheless very cordial and inquired about her family, even remembering the name of her son. After the consultation, we conversed with the lama about my research, and I asked him about his background, studies, and work. It came up in the conversation that he, like Gerelma, was from Kizhinga District. After leaving his office, Gerelma could not hide her wide smile; she was happy about the fact that he was also her zemliak. She had always liked him but never knew that they came from the same district. Perhaps their shared roots are in fact the reason why she liked him so much, she speculated. I asked Gerelma why sharing a home district with the lama was important to her, to which she replied that zemliaki were "closer to one's heart" (Rus., *blizhe k serdtsu*), and they understood her better. Connections with the land and social and cultural proximity appear to be important factors in maintaining the relevance of rural Buddhist links in the city.

Another important way of imbuing the urban Buddhist setting with rural Buddhist potency is through direct exchanges with the countryside by the consumption of its products. Milk, vodka, grain, and other products are abundantly used in ritual contexts in Buryat Buddhism. While, at least during my fieldwork, cheap imported goods were typically used, several local lamas and activists spoke to me about trying to reestablish local production so that local products could be used in ritual settings. According to my interlocutors, this would have several effects, one of them being that sacrifices would be more productive—surely local spirits would prefer local products. Another benefit would be that the profits would stay in the region and help to ensure its economic improvement. While at least one urban datsan shop was selling some regional products, like fermented milk vodka (Bur., *arkhi*), the effort was not widely known about or particularly popular among customers, likely because of its small scale and the higher prices than those of imported products in supermarkets.

Rural power was also channeled to the city through several popular advanced urban lamas who went to the countryside for extended periods to meditate and undertake retreats, only to come back to the city recharged. The calm and quiet, as well as the difficult physical conditions under which these retreats would take place, were deemed by my lay interlocutors to lend special power to these lamas. Such retreats in the wild would render these lamas ritually more powerful as well as draw renewed attention to their teachings. A popular tantric practitioner, Lama Amgalan, would disappear into the countryside for much of the summer. While this complicated the running of his small urban temple—khurals would often fail to take place according to schedule, and either a novice would consult with people in his stead or the temple would be closed for extended periods—many of his lay clients considered these unannounced, unpredictable retreats to be an important marker of the lama's advanced practice and power.

In the summer of 2016, I took part in an urban oboo ritual—perhaps the only one taking place within the confines of the city. Oboo rituals take place once a year, usually in June, and are dedicated to local spirits and deities. Oboo sites are distinguished by a heap of stones, and while similar rituals were conducted by shamans in the past, today they are often performed in Buryatia by lamas. Before the ritual began, the leading lama briefed the participants as to its significance. He explained that the hill on which it took place was a site of worship for the Buryats before the lands were seized by Russians and the Buryats were pushed out. "These lands have always been Buryat," the lama stated, and even though little is known about this oboo site, he explained that it was important to sustain the traditions of the Khori Buryat tribes that resided there before the Russians. The lama claimed continuity for the ritual, as some of the elderly laity performed it in secret during the Soviet period. This urban oboo ritual may be seen as part of the effort to "naturalize" Buddhism in the urban context, smoothly connecting the past and the present, and mark a direction for the future of urban Buryat Buddhism with deep historical roots.

The various practices described above aim to reshape the ostensibly religiously empty urban setting. Seen as essentially devoid of spiritual or supernatural power and historical resonance, the city is recoupled to Buryat religious histories and embedded within Buryat sociocultural networks. Discursive adjustments, ritual interventions, and practices of consumption selectively imbue the city with the

FIGURE 8. Urban *oboo* in Ulan-Ude, 2016. Photo by author.

power of rural Buddhism through reterritorialization. Lamas and laypeople creatively bridge the physical as well as symbolic distance between the rural places of power and convenient settings of everyday dwelling, drawing from the longstanding sources of power and efficacy to be found in rural Buddhist settings.

Such mediation between the city and the remote, rural or wild, sites of power is in fact far from unique among Buddhist contexts. In each case, it taps into and shapes local religiopolitical constellations. Notably, it is a key part of Thai Buddhism, where ascetic forest monks are seen by many to be especially reputable and powerful. As a consequence, while they often gain popularity among urban followers wishing to associate with their perceived sanctity, the state-supported Buddhist administration can also attempt to legitimize itself by piggybacking on their renown, establishing regular monastic structures on such sites of power and thereby spoiling the untouched and pure qualities that are the source of their efficacy (Taylor 1993). Early Indian Buddhism provides another example. As Greg Bailey and Ian Mabbett (2003) have argued, it was mediation between the city and the sources of power outside of it that ensured the popularity of early Buddhist monks, leading to the eventual expansion of Buddhism. Buddhist monks traveled extensively, spending time in remote settings as well as in communities on the peripheries of the expanding urban polities. At the same time, they were also expert in navigating the new urban centers native to many of their patrons. This very ability to navigate contrasting contexts, providing a spiritual and cultural bridge between them and transferring rural/wild powers to the urban setting, proved to be key to Buddhism's early spread. Such mediation was especially crucial given the political context of the time, where urban expansion was part and parcel of the increasingly centralized urban-based state, gradually incorporating rural areas into its purview. Like in Buryat Buddhism, rural and urban religious contexts are distinct in their sociopolitical constellations but are in a dialectical relationship mediated by the Buddhist sangha.

Caroline Humphrey (1999) has argued that urban shamanism in Buryatia in the 1990s performed the important work of imbuing the city, a Soviet secular space typically bereft of religious efficacy, with meaning and power through narratives and rituals. Urban shamans, she argues, "vitalize urban contexts by transmogrification, re-envisioning them in relation to other spaces and times, and turning them into sites of energy where social relations are re-fashioned" (4). This may mean conjuring powerful shamanic spirits in urban rituals or narrating mundane urban spaces like bus stops as sites of magical happenings. Ultimately, such acts relink the city with sites and sources of power more typical to Buryat shamanism and Buryat culture more generally, not just integrating the city into their framework but reworking the long-problematic urban-rural divide in Buryatia. In the 1990s, described by Humphrey, this occured at an important shift in urban-rural relations. Not long before, the city had often experienced shortages of food and other basics, and the countryside was the provider. In late Soviet and post-Soviet times, the city is fuller of necessary goods and resources, as dependency has shifted the other way. Today in Buryatia, the politico-economic scales remain tipped in favor of the urban, while the sources of power and historical strength of Buryat Buddhism lie, like with shamanism, in its rural surroundings. Urban Buryat Buddhism today accomplishes the important work of not just connecting the rural and the urban but, as Humphrey suggests in the above case, "re-calibrate[ing] the city in space and time; . . . re-chronologiz[ing] in relation to ancestral time" (5).

The continuing relevance of rural Buryat Buddhism is culturally and politically consequential. Traditional Buddhist institutions have long provided alternative sources of authority and community to those offered by the Russian state. Formerly key educational and cultural centers to nomadic Buryats, Buddhist institutions remain important and authoritative local institutions, despite centuries of persecution and undermining by the Russian and Soviet states. Not only is continuity with historical Buryat Buddhist sources of authority being creatively revived; it is also being imprinted onto the novel urban setting. More than this, as I have explored elsewhere (Jonutytė 2020c), the efforts of the Buryat sangha to reclaim the status and power of traditional rural Buryat lifestyles constitute a renegotiation of fields of religion and politics in contemporary Russia. This reclamation of traditional Buryat Buddhist sources of power and potency remains relevant in the city, where it is creatively connected to the new urban setting. As such, the changing religious topographies of Buryat Buddhism provide a fertile infrapolitical field.

Diverse Sources of Power in Urban Buddhism

Not all Buryat Buddhists subscribe to the vision of the countryside as an idealized source of power and inspiration. The urban context provides an alternative vision for Buryat Buddhism in the contemporary period, especially among the urban Buryat intelligentsia, which is often critical of the BTSR, and among some lay groups. As one prominent Buryat lama succinctly put it when talking about the Buddhism propagated by the BTSR: "It is all becoming some sort of a Soviet collective farm [*kolkhoz*]. . . . Clearly too crude! [*Grubovato, konechno*]." He invoked the negative, overly pragmatic connotations of Soviet collective farms to contrast with the more spiritual and religious pursuit that Buddhist institutions should, in his opinion, pursue, independent of the Buryat countryside. A vocal critic of the BTSR, he stressed the fact that he had invited highly esteemed Tibetan monks and incarnate lamas to Buryatia and that, as rural datsans do not do the same, Buddhism does not prosper there. Another urban lama echoed a widespread sentiment when, in an interview, he argued that the "dark" countryside was fast degrading due to joblessness and alcoholism and claimed that Ulan-Ude is the only place where there is still hope that Buryat Buddhism will really revive. As we spoke in the mid-2010s, he pointed to the Buryat-language courses that were organized in the city, a new Mongolian art gallery, public Buddhist lectures, and young urban Buryat intellectuals as proof that the future of Buryat culture—and Buddhism—is in fact located in Ulan-Ude.

While the Buddhist scene in Ulan-Ude is constantly changing, in the 2010s there were approximately a dozen prominent Buddhist datsans dotting the cityscape both near the city center and on the outskirts. There were also at least several dozen inconspicuous, smaller temples and lama offices spread across the city. In addition to datsans, individual temples, and self-employed lamas, there are also international and local lay organizations, as well as loosely structured lay groups that assemble for the teachings of a specific lama. There are several Tibetan temples, opened and run by Tibetan lamas, some of them hosting local Buryat lamas as well. Both the international organizations and the Tibetan temples are somewhat marginalized in the hegemonic Buryat Buddhist milieu

FIGURE 9. A small Buddhist temple in Ulan-Ude's old town, 2016. Photo by author.

where isolationist tendencies prevail in line with broader political trends in Russia. Despite this marginalization in the discursive and political fields, they find ample followers in the diverse and populous urban religious scene where, despite surface appearances, not all subscribe to the official line of BTSR religiopolitics.

Similarly marginalized from Buryat Buddhist orthodoxy, there is also one "female" datsan (Rus., *zhenskiĭ datsan*), Zungon Darzhaling, in Ulan-Ude, the only Buddhist temple in Buryatia where female lamas work.[5] It was opened following the advice of the Fourteenth Dalai Lama during his visit to Buryatia in 1992 and with the help of India's ambassador to Mongolia, the Nineteenth Kushok Bakula Rinpoche. The temple was opened in 2000 and has since been run by Buryat and Mongolian female lamas, usually only a few at any one time. The temple is evidently not one of the more popular or wealthy ones in the city, but it does have its circle of lay followers. Some of my interlocutors chose to frequent this temple and claimed that female lamas may even possess superior insight for divination due to their higher empathy and intuition. Many Buddhists, however, look down on female practitioners as unorthodox and therefore suspicious.

This is hardly surprising, given the masculinist and often sexist attitudes of some Buryat lamas, most notably the Khambo Lama. He has claimed, for instance, that the greater female presence in Buddhist temples is a "tragedy" and has argued that, "from the Buddhist point of view, if a woman has five children, she is going to paradise. . . . This has been the great value of women since time immemorial" (Bernstein 2013, 148), contrasting this to more arduous requirements for male Buddhists.

In the religious market of Ulan-Ude, Buddhist institutions and actors coexist with other religious professionals, including shamanic specialists, Russian traditional healers (Rus., *babki*), and priests of various branches of Christianity. Religious practice is often eclectic, and a layperson may turn to several religious professionals of the same or of different religious traditions with the same issue. There is a general sentiment that seeing several specialists "will do no harm" (Rus., *khuzhe ne budet*), and while some religious professionals criticize such an eclectic approach, others are tolerant or even supportive of it. Among the many Buddhist lamas in the city one would perhaps expect competition. However, while lamas sometimes speak critically of other temples or members of the sangha, there is little outright contest and disparagement or attempts to poach clients.

This diverse Buddhist milieu has gradually emerged in the city since the late 1980s. The most prominent Ulan-Ude Buddhist centers are Ivolginskiĭ datsan, Rinpoche Bagsha datsan, and Datsan na Verkhneĭ Berëzovke. Ivolginskiĭ datsan was built in 1948 and has since been considered by many to be the focal point of Buddhism in Buryatia. The residence of the Khambo Lama is located in a humble wooden house within the datsan compound. Even though it is located some thirty kilometers outside of the city, most locals still consider it an essential part of the Ulan-Ude Buddhist milieu. In contrast, Rinpoche Bagsha datsan looks over the city from a high and prominent hill. In addition to being highly visible, many locals value it for the surrounding greenery, which lends itself to weekend outings, as well as for the lavish and impressive architecture. This datsan was established in 2000 by a Tibetan lama, Yelo Rinpoche, who is very highly regarded as an incarnate lama and a celibate, well-educated Tibetan monk. The third urban Buddhist center is Khambyn Khurė datsan, better known locally as Datsan na Verkhneĭ Berëzovke. It was established in 1994 as the urban datsan of the BTSR, now well attended by locals and tourists alike. The latter two datsans were initially built on the outskirts of Ulan-Ude, but fast-paced urbanization has caught up with them and absorbed them into the city, if its greener and quieter parts. Not least, this happened because of the infrastructural extensions built for the datsans, including electricity, sewage, and public transportation.

Apart from the several prominent Orthodox churches and Buddhist temples scattered throughout the city, the lively religious scene of Ulan-Ude is not immediately obvious to an outside observer. The Christian churches are mostly located more centrally, while the bigger and more visible Buddhist temples are rather on the outskirts of town. Other than these few outstanding temples, one has to pay close attention to notice most religious spaces in the city, tucked away in regular buildings, often away from busy streets, with only a small signboard to distinguish them, if that. While these temples are open to all and do entice one-off random visits, they typically attract a clientele that learns about them either through finding them located close to their home or workplace, through seeking out a particular lama, or through a recommendation. Many small temples and lama offices are only partly accessible not just because of invisibility but also due to their location in parts of town avoided by outsiders, be it because of their reputation of high crime rates, distant location, or disorienting space of unauthorized settlements.

In these and other urban Buddhist settings, beliefs and practices associated with "traditional" Buryat Buddhism mix with "modernist" influences. As David McMahan puts it, a "modernist" trend in Buddhism has become especially prominent outside historically Buddhist regions and among the educated middle class in Asia. It "involves fewer rituals, deemphasizes the miracles and supernatural events depicted in Buddhist literature, disposes of or reinterprets image worship, and stresses compatibility with scientific, humanistic, and democratic ideals" (McMahan 2008, 5). Perhaps the best-known example of this trend is what Richard Gombrich and Gananath Obeyesekere (1990) explored as a "Protestant Buddhism" movement in Ceylon at the turn of the nineteenth century, led by Anagārika Dharmapāla. They argue that it emerged in a colonial dialectic, wherein the relevance and value of Buddhism had to be proven to both the British regime and to the educated middle classes who were turning to Christianity. Not only Dharmapāla's movement but also similar ones elsewhere have been extremely influential in rethinking what Buddhism is and should be and have fed into the understanding and practice of Buddhism worldwide.

In postsocialist settings, researchers have drawn attention to two strands of Buddhist activity, adhering broadly to the lines of "traditional" and "modernist" (Abrahms-Kavunenko 2012; Elverskog 2006; Sinclair 2008). Such trends are also recognized locally in Buryatia, one being "traditional" (Rus., *traditsionnye*) Buddhists and the other variously referred to as "neophyte" (Rus., *neofity*), "Buddicising" (Rus., *buddanutye*), and "fanatical" (Rus., *fanatichnye*), among other terms. Given the context of Vajrayana Buddhism in the region, these active, modernist-leaning lay Buddhists are usually aspiring practitioners of tantra. While a division of lay Buddhists into two groups may initially seem applicable in Buryatia as well, I often found the two trends hardly separable and more present as leanings or layers of belief and practice than as two distinct groups of people.[6] I want to convey some of this complexity through brief biographies of two urban Buddhists.

A laywoman in her forties, Sesegma grew up in a Buryat village in a mountainous southwestern region where both Buddhism and shamanism are widespread. She comes from a family living on a collective farm that was not particularly religious but who tried to preserve Buryat traditions, including the occasional, although rare, shamanic ritual. Sesegma rarely took part in these as a child, since her parents wanted to protect her from the potential trouble with officials that religious practice might bring. As a consequence, religion played a very minor role in her life up until the early 2000s when the Buddhist revival was already well underway. Having moved to Ulan-Ude by then, she frequented Buddhist temples with her colleagues and at one point regularly visited lectures given by a popular Tibetan lama, Geshe Jampa Tinlay, as well as those by the Tibetan Yelo Rinpoche. While she attempted to deepen her understanding of Buddhism and even accepted tantric vows at one point, she only sustained this intensive practice for a short period. Since then, she has only turned to Buddhism, as she put it, "when in need," which involves consulting lamas and visiting temples mostly when asking for divine help. More recently, as she narrated, she started relying on herself more than on divine support, since this constitutes a more "correct" form of Buddhism compared to the "utilitarian" form that she had been practicing.

Sesegma's religious practice changed further over recent years due to her marriage to a Shènèkhèn Buryat (Rus., *shènèkhenskiĭ burĭat*) man from Inner Mongolia, a descendant of Buryats who had fled Russia in the early twentieth century. Through private and collective rituals, as well as donations to temple building and other Buddhist causes, she has entered a religious milieu somewhat different from her previous one. Her religious ties have become bound more strongly with those of Shènèkhèn Buryat Buddhists, including temple visits to Sesegma's husband's home region in China. Since Shènèkhèn Buryats are typically considered more traditional, she has had to immerse herself in a more conservative religious setting, as compared to her previously eclectic urban Buddhist practice. At the same time, due to her roots in one of the mountainous regions in southwestern Buryatia where shamanism prevails over Buddhism, she continues to occasionally attend shamanic rituals.

A layman in his mid-forties, Rinchin grew up in a Buryat Buddhist family in the remote northern region where his parents worked. Few Buryats lived there, as this district is historically inhabited by the Evenki minority. A mix of ethnicities was present in the area because of their involvement with the building of the Baikal-Amur branch of the Trans-Siberian Railway line, as well as resource extraction. Upon finishing high school, Rinchin moved to Ulan-Ude to study. After graduating from the university, he stayed on, with religion playing only a marginal role in his life. As he reflects, this was in large part because of his atheist upbringing by Soviet-educated parents in a Buryat-minority region. Now he is an active Buddhist layperson, while his brother is studying to become a lama.

Following his move to Ulan-Ude, he sometimes attended Buddhist rituals in the company of his parents and later his wife, and he enjoyed them but did not understand much of what was happening. He was always curious as to what all the beautiful sights and prayers in temples might mean but was ignored or sent away by lamas when he tried to "dig deeper." To learn more, he would occasionally read articles about Buddhism and engage teachings on the internet. Later he came across a lay Buddhist group in Ulan-Ude, which he subsequently joined. While the lay group is international, and their practices and ideas are quite different from traditional Buryat Buddhism, he sees the two as complementing each other.

Some members of the lay group feel strongly about the superiority of their practice compared to that of most Buryat Buddhists. After all, they have consciously selected to practice this style of Buddhism; they read books on Buddhism, listen to lectures, go on retreats, and meditate. Many, if not most, of the members of this Ulan-Ude group are not Buryat. Nonetheless, Rinchin continues to firmly identify with traditional Buddhism and sees the lay group as helping him practice it better. He does not draw a clear boundary between the two kinds of Buddhism—the traditional Buryat one and the international lay group—and explains that lamas in Buryatia are not very knowledgeable today due to the Soviet repression of Buddhism. He insists that the situation is getting better, and soon Buryat lamas, especially those who have studied in Tibetan monasteries in India, will be better able to explain Buddhist philosophy to people like him. He sees his own quest for answers as being somewhat unusual among the laity but does not feel that other lay Buddhists should necessarily bother themselves with it unless they feel the need.

These are just two of the many complex religious biographies of Buryat Buddhists in Ulan-Ude. They point to the ways in which the religious lives of post-Soviet Ulan-Udensians cannot be exhaustively determined by categories like "traditional" and "modernist," "Buddhist" and "atheist." Sesegma and Rinchin pick and choose, try and change, and even simultaneously partake in what would seem to be very different religious settings. Their religious orientation changes over their lifetimes. In contemporary Buryat Buddhism, categories intertwine and cojoin in an eclectic religious milieu. It has been argued that urban religion moves "from ethnics to ethics," or from ethnicity-based belonging to that relying on universal ethical propositions (Blom Hansen 2005, 375). The Buryat case complicates this picture, both with the continuing relevance of the "ethnic" part of religion and with the entwinement of the "ethnic/traditional" and "ethical/

FIGURE 10. A khural at Datsan na Verkhneĭ Berëzovke, 2019. Photo by author.

modernist" strands. In a society marked by rupture and facing ongoing Russification, an alternative authority rooted in the past remains an important resource in maintaining a distinct identity and establishing legitimacy today. At the same time, the social and religious diversity of the city has opened up space for alternative religiopolitical constellations in Buryat Buddhism, where parochial, conservative, and isolationist tendencies are challenged by alternative sources of authority and power, be they transnational, unorthodox, or otherwise divergent.

Buddhism and Urban Aspirations

Peter van der Veer (2015) has argued that urban aspirations are an important part of urbanity, yet they remain underexplored in the social sciences because of the often materialistic focus of urban studies. It is not just the concrete present setting that defines our worlds and experiences but also our aspirations, hopes, desires, and efforts for a particular kind of future. Such emphasis on the would-be, van der Veer (2015, 3) claims, "does not distract from the materialities of social life but rather allows us to consider the material effects of social imagination." In addition, it destabilizes the seemingly static conception of identity. To van der

Veer, religion is a key lens through which to view urban aspirations, as it shapes personhood and social imaginaries in significant ways. The intertwinement of religion with urban aspirations is clearly visible, for instance, in the bazaars of Dushanbe, where Islam provides an important resource in attaining moral and virtuous personhood working toward a financially and spiritually prosperous future (Stephan-Emmrich and Mirzoev 2016).

Cities are often sites of hopes and desires, in particular, of opportunities for a better future, be it wealthier, more comfortable, more virtuous, or more intense and exciting. Around the world, urban migration is fueled by these aspirations. Yet urban migrants often find a disappointing reality in cities rather than endless opportunities they desired. Be it in Astana (Laszczkowski 2011) or Hanoi (Karis 2013), high expectations of urban well-being are met with inadequate infrastructure, social and economic inequalities, second-class citizenship, and the burden of relocation costs, both financial and otherwise. This is especially so in post-Soviet and more broadly postsocialist contexts, where the city is a key site both symbolically and economically of the promise of progress and desirable modernity, largely unfulfilled (Collier 2011; Rubin 2016; Schwenkel 2015).

In Buryatia, too, the city remains an important site where urban aspirations meet limited opportunities in real life. Many urban migrants hardly find the better future they are looking for in the capital city. Often the poorer newcomers settle in the further removed outskirts of the city, sometimes in illegal settlements (*nakhalovki*). In most cases, urban migration in the region is economically driven, and its outcomes are mixed (Breslavsky 2014). Newcomers tend to find jobs and material conditions that may be less than desirable, and the suburbs have few comforts, just like village housing. At the same time, the city offers better social services, especially in medicine and education, as well as opportunities for consumption and leisure. While religion may seem marginal to these urban aspirations, it is often intertwined with urban migration and everyday life.

For instance, the Zhamsanov family moved to Ulan-Ude from Aginskoe in search of better educational and career opportunities. After Aga-Buryat Okrug was merged with Zabaykalsky Krai, the region had a lot less to offer economically than before. However, the move was more difficult than they had anticipated—the father could not find a job with sufficient pay for the family to get by, and rent was more expensive than they had anticipated. In Ulan-Ude, the mother visited three different lamas and shamans to conjure some luck in establishing themselves in the city and figure out the source of their misfortunes. The search was exhausting, and she was struck and somewhat amused by the eclecticism of the urban religious field: one lama she saw required her to bring RUB 3,333 to pay for the ritual. She was told the number itself would add to its efficacy. Since these interventions did not seem to improve the situation, the father went back to Aginskoe to see their family's regular lama about this problem. He established that the time and direction for the move had been inauspicious and ritually removed obstacles for their further undertakings. The family was hopeful that things would get better after this visit, and weeks later, they continued to feel positive about their future in Ulan-Ude. As such, religion continues to provide an important resource, guiding and helping to fulfill the urban aspirations of contemporary Buryats.

It would, however, be incorrect to see religion merely as a coping mechanism for addressing urban problems. Certainly, the city is today the site where most Buryat Buddhists reside, and they do regularly turn to religious resources for everyday problem-solving. Yet beyond that, religion is at the core of pursuing a meaningful and prosperous living in the city. In this, it provides an alternative not just to the otherwise powerful Soviet secular modernity project but also to idealized imaginaries of traditional pre-Soviet Buryat life, as well as to current Russo-centric mainstream visions of the good life in the city. It is in settings like Buddhist consultations, discussed in the next chapter, that the role of religion in urban aspirations is clearly visible on the individual level, where Buddhist ethics and rituals mold the agentival capacities of local Buddhists. On a larger scale, Buddhism becomes crucial in negotiating and asserting group urban aspirations through visions of equality and fair representation in the city, as I outline in what follows. In these cases and many others, Buddhism plays a key role in urban aspirations and their pursuits rather than playing an ornamental role to the seemingly more concrete materialities of the city.

Urban Buddhism and "Normal Human Needs"

In Buryatia, many Buddhists consider temples, the religious expertise within them, and other components of the Buddhist revival to be essential religious infrastructure that should be available to all. Many locals see this as indispensable and as something that both personal and collective well-being hinges upon. Some of my interlocutors reflected that temples are a necessity, and so they—like hospitals and schools—should be built in every district of the city to be easily accessible to all urbanites. One interlocutor, for instance, compared Buddhist temples with their religious facilities to public toilets. In her view, they are necessary in order to meet "normal human needs" (Rus., *normal'naia chelovecheskaia potrebnost'*) and should therefore be widely available to all. Part of the "normal human needs" in the Buryat context is the management of divine and supramundane presences and the ensuring of their benevolence, as discussed earlier. In addition, public and private ritual services provided in Buddhist temples ensure divine support in particular areas of life (health, education, etc.) depending on the khural, as well as generating blessings and producing merit for individuals and the wider community, up to and including all sentient beings.

An equally important "normal human need" temples provide is access to Buddhist counseling. This is a kind of conversational and ritual individual support that lamas provide for the laity, which is usually reimbursed by a donation. Lay Buddhists always leave money for these consultations, as some put it, "as a sign of gratitude," "to thank for their work and knowledge," "because he spent time and effort on me," or for other similar reasons, but stressed that this was not mandatory. As one interlocutor put it, "Imagine if someone is really run down and has no one to turn to and no money left. This might be his last resort, and it might actually help him. So, they should be entitled to this help from a lama whether they have money or not. And when they do, when they've stood back up on their feet, then they can give back."

Buddhist counseling in Ulan-Ude is seen as a vital resource for those who are down-and-out, with no one else to turn to but a religious specialist. Consultations must be available to them as a last resort, an essential infrastructure in an uncertain and often rough urban life. This is why, although many insist one does not have to give money for a consultation, they always do—it is both a local relational "enactment" (Sneath 2006), an appropriate form, and a way to contribute to the existence and continuation of this religious infrastructure of help for those in need.

Such solidarity is unsurprising in a region where the lives of many have been shaped by precarity and uncertainty. These difficult experiences of the post-Soviet transition are still fresh in people's memories. In addition, political-economic crises appear to be a constant in Russia over recent years, exacerbated by its increasing isolation and militarization. People still in Buryatia and those who have recently left speak of a newly booming religious market in Ulan-Ude since the start of the full-scale war in Ukraine, as people seek support in the highly fraught social, political, and economic situation that is today's Russia (Namsaraeva 2024, 139). In this context, the need to maintain the possibility of a last spiritual retreat is a sign of acutely felt solidarity.

Who is responsible for maintaining this infrastructure that supports "normal human needs"? This is where the political potentialities of urban religion become especially visible. Many of my interlocutors felt that it was the responsibility of the state to ensure that temples and lamas are sufficiently supported. They reflected on the issue of rebuilding Buddhism, comparing it with Orthodox Christianity: Since so many Christian churches have been rebuilt in Russia, many sponsored by the state, Buddhist temples should be accorded the same consideration. In a multiethnic and multireligious formally secular state—where Orthodox Christianity nonetheless entertains close relations to state powers (Richters 2013)—seeing to the equality of religious infrastructure is recognized by many as a way of ensuring peaceful coexistence between the different religio-ethnic groups.

Despite this expectation of a caring state, providing equally for all its citizens, the reality on the ground is quite different. It appears that the state does not support Buddhist infrastructure and, more than that, in some ways even creates obstacles for it to appear. While municipal authorities have provided land for some Buddhist temples, I have not heard of cases where the construction or maintenance of urban temples or other Buddhist structures was supported by the state. Temple building is usually funded by donation, either by wealthy sponsors or through mass collection drives soliciting small contributions. This form of funding is typical throughout the Buddhist world, as donations to temple building are prominent sources of merit making. Through donations for temple construction and maintenance, laypeople in Buryatia, as elsewhere in the Buddhist world (Abrahms-Kavunenko 2015; Bowie 1998; Heim 2004; Sihlé 2015), seek to act meritoriously in a number of domains: accruing merit, contributing to their communities, and developing as Buddhists through the practice of generosity.

Lama Samdan, a prominent Ulan-Ude lama, initiated the construction of a large Buddhist prayer wheel (Bur., *khurdė*) in the city center (Jonutytė 2022). He had seen similar religio-ethnic interventions into urban space in Elista, the capital of the Buddhist region of Kalmykia in southwestern Russia, as well as abroad. They left a lasting impression on him, and upon return to Ulan-Ude after monastic studies in India, he initiated a similar project of religious beautification for the city. The aim was twofold. The lama sought to improve the karma of the city and its inhabitants through the prayer wheel as a religious device. Once turned, it would produce merit for individuals and communities in the city. This was seen as a much-needed intervention in a city with a complex history, represented in the environs of the proposed location of the prayer wheel by a Second World War memorial and a cemetery rumored to host the remains of victims of Soviet repressions. Yet the prayer wheel would also represent a Buryat Buddhist presence in a city that otherwise remains a space architecturally and monumentally like many others in Russia.

As Lama Samdan explained:

> I thought, something is lacking here. . . . You look elsewhere in Russia, all cities are analogous: dilapidated, factories are closed, dismantled and suchlike. And then I was lucky enough to go to Kalmykia [a Buddhist region in the European part of Russia], Elista [its capital]. And there I saw City Chess [a large, expensive complex built for chess competitions] that creates a good mood in the city. In the city center—and they live in

the West—all beautiful colors of Buddhism: pagodas, pavilions. Oh, I was inspired by that; my soul was touched.

Other volunteers with the *khurdė* project agreed. One participant told me she wanted a Buddhist prayer wheel in the city center because it would beautify the city and make it look more Buryat. She was embarrassed in front of visiting Mongolians who saw Buryats as Russified and Ulan-Ude as a largely Russian city, compared to the visibility of Mongolian material culture in Ulaanbaatar. Another volunteer shared with me that she was excited about the prayer wheel beautifying her home city and looked forward to recognition from her friends and family, with whom she planned to share her contribution in a picture on social media of the opening ceremony.

The khurdė initiative ended up being fully organized, financed, and executed by the lama and lay Buddhist volunteers who also did most of the manual labor. While the local government at times led the organizers to believe that some money would be allocated from funds for tourism-related activities or as part of the Altargana all-Buryat festival organized in Ulan-Ude in 2016, the promises were never acted on and the khurdė ended up as a "people's project" (Rus., *narodnoe stroitel'stvo*), a colloquial term implying that it was financed and executed with-

FIGURE 11. The completed prayer wheel in front of the Buryat Drama Theater, Ulan-Ude, 2019. Photo by author.

out official support. Money was collected through donation boxes in temples, during Buddhist lectures, and in several other spots, such as the Buryat drama theater. The lama himself also went around to institutions and offices gathering donations. As another participant stressed after weeks of intensive fundraising, this prayer wheel was especially "of the people" (Rus., *narodnoe*) because the rich businessmen did not contribute to the project as much as expected. He said that they would complain about the economic crisis, give RUB 1,000, and feel as if they had contributed a lot while some common people donated as much as RUB 5,000 and helped with manual labor. These comments point to morally laden judgments concerning proportionate contribution to a collective cause.

Fragile Diversity: Religion, Ethnicity, and Representation

Unexpectedly, a local Russian Cossack, Pavel, with whom I discussed the prayer wheel, also stressed the importance of the fact that it was a "people's project." So would be their long-awaited memorial statue to the Cossack founders of the city. At the time of our conversation in 2016, the project had finally received authorization, albeit not in the location of the original Cossack outpost, in slightly modified form, and without official funding.[7] Pavel, an active member in the local community, saw this as a blessing rather than a curse. He explained that memorials initiated from above are of no interest to people; they are not, in his words, "alive." In contrast, when people contribute to a project financially or otherwise, they genuinely care about it and support it, and fundraising is also a good opportunity to popularize the project. While the Cossacks spreading the word about the memorial is also a way to propagate their long-awaited victory in the battle over memory and heritage, the Buddhist khurdė constitutes a similar, albeit locally less controversial, struggle over representation in the city and its material makeup. The difficulties encountered in the project brought Buddhists together to overcome bureaucratic barriers, lack of funds, long hours of manual labor, and repeated delays of the opening ceremony. To the relief of many participants, the prayer wheel was unveiled in October 2016, complete with a ritual of sanctification, a yoga session, a buffet reception, and the handing of diplomas to those that contributed the most.

Meanwhile, the Cossack people's project continued to struggle through societal, bureaucratic, and political resistance. The struggle for the memorial started in 1991, when the local Cossack group expressed a wish for such a memorial.[8] It met with firm resistance from a significant portion of Ulan-Ude's urbanites. As in essence a monument to the colonization of the region, it represents a problematic heritage to many Buryats. Despite the fact that the colonization of Buryatia is presented as a peaceful and voluntary incorporation in Russia's official narratives, historians highlight its less publicly touted violent nature, with numerous deaths, plentiful violence, and substantial local resistance (Chimitdorzhiev 2001; Forsyth 1992; Sablin 2017; Schorkowitz 2001b). The monument therefore met numerous rounds of resistance and for many years did not materialize amid the cityscape of Ulan-Ude.

All this changed in November 2022. A memorial to one of the Cossack founders of the city, Gavril Lovtsov, was erected on the grounds of a private museum. The local media credits a local businessman and the founder of the only private museum in Buryatia, Lev Bardamov, with the initiative. The monument stands within the compound of the museum, in front of a reconstructed Cossack outpost, including a tower and a fragment of the wall. The monument portrays a Cossack state servant in an old caftan, with a firearm in one hand and an axe in the other, standing on a pedestal reminiscent of a large rock. He gazes into the distance, presumably surveying the lands yet to be conquered. A carving on the pedestal reads: "To the founder of Verkhneudinsk Gavril Lovtsov." An antique cannon in a wheeled carriage stands next to the monument.

The long-desired Cossack monument has thus found a place in the city—if far removed from the people's project vision. A controversial memorial successfully kept out of public space for three decades by Buryat activists quickly and quietly found its place on private museum land while more pressing issues were shaking the region in 2022. Fenceless and freely accessible, however, it is visually reminiscent of any other public monument in the city. The seemingly smooth emergence of the new monument became possible through the deliberate delineation of the boundaries of the purview of the state. The state here delegated a controversial political issue to being a distinctly private matter for the museum. Both the seemingly successful boundary work of the state and the tense political moment during which it appeared prevented public discontent.

In contrast, the Buddhist khurdė did receive a spot in a relatively prominent public space, if not the one originally chosen by its proponents. They initially wanted to build the prayer wheel by the Second World War memorial, next to an imposing tank from the period. The local government, however, denied this request. Rumors have it that they found a Buryat Buddhist intervention inappropriate at this sensitive memorial site and eventually agreed to a more "appropriate" spot in front of the Buryat drama theater. One of the contributors to the prayer wheel explained that the already existing Buryat character of the place determined the approval of this location. While Buryat cultural and religious expressions must have a place in the city, they also have to be contained. Containing the potential spillage of Buryat spaces into Russian or Soviet ones, like the Second World War memorial site, emerges as a way of managing diversity in multiethnic Ulan-Ude. The post-Soviet city thus appears to be akin to a "communal apartment" (Jonutytė 2022), wherein each ethnic group has a room, or a designated space, of its own. A sort of equality is seemingly upheld, but so is boundary work, ensuring the appropriate placement and reach of the identity politics of the permitted groups.

The fact that the Buryat monument received public space in the city center while the Russian one did not may appear counterintuitive, considering that ethnic minorities are deemed a "security threat" (Prina 2021) in Putin's Russia and given the long-term tendency of Russification in the country. However, this outcome confirms Federica Prina's (2018) suggestion that "cultural" institutions appear in Russia to be removed from the political sphere, despite the actual intertwinement of the two (see also Stewart 2023; Yusupova 2021). Moreover, religious expression is a particularly sensitive field in Russia, with "offence to the rights of believers" (Rus., *oskorblenie chuvstv veruîushchikh*) considered a violation under the Russian criminal code and official discourse highlighting the proudly multireligious character of the country. In contrast, the Cossack monument, without directly addressing politics, references a controversial, violent aspect of the region's past. Even in contemporary Russia, bringing the controversy over the colonial past and present of the region into public space may have involved walking on a little too thin ice, so the yard of a private museum must have appeared a permissible compromise. Here, again, urban Buddhist contributions emerge as an important infrapolitical force, combining ethnic and religious appeals to minority representation and visibility in a diverse setting.

Religious interventions into urban space are a prominent—and controversial—issue in many contemporary cities. Novel religious interjections are especially contentious in ethnically and religiously diverse contexts. In the postsocialist context, there is often an unresolved tension between the largely secular urban space and the newfound urgency for religious representation. During over three decades of religious "de-privatisation" (Hann 2000), both new and repurposed religious spaces have mushroomed in postsocialist cities. In this process, they have met with contestation and resistance from various groups, including urban planners, atheists, and others. While in some postsocialist cities, like Bucharest, majestic new churches demonstrate the unassailable domination of the majority religious group (Tateo 2020), in others, like Yoshkar-Ola, in Russia's Middle Volga region, minority religious groups retreat to "recycling" and appropriating existing spaces (Luehrmann 2005). They repurpose old nonreligious buildings like cinemas to be able to gather and practice religion and thereby avoid standing out and attracting unwanted attention.

Gareth Fisher (2008) discusses temple building in contemporary China, where monks and nuns travel across the country and abroad to collect donations for the establishment of new temples. These temples "become a powerful outward symbol of the religious community" of Buddhists and are "a powerful testament to the efficacy and rightness of the practitioner's belief in a country where Buddhism—and religious practice in general—is still often criticised" (Fisher 2008, 148). In Chinese cities, Buddhist temples constitute "islands of religion" (Fisher 2014, 204): While religious expressions, including sanctioned minority ones, are allowed to take place within the clearly defined bounds of urban temples, churches, and other religious structures, they must not spill out either spatially or socially. Since religion does provide a socially productive field of critical engagement with the "moral breakdown" of contemporary Chinese society, politics, and economics, the state attempts to keep all its public expressions contained and manages to avoid their spillage into the public urban sphere (Fisher 2014).

In Buryatia, Buddhist interventions into urban space—undertaken by lamas and laypeople alike—constitute a means for publicly expressing the strong continuing presence of Buryat religion, as well as the ethnic identity with which it is intertwined, in the context of an increasingly centralized Russia and an increasingly Russified Buryatia. Whether intentionally or not, practices of religious intimacy, such as religious placemaking, are a significant way to invigorate distinct group identities and particular ethical and social constellations, which almost invariably constitute a critique of society. As minority religion and ethnicity tend to go hand in hand in the Russian context, these religious interventions form a powerful infrapolitical terrain.

4

BEING A PILLAR
Buddhist Counseling

A *biznes-tsentr* like many others is located not far from Ulan-Ude's city center on a busy street.[1] Bearing a French-inspired name tapping into the symbolic capital of the "imaginary West" (Yurchak 2000, 415–16), it seeks to carve out a businesslike, professional commercial space in its surroundings of residential multistory buildings, the spacious sandy yards between them, and crumbling sidewalks sunk beneath dirty melting snow. Upon entering the building, one sees a range of businesses all contained within near-identical booths: a pharmacy, kiosks with an array of bits and bobs stacked into glass showcases, a tutor's office, a sewing workshop, a lawyer's bureau, a small technical college, and a selection of other shops, as well as empty booths. A wall directory lists all the companies located in the building, although there seem to be suspiciously few entries, owing perhaps to the fact that many of the occupants are likely not officially registered companies. On the second floor, beside a café, a photography studio, and a loan collector's office, there is also a small Buddhist temple across two booths and an unidentified office outside of which a number of people usually wait at any time of the day. This office is in fact the workplace of Lama Amgalan, a popular middle-aged Buryat lama who offers counseling and ritual services to his many clients, both devoted lay Buddhists and first-time, one-off visitors who hear through the grapevine about the tantric specialist.[2]

On a Monday morning, a regular workday was underway at the biznes-tsentr. As I arrived, a queue was forming to see Lama Amgalan. An elderly woman had been waiting since nine a.m., knowing that the lama usually arrives around

FIGURE 12. A Buddhist temple in a biznes-tsentr, Ulan-Ude, 2016. Photo by author.

FIGURE 13. The interior of the biznes-tsentr temple, Ulan-Ude, 2016. Photo by author.

ten—the queue forms quickly here, she explained. By ten thirty, she had already phoned the lama twice, to hurry him along, and he arrived soon after and invited her in. He performed a purification ritual, which had been previously planned. The woman had brought with her the required offerings, including milk, kefir, sweets, and grain. In the one and a half hours that the ritual lasted, I sat in the corridor with other clients who gathered gradually: a young man with his grandmother who were regulars, a mother and her son who were there for the first time, and an elderly woman who was also a regular. The two elderly women turned out to be *zemliaki* and had much to discuss during the long wait, while the first-timers were visibly annoyed with the hours lost in the queue. The man and his grandmother were then let in for a consultation and a ritual that lasted about forty minutes. Afterward, the lama let me observe the following consultations, with the clients' approval. He called the mother and son into his office and immediately disappeared for about half an hour to have lunch with a lama friend who had dropped by.

When Lama Amgalan returned, he asked the waiting clients why they had come to see him. It was because the son was planning a stint of (unauthorized) work in South Korea and wanted to consult with him about it: Would he get there safely, or would he be rejected at the border? Would he find work and be paid for it? After several questions—whether he already had tickets, when he wanted to go, how long he planned to stay there, as well as what his name, birth year, and home district in the Buryat region were—Lama Amgalan started a divination. He repeated the given information, translating it from Russian into Buryat, hummed and chanted, and twirled rosary beads with his fingers.[3] Afterward, he said that the divination indicated uncertain success, and the young man might even be stopped at the border. Then again, if he was determined to go, the "road is not fully closed" (*doroga ne sovsem zakryta*), and Lama Amgalan could perform a ritual to further increase the likelihood of success. As the clients confirmed that they would like that, the lama wrote down the names of five khurals on a piece of paper, as well as offerings they had to bring, and told them to come back another time. Perhaps sensing slight dissatisfaction, he tried to reassure them: There was nothing to worry about, obstacles could be removed, and everyone that he had consulted went to Korea successfully. After a consultation of about fifteen minutes, the pair thanked the lama and bowed respectfully, and the mother left a small remuneration (RUB 100) on the lama's desk.

Next, an elderly Buryat woman came in. She knew Lama Amgalan from their home district, and the exchange seemed more cordial than with the previous pair. At the same time, an air of reverence was very much present during the consultation, to an extent I only witnessed when very old people visited lamas. The woman slowly walked up to the lama's desk with her head lowered and her hands placed together in prayer, bowed three times in front of the lama touching the desk with her forehead, and then presented a RUB 500 note as an offering with two hands, again bowing. In turn, the lama lowered his head slightly and put his hands together, accepting her offerings, but also showing respect to the elderly as is customary in Buryatia. During the session, the woman inquired about the horoscope reading in Mongolian or Tibetan astrology (Bur., *zurkhaĭ*) for herself and five of her close relatives for the upcoming year.[4] Lama Amgalan divined and consulted an astrology book and talked briefly about each person's horoscope, pointing out probable difficulties and how to prevent them and addressing specific questions that the woman had about each person regarding the plans for the year. He recommended khurals that should be ordered and then fulfilled the woman's request for a ritual blessing at the end. After a session of around twenty minutes, the woman offered another RUB 100 with a bow, briefly discussed the fact that she would invite him to their home to read the prayers he had recommended, and left the room walking backward—thereby showing him utmost respect by not turning her back to the lama.[5]

The next consultation provided quite a contrast in terms of both tone and content. A middle-aged Buryat woman marched into the room with little hesitation, took a seat before the lama could invite her to sit, and went straight to the matter. She had visited the lama several days before to ask whether or not her husband was cheating on her. While Lama Amgalan had established by divination that he was not, the woman wanted to double-check, since some of her friends and relatives were convinced otherwise. After a brief conversation and a divination, the lama confirmed that her husband was faithful. The woman seemed relieved but reiterated that people close to her doubted the fact. Lama Amgalan then assured her, stressing that during the divination the beads had always landed in threes, which indicates a sure outcome. Rather cheerfully, the woman thanked the lama and left some money on his desk for the brief consultation.

A man in his twenties with a slightly older couple—likely his parents or other relatives—came in next. Clearly friends and zemliaki, they all greeted each other cordially and discussed news about their mutual acquaintances, as well as from their own lives. Through this informal chatting, they came to the question that had brought them to see Lama Amgalan. The young man was looking for a Tibetan or Buryat-Mongolian medicine expert (Bur., *ėmchi, ėmshėn*) in Ulan-Ude. While there are many such experts in Ulan-Ude, he wanted to find a reliable and efficacious one. Lama Amgalan recommended an experienced and powerful (Rus., *moshchnyĭ*) zemliak, and they also discussed another specialist that had been recommended to them. Lama Amgalan's divination confirmed that this doctor would also be good and said it was up to them which one they selected. A further friendly chat ensued, during which it transpired that the man needed a doctor because he was a contract soldier who took part in the militant actions in eastern Ukraine. The health problems he was facing as a result of his work were not treated adequately in a polyclinic. With warm goodbyes and a small remuneration left on the table, the group left. Following this, the lama excused himself as he needed a massage, complaining that his back was in pain these days due to him having to sit so much. As we went out into the corridor, lunchtime smells wafted from the café, and the loan collectors several offices down were shouting loud threats and curses into their phones.

The potpourri of sounds, smells, and people going about their business in a nondescript, bland and windowless corridor of a biznes-tsentr might seem an unusual setting for a temple and an odd waiting room for people seeking advice from a religious specialist. This is especially so since this advice often pertains to hope and the future, sense and meaning, relationships and the social worlds of the people in need of support. While Buddhist counseling can and does take place in the more conventional setting of temples as well, this description of Lama Amgalan's workplace epitomizes much of what such Buddhist consultations achieve and how they achieve it. Namely, Buddhist counseling is a practice that combines the religious and the secular, a heightened ritual setting and bleak office space, dealing with spirits and "commonsense" advice, conjuring the help of deities and solving worldly problems. The help sought pertains to issues both local and global, religious and secular, mundane and lofty.

Images of the Khambo Lama parading next to Putin and narratives of the long-term synergies between Buddhist and Russian powers are conspicuous and intriguing. They easily attract attention and debate and have come to dominate discussions of Buryat Buddhism both locally and from without. However, the everyday settings and interactions that constitute the Buddhist field in Buryatia are significantly removed from this lofty backdrop. Much more often, they are based in contexts of urban religious intimacy. Buddhist counseling provides just such a setting that may unsettle grand representational narratives and provide a window into everyday negotiations of religion, identity, and agency. These consultations reveal the local hardships experienced by laypeople as they try to assert their agency and muster divine support. Precarious jobs, labor migration, pressing loans, health problems—these are just some of the grievances managed through Buddhist interventions in Ulan-Ude. Very often, these problems stem from or are aggravated by the felt neglect of the state: inadequate health care, joblessness, poverty, and attempts to deal with them. Alternatively, they demonstrate the continuing relevance and authority of traditional Buryat institutions, for instance, when lamas are consulted about relationships or family matters. The efficacy and reliability of lamas in such settings establish the sangha as one of the main pillars of Buryat society. Acting as an alternative source of power and authority, this pillar constitutes a challenge to the hegemony of the Russian state. This setting of religious intimacy and alternative ethics is all the more important today when Buddhists in Russia are being subject to the profound violence of the state and are seeking everyday support in coping with its effects, all while avoiding the considerable dangers of engaging in direct, open means of resistance.

Buddhist Counseling

> Whether we [religious professionals] want this or not, we must take an active part in all spheres of life of the people. Otherwise, we move away from the people.... Give your every day after the morning khural to the believers, with as little concern for yourselves as possible, because caring about one's own well-being is a false path. And woe to the lama to whom laypeople do not come for consultations (Ayusheev in Makhachkeev 2013, 15).

To a considerable extent the relevance and esteem of the sangha in Buryatia is affirmed and reproduced through the individual interactions between lamas and laypeople that I call "Buddhist counseling."[6] Consultations with lamas are one of the main occasions of lay engagement with Buddhism in Buryatia and therefore constitute important sites where Buddhist institutions and efficacies are experienced. More than khural public religious service, this engagement is mutually constituted, active, and less formal than most religious interactions in Buryatia.[7] Not only does the layperson "speak with Buddhism" by asking for help, receiving bits of teachings or giving offerings, but Buddhism also "speaks to them" through the encounter with a lama who in a conversation approves, condemns, and shapes one's lifestyle, choices, opinions, and actions, as well as teaches and advises. As such, consultations are exercises in mutual legitimation and in mapping out the potencies of such Buddhist exchange. After all, as David Zeitlyn (2012, 537) suggests, "the evaluative test for diagnosis (and divination generally) is not whether it is correct but whether it helped." These everyday interactions and the mutual feedback system they provide are a good entry point for the study of contemporary urban Buryat Buddhism—and the everyday exchanges between the laity and the sangha that it entails.

In consultations, laypeople see a lama to ask for help with whatever issues they are facing, be they related to economic matters, travel, life cycle rituals, relationships, or other topics. The lama responds using various means such as divination, the astrological calendar, common sense, and their own life experience. The means selected depend on both the question asked and on the preference of the lama. A ritual may or may not be performed during a consultation as well. Such consultations take place in temples, either in designated spaces in the main prayer hall or in other premises within the temple complex. A smaller number of lamas are based in "offices," either their own or shared, that specialize in consultations.[8] These are premises in a rented office or similar space where public service and public rituals are not usually held—such as Lama Amgalan's office-temple in the ethnographic excerpt above. Still other lamas receive people at home or only do home visits to the laity without having a fixed base. Temple-based lamas spend much of the day counseling laypeople privately, in addition to performing one or two khural services a day. This is partly a matter of devotion to the laity and a wish to help them and partly a necessity, as remuneration for consultations constitutes a substantial part of any lama's income.[9]

Laypeople tend to consult lamas when they are facing a pressing issue, have an important decision to make, or need a ritual or divination performed. The problems discussed in such consultations often reflect the dominating societal and economic problems in contemporary Ulan-Ude, including precarious jobs, poverty, and various misfortunes. Some may consult a lama every few months, while others have only done so a few times in their lives. Many visit lamas yearly at the start of the Buddhist New Year to receive an astrological prognosis and learn what rituals are due that year, in addition to one-off consultations. While Buddhist counseling can take the form of one-on-one sessions with a lama, it is also common to bring family members or friends along. These occasions are usually deemed a rather private matter as the questions discussed are often of a personal kind. However, since they generally take place in a public or semipublic space, often hidden only by a curtain in a quiet temple, people are aware that their conversations are often listened in on by others in the queue, as well as by other lamas and visitors present. Many interlocutors confessed that when queuing to see a lama, they eavesdrop on what is being discussed by other clients, judging the lama's skill and trustworthiness by his questions and advice.

Consultations with lamas are not unique to Buryat Buddhism. Similar kinds of engagements with Buddhist specialists exist in different forms throughout the Buddhist world, although they typically do not enjoy the spotlight in the literature on Buddhism. In Ulan-Ude, a layperson may simply drop by a temple and talk to any lama during opening hours rather than turning to a Buddhist specialist they know. Consultations are not a new phenomenon in Buryatia, although they seem to have changed somewhat when compared to the pre-Soviet period. Previously it was common for a layperson or a whole family to return to one lama

FIGURE 14. Queueing for a consultation with a lama, Ulan-Ude, 2015. Photo by author.

regularly with questions and requests for rituals and offerings. He would be a guru throughout one's life. While having such a guru lama is seen today by many as virtuous and desirable, this practice is not strictly followed. In the urban context, some laypeople have one or several lamas whom they prefer over others that they seek out when in need of a consultation. Such lamas may be relatives, share a connection to the same part of Buryatia (*zemliaki*), or have proven pleasant and efficacious in the past. However, many laypeople simply drop by a temple and consult any lama there or rely on advice from friends, relatives, or social media to find a powerful lama.

In the religious scene of Ulan-Ude, people approach not just Buddhist specialists but also those of other religions with similar queries. While lamas are popular and easiest to approach, shamans have become prominent in the city in the post-Soviet period (Humphrey 1999; Shaglanova 2012). Like lamas, they consult clients and provide ritual help in private consultations, and several shamanic centers have opened in Ulan-Ude for this purpose.[10] Sociologists Timur Badmatsyrenov and Sanzhida Dansarunova (2015, 53) identify the most common consultation questions to shamans in Ulan-Ude as addressing (in decreasing order of frequency) family, work, financial issues, personal life, spiritual matters, studies, important events, alcohol abuse, and the death of a relative.[11] Most of my interlocutors had consulted a shaman at least once in their lives but turn to lamas more regularly. As many explained, they go to see a shaman when they have a "more serious" issue, one where a lama is unable to help, or something related to spirits and nonhuman beings: Serious illness, curses, and spirit attacks are some examples. Many consider shamans to be more powerful but also more hit-and-miss; gossip regarding fake shamans and "not-quite-shamans" (Pedersen 2011; see also Buyandelgeryin 2007) is abundant. In contrast to lamas, they are seen as morally dubious, dangerous, and greedy. In turn, most deem lamas to be predictable, perhaps less powerful, but reliable and harmless. While some feel strongly about choosing a religious specialist of one kind or the other, many are flexible and even forget what kind of specialist they consulted on a past occasion. Religious specialists from different traditions may also refer clients to one another.[12]

It is likely that over centuries of side-by-side coexistence in the Buryat lands, Orthodox Christianity, shamanism, and Buddhism have shaped one another, and comparable consultations exist today in all three religious contexts. An excellent example of this is the opening of a shamanic temple in Ulan-Ude in 2019 for rituals and consultations—a common occurrence in Orthodox Christianity and Buddhism but hardly typical in shamanic practice, which is usually more individualized. Despite isomorphic qualities among the different religions in the region, as becomes clear in what follows, Buddhist counseling makes a unique contribution in this field. Laypeople often learn about Buddhist ethics and cosmology in this setting and apply them to their lives, seeing themselves through a distinctly Buddhist lens as a consequence of the interaction with the lama. They also engage with the Buryat Buddhist tradition, and through it the past, and lean into the alternative source of authority and power provided by the Buddhist sangha in contemporary Russia. Finally, they partake in a mutuality of religious intimacy, enacting a religious community bound by imperfections but also hope and tenacity.

Arthur Kleinman ([1980] 2003) has claimed that similar religious and religio-medical counseling in Taiwan constitute a "health care system," deeming consultations on a broad range of nonbiomedical issues to be nonetheless medical, albeit in the widest sense of the term. Martin Mills (2003, 168) has similarly considered a wide range of Buddhist consultations in Zangskar to constitute a "series of differential fields of relationships designed to mediate, interpret and ultimately ameliorate illness," with illness being a cultural experience rather than a biomedical one. Indeed, some of the Buddhist counseling in Buryatia is also health-related, preventative, or reminiscent of psychotherapy. However, I want to diverge from medicalizing the practice of Buddhist counseling to see it in context as part of the broader negotiation of support, care, and belonging. Those who make use of Buddhist or shamanic consultations in Buryatia may use medical comparisons and metaphors themselves, comparing consultations and rituals to medications, psychological and psychiatric counseling, doctor's consultations, and the like. As in other precarious contexts in post-Soviet Russia (Chudakova 2021; Lindquist 2005; Quijada 2012) and beyond (Buyandelgeriyn 2007), the failures of biomedical health care, alongside other forms of social and physical care by the state, are a contributing factor in people's search for alternative systems of protection, attention, and guidance. Furthermore, particular kinds of religio-medical treatments are seen as being particularly effective on particular bodies, and Buryat Buddhism and its attendant Tibetan-Buryat healing are seen as essential within local constellations of health and well-being (Chudakova 2021). However, as I detail below, the scope of Buddhist counseling extends well beyond the medical field (however broadly defined), encompassing crucial dimensions like power, agency, and belonging.

From Labor Migration to Spirit Attacks

Almost all the lamas I talked to in Ulan-Ude highlighted labor migration and loans as the dominant themes in Buddhist consultations during my fieldwork in the mid-2010s. This is perhaps unsurprising considering that Buryatia is a fairly poor region and, along with the rest of Russia, has suffered from the ebbs and flows of the post-Soviet economy. During my time in Buryatia, many acutely felt the impact of the 2014–16 economic crisis that followed Russia's annexation of Crimea. Labor migration has provided one of the main ways, in addition to work as a contract soldier (Rus., *kontraktnik*), in which Buryats have dealt with economic difficulties. Most commonly, this meant illegal short-term stints of manual labor in South Korea and longer-term recurrent movements to the larger Russian cities or to the resource-extracting plants in the North (Rus., *vakhta*). In such cases, one commonly consults a lama regarding an auspicious date for travel or to divine whether the migrant will successfully cross the border and whether one will be cheated by their employers. Taking out a bank loan is a strategy that is often combined with labor migration. Many consult lamas before taking a loan and ask for practical advice, such as where to apply for it, how large it should be, or how to deal with the inability to pay it back.

To answer such queries, lamas combine a variety of methods. They typically use divination, though several lamas confided that it is not always necessary and sometimes has a more performative than utilitarian power. What often plays a defining role, according to my lama interlocutors, is the practical circumstances of the person in question. Lama Daba explained how he advises people regarding labor migration. He first asks whether the person has a job, how much they earn, and how stable their position is. He then asks if they are married, whether they have children, and how many people depend on their wage. He also considers the person's age, health, debts, and other significant factors. If he sees that the person is better off staying put, he explains that it would be unwise to take on the risks involved for the sake of some extra cash. Only if the person insists does Lama Daba look up their horoscope, divine, and advise them further. In case of doubt, he lays out the uncertain factors to the client and offers several possible courses of action.

Lama Daba also walked me through how he advises teenagers who are not sure what they want to study at university. He first gets them to talk about their hobbies, wishes, and priorities and inquires about their school results. If the client has several options, he advises which one seems to suit them best, also consulting the person's horoscope. If the student-to-be does not have any particular inclination, then, as Lama Daba sees it, the best option is to study medicine: at least then they will be of help to other people and do something meaningful. This, in his opinion, will likely lead to happiness in the long term if the person is able to endure the tough studies.

For Lama Daba, this one-size-fits-all approach reflects his understanding of Buddhism as a rational, sensible outline of how to best live one's life and be of use to others. In contrast, some other lamas stressed psychology and adapting to each individual as being key to their work. As the very popular Lama Mergen told me, it is first and foremost crucial to understand the person who comes to see him. He starts analyzing the person when they enter the room, using his common sense, empathy, knowledge of psychology, and tantric insight.[13] In the short span of a consultation, he tries to understand not just their query but also their character, which provides insight both into the problems they are experiencing and the solutions that might best suit them.

Lama Mergen gave the example of a woman whom he consulted regarding her multiple misfortunes over the last few years. She had had a good job but decided to quit it due to a conflict at work. The woman was then unable to find a new job and moved to a different city. She settled there and started a family with a newly met man, but it soon turned out that the marriage was ill fated. After a divorce, the woman struggled with depression and eventually came back to Ulan-Ude, where she saw the lama. During the long and emotional consultation, Lama Mergen saw that a purification ritual was needed. As he later explained to me, he could have done it there and then in the temple office, but he decided instead to take the woman to a river nearby and perform the ritual there. While it was not necessary for the ritual itself, the special setting—pregnant with symbols—and the effort involved would make for a significant, even life-changing event. This would enable the woman to make a fresh start. Put in other words, Lama Mergen stressed the performative aspects of ritual (Tambiah 1979, 119) and hinted at the power of what can be called ritualization, which sets "some activities off from others, for creating and privileging a qualitative distinction between the 'sacred' and the 'profane,' and for ascribing such distinctions to realities thought to transcend the powers of human actors" (Bell 1992, 74). It is through such setting apart that people may be moved by the ritual and subsequently transform their lives.

Similarly, Lama Mergen argued, giving the lama a large remuneration after a consultation may add to its efficacy, because the client then feels that it was important and meaningful and is more willing to follow the lama's advice and change their ways.[14] While Lama Mergen does not ask for a particular sum of money, he understood the significance of large donations from having once declined one. At the time, he was uncomfortable with taking such a large sum of money (RUB 5,000) but later regretted not taking it as he understood that this gesture would have helped the client make a fresh start.

Lama Amgalan, from the introductory vignette, highlights the significance of his own life experience in consulting with laypeople: he considers himself to be particularly good at answering questions regarding economic matters because he has had many different business ventures himself. He is, however, not just a business adviser but combines his practical knowledge with expertise in Buddhist philosophy and ethics, as well as tantric insight. As an example, he recounted the case of a woman who had recently come to consult him about exhaustion and volatile luck in her several business ventures. Based on his personal experience in business, as well as his understanding of Buddhism, he advised her to scale back her enterprises and stick to just one of them, investing all her energy and resources into it. He argued that this would eventually be more financially profitable and better for her well-being, and it was in line with Buddhist teachings.

Consultations are often pragmatic in tone, and they rarely include extensive or abstract teachings on Buddhism. But they may nonetheless provide an occasion for learning about Buddhist philosophy, ethics, and cosmology, through, for instance, reflecting on their life situations using such concepts as interconnectedness or karma. When interpreting the presented issue, lamas may reflect on the "Buddhist way" (Rus., *po-buddiĭski*) of interpreting and solving it. They may highlight the significance of according with the astrological calendar or holding to traditional Buryat -Mongolian ways. For instance, Lama Daba recounted a consultation in which a man who was working for an illegal logging operation complained about his and his family's ill health, as well as financial problems. After learning about what the man did for a living, Lama Daba explained that the problems likely arose from the fact that his activities bothered the forest spirits and triggered their attacks. The lama used the setting of the consultation not only to conduct the appropriate rituals to remedy the situation but also to teach the woodcutter that Buryats used to condemn behavior that is harmful to the environment and its nonhuman inhabitants. Here, too, the illegality of the operation and the grim ecological situation of the forests in the region added to the severity of the situation, and Lama Daba encouraged the man to rethink the morality of his choices and potentially seek a new occupation.

Buddhist counseling therefore does not just resolve the question at hand but further guides laypeople's actions in daily life through small teachings in being a "good" Buddhist and Buryat and a moral person in particular ways. These are especially powerful in a context where many feel insecure in their Buddhist knowledge and practice. Such guidance can be overt, like in the consultation above, or it may be implicit, as in the case in the introductory vignette, where Lama Amgalan tried to convince a laywoman that her husband was not cheating on her. I was hesitant to press Lama Amgalan further as to what led to the outcome of that particular divination, but it seemed likely to me that in this situation—like in many others I heard about—it was not only the way that the prayer beads landed that shaped the divinatory outcome. Similar to Theodor Adorno's (1957) diagnosis of a newspaper astrology column, in consultations, lamas' moral and ideological convictions, as well as their visions of the best result for everyone involved, guide the outcome of the consultation as much as the divinatory process itself.

In some cases, the power of the sangha can be very pragmatic. My interlocutor Radna recounted how a lama once helped him avoid the military draft. After graduating from university, Radna was drafted for mandatory service before he could apply for a PhD program, as he had intended to do to avoid serving in the military. While his parents tried to use their contacts and think of other ways to save their son from the army, they failed. Several days before Radna was to start his service, his mother took him to see a zemliak lama. Although they did not have a close tie to him, he was the highest placed lama they could think of that they had any connection with. They said they wanted the lama to pray to ensure Radna's service went smoothly. But upon hearing the story, he responded: "Sometimes, there is no need to pray." He gave them the number of a high-ranking official in the military commissariat (Rus., *voenkomat*) who was also their zemliak, suggesting they give him a call and hope for the best. The official was willing to help but said there was not enough time to change anything. On the morning Radna was supposed to go away, he woke—terribly hungover from what he thought was his last night out before starting military service—to a call from the conscription service. His service had been moved by half a year, which gave him time to apply for a PhD and hence to avoid it altogether.

While Radna's story is a decade old, questions of conscription and military service are especially pertinent in Buryat Buddhism today. Since Russia began waging a full-scale war on Ukraine in February 2022, Buryatia appears to have suffered disproportionate losses compared to most other regions of Russia (Vyushkova and Sherkhonov 2023). As is typical in the region, people have turned to lamas to find solutions, as well as comfort in this unusual and difficult situation. As lamas based in Buryatia and in diaspora have told me, laypeople now seek them out to conduct rituals for their sons fighting in Ukraine, to divine in case they have not heard from them in a while, and to conduct mortuary rituals for those who died in the war to ensure their auspicious rebirth. If mortuary rituals are not conducted, they could end up as hungry ghosts in a land far from home, bound for an unknowable period of suffering. Since the draft, many also consult lamas about whether to submit to the draft, whether to flee Russia, or how to best avoid military service.

Here, as in Buddhist counseling in general, the same principles apply. Some lamas are guided by their understanding of Buddhist philosophy: One lama I met in Ulaanbaatar postmobilization told me he advised men to avoid the draft in any way they could. After all, he explained, one of the main Buddhist principles is not to kill—so how could Buddhists go to war? This is especially so since this war is not one of self-defense but of unprovoked aggression, invading a foreign country, he noted. When he consults laypeople about this, he said he tries to brainstorm with them all the possible routes for avoiding the draft: Do they have any medical conditions? Dependent relatives? Can they go away to a village for a while and lay low? Another lama who fled Russia himself said his go-to advice is for men to retreat to a forest for some time. He claims that fleeing abroad is not an option for many, since it is expensive and difficult, but living out in the woods is free, and most men in Buryatia have some familiarity with rural life, so they could certainly survive out in the wild. I also heard from my lay interlocutors about lamas in Buryatia who have gone to the war as volunteers or who encourage their clients to submit to the draft or go as volunteers. Just like with other questions in Buddhist counseling, the lama's views and previous experience shape their interpretations of Buddhism and hence influence in part the outcomes of their consultations.

Several insights can be drawn from the discussion so far. First, lamas are not simply mediators of Buddhist expertise and divine power but actors who shape people's engagement with Buddhism through their own experience and choices. Second, multiple logics and ideologies are at work in Buddhist counseling, whether competing or complementary: secular and religious sensibilities, grounded in psychology and astrology, along with calculated probabilities and divine guidance. Third, Buddhism is not, as Weber ([1916] 2009) contends, a religion intrinsically oriented toward otherworldly matters. Instead, it is a religion that informs and influences the decisions and actions of Buddhists in everyday life, including in social, economic, and political matters, and is often directed toward this-worldly goals. Overall, this kind of intertwinement of Buddhism and utilitarian matters is not seen by most Buryat Buddhists as inherently problematic: Lamas have traditionally guided the laity in important life events and decisions. In fact, such entwinement is often seen as desirable, as Ayusheev's quote in an earlier section indicates. Religion in general and lamas' counseling in particular are locally valued as providing a moral compass, as well as a practical pillar for society.

Much of the discussion above stems from interviews and conversations with lamas, who perhaps predictably stress their own role in determining the outcome of the consultation. In contrast, laypeople's accounts can give the opposite impression. I repeatedly heard from them that before visiting a lama to ask a question, they often already know the answer, or at least they are predisposed to one solution or another. While they are respectful of the lama's suggestions, if they do not coincide with their own vision of the situation, they may politely, sometimes indirectly, insist on their own course. In some cases, this may be straightforward, like when parents dislike the name a lama suggests for a newborn and request another option. In other cases, it requires more subtle navigation of the client's (often unsaid) preferences, premonitions, inclinations, and even dreams. Who is it, then, that leads consultations: the lama, the deities, Buddhist astrology and ethics, the layperson? Even objects used in divination exert a particular kind of agency (Swancutt 2012, 154–84). Or is it a combined effort? And if, as some laypeople claim, one does not necessarily seek a novel solution but sometimes only the confirmation of an expected outcome, then why consult a lama at all?

Negotiating the Outcome: Agency in Buddhist Counseling

One session I observed at Lama Amgalan's office provides insight into the dialogic nature of consultations. A middle-aged Buryat woman whom the lama knew from their home district dropped in. She first asked about her business in the city market, which was not going well. Due to the economic crisis, she complained, people spent little money, while those who had it shopped elsewhere. As the woman was explaining her problem, Lama Amgalan nodded, sighed with empathy, and asked several questions for clarification. He then started to divine, moving the prayer beads quickly in his hands and recounting in Buryat the main details of the client—name, year of birth, city of residence—as well as her question, namely, whether business would improve and when. The answer was somewhat vague. Yes, the business would improve, but things would remain difficult for a while. Clearly disappointed with the reply, the woman pressed him further. She told the lama that, as he knew from her previous visits, she had a friend in St. Petersburg who had a good job at the post office and was willing to put in a good word for her so that perhaps she could also get a job there. The friend had been inviting her for a while, and it seemed like a good option in the current economic climate. The lama then started divining again, asking her additional questions as he twirled the prayer beads with his eyes closed: "How is your mother's health? Would she stay here alone if you left?"

The lama's face after he put his beads on the table was telling. The woman asked, "It [the divination outcome] is not looking good, right, *lamkhaĭ* [respectful address to lama in Buryat]?" The lama replied that indeed it was not and started consoling her—she would not like St. Petersburg anyway, as it is cold, humid, and gloomy. Besides, leaving her mother alone and in poor health would not be right. As the woman nodded, her disappointment was clear, so much so that the lama eventually gave in. He conceded that if she truly wanted to go, she could give it more thought and come back another time—after all, most obstacles could be removed, especially if she got a good job offer or if business here kept declining. After several more minutes of nodding and reiteration, the woman was still reluctant to leave and mused out loud that perhaps she could call her friend and try to find out whether the offer still stood and what the particulars were. The lama read the fortune again and said that she could do so if she liked. Much relieved, the woman stood up to go, leaving a small donation on the table, and on the way out she asked one last question: What time should she make the call? Closing his eyes and pressing the beads, Lama Amgalan replied: After lunch would be a good time, since no one likes to receive calls while they eat.

This consultation demonstrates a mutually sculpted divination, which is quite typical based on my data. While the layperson needs affirmation and support, and a consultation with a lama is an established practice in such cases, this does not mean that the lama alone decides the solution to the layperson's question. Laypeople negotiate the outcome of the consultation and in a way bend divine power toward their—somewhat vacillating—premeditated preference. A lama, for his part, reads the unspoken inclinations of the visiting layperson, consults divine powers, and evaluates the practical circumstances affecting the question. Writing on Buryat shamanic divination in Inner and Outer Mongolia, Katherine Swancutt (2012, 47) also points to what she calls "nearly egalitarian dynamics behind the Buryat divination." Having undertaken divination herself as part of her fieldwork, Swancutt saw, both in her own sessions and those she observed, that rather than being docile receivers of knowledge, Buryat inquirers in fact volunteer their interpretations, presentiments, and speculations to the diviner and thereby shape the outcome.[15]

It is this combination of ritual, theoretical and practical considerations, receptiveness, empathy, and social skills that are valued in a lama by many laypeople. The dialogic character of Buddhist counseling is part of what makes it relevant and popular. Moreover, and significantly, the mutual construction of the result may often be where the real strength of the process lies. Not only are laypeople supported and encouraged in their endeavors, they are also coproducers of the outcome itself. After all, what is more likely to assure divine support and protection for a desired outcome than being a proactive agent in the summoning of said support?[16]

Why do people involve Buddhist counseling in a wide variety of scenarios, even when they might already know their preferred course of action? In her extensive work on magic and the market in Moscow in the late 1990s, Galina Lindquist (2006, 199) explores the work of magic as "an aspect of the existential safety net operating in conditions of precarious presence," which "can work to augment individual human agency in a society where formal channels of agency are limited." The consultations that Lindquist describes differ from Buddhist ones in Ulan-Ude in significant ways. Buddhist consultations are a long-standing tradition, even though they have changed over time and in the urban context. Unlike magi, lamas are not marginal but instead well respected and trusted. Their education and the methods employed are fairly standard, and while a personal touch is certainly present, their consultations are quite orthodox compared to the bricolage of magical practice in early post-Soviet Moscow.

Crucially, there is a similar impetus that lies behind many consultations. There are economic, political, and social uncertainties that many feel unable to control. They feel themselves falling through the cracks of the uncaring, incapable state and so turn to lamas in search of advice, support, and inspiration. Many rely on the sangha as a source of hope and coherence to aid in muddling through difficult situations in everyday life, as well as moments of crisis. People also turn to the sangha as a pillar for support during significant events in their life, like a birth of a child or a new job. There is in turn a similar impact that consultations often bring: a fostering of hope and a reinforcement of agency, be it by means of divine help, sensible advice, ritual enchantment, or—as discussed above—coproduction of the outcome.

In Ulan-Ude, many relate the prominence of consultations to the difficult socioeconomic situation in the post-Soviet period. Lama Amgalan, for instance, stressed two factors as being key to people's propensity to consult lamas: the difficult life in contemporary Buryatia and the lack of decision-making skills and self-reliance. As he explains, in the Soviet period, one was well cared for and had to make few choices in life, and most people had similar earnings and lifestyles. The workplace and the state made most decisions for people, and life paths were quite clear: school, studies, family, work. In the post-Soviet period, when subsistence is precarious and dependent on one's skills, background, and choices in life, many are lost. They are not used to making decisions that determine their livelihood. Hence, Lama Amgalan suggests, people rely on lamas to make these decisions for them. This explanation, along with the variations on this general theme that I heard from many interlocutors, is certainly simplified. One could critique the too direct linking of the consultations and the socioeconomic situation, and the idealization of the sangha. Such post-Soviet problematics might be applied more readily to the 1990s and the then-ubiquitous issues with crumbling infrastructure (Humphrey 2003), crime and corruption (Humphrey 2007), and mistrust and a sense of crisis (Humphrey 2007, 180; Shevchenko 2009). However, in the ebbs and flows of the post-Soviet decades, Lama Amgalan's observations about social and economic difficulties still ring true in Buryatia today, as a sense of continuous crisis and precarity persists.

As I have attempted to show, the link between Buddhist counseling and socioeconomic uncertainties is more complex than such explanations suggest. Consultations not only have a long history in Buryatia and elsewhere (and are not simply a reaction to the post-Soviet condition), but they are also contingent on the historical, social, and religious context. They occur not only at a time of difficulty but also at other times where Buddhist support feels appropriate, like important family occasions or setting a positive tone for the upcoming year. But Lama Amgalan's explanation above—if involving little nuance—points to one of the key issues in play: the fact that consultations are often a means to reinforce one's agency when it is lacking. A layperson gains encouragement, advice, and ritual support, as well as a forecast of what lies ahead, to be better able to anticipate and potentially change it. Moreover, the client is an active participant in the consultation and in bringing about a desired outcome.

Also supporting the contention that agency is molded in consultations is the fact that I did not hear much complaint about lamas giving bad advice or divining inaccurately nor people blaming them for an undesired outcome in a problematic situation—both of which would have pointed to a sense of a lack of agency. On several occasions, laypeople told me about lamas who negligently read sutras and rushed through them or those who behaved inappropriately during rituals by, for instance, showing up inebriated to perform a ceremony. However, in typical consultations, when rituals seem to have been properly performed, laypeople see themselves as primarily responsible for any actions they take following the consultations.

In discussing Senegambian divination, Knut Graw (2006, 81) offers a detailed analysis of the beginning of divinatory consultations, arguing that they open up an "intentional space" for "articulating and dealing with personal intentions and desires that not only reflects the intentional nature of a human being but responds to, negotiates and transforms the subject's intentional position by allowing him to engage actively with his longings and afflictions in a changing and challenging contemporary world." In other words, by initiating a consultation and stating intent, the consulter recognizes themselves as an active player, and the divinatory process thus orients the intentional situatedness of the subject regardless of the outcome. In Buryat Buddhist counseling, too, such a shift is usually present, rendering it a shaping—and even transformative—space. More than that, in the Buryat case, this intentional space is not only present in the beginning of divinatory consultations but also throughout them, as the layperson repeatedly shapes and directs the outcome. Finally, Buddhist consultations and rituals imbue simple everyday settings of urban dwelling with potentiality. Be it through ritual scent and sound spilling into the biznes-tsentr or through "opening the road" for opportunities at work, Buddhist contributions to the city often lie beyond the surface but contribute hope, possibility, and a reinforcement of agency to contemporary Ulan-Udensians.

Support, Authority, and Agency of the Sangha

The range of questions that lamas deal with on a daily basis is striking. Why would laypeople rely on a single kind of expert for anything from establishing the fidelity of a partner to cleansing oneself of misfortunes? Other consultations I have witnessed involved healing, making business decisions, naming a baby, and coping with grief, along with many more questions. It is not like all of these questions require just one kind of solution, say, divination, or one particular area of ritual expertise. They may involve a range of techniques, including these, but also teachings in Buddhist ethics or philosophy, practical advice, or a great variety of Buddhist rituals. Wherein lies the authority of and trust in the sangha to effectively provide help with such a variety of issues? Ultimately, the answer lies not just at the intersection of efficacy and the reinforcement of agency but also in authority.

The sangha is at the receiving end of considerable critique from the laity in contemporary Buryatia. Lamas in Buryatia are criticized for their questionable motivations and perceived lack of education, expertise, devotion, or discipline. However, such appraisals are often directed at individual lamas rather than the sangha as a whole, which by and large remains very highly esteemed in Buryatia. Sustained critique, coming especially from the urban intelligentsia, is also directed at the person of the Khambo Lama Ayusheev or sometimes the whole institution of the Buddhist Traditional Sangha of Russia (BTSR). As explained earlier, both Ayusheev's crass character and his pragmatic approach to Buddhism, as well as the BTSR's loyalty to the Russian state, are cited as causes of laypeople's dissatisfaction. Yet Buddhism and the sangha as a whole remain very highly valued and trusted. Given the prominent suspicion toward politicians and the pervasive mistrust in bureaucracy, the sangha often emerges as a reliable source of support and power.

In Buryatia, both lamas themselves and laypeople often refer to the sangha as a pillar (Rus., *opora*) that the laity relies on in their day-to-day lives, especially in difficult times. This alludes to the ritual support they provide to the laity during public services, as well as privately in the form of Buddhist counseling. Sometimes, the charisma and efficacy of an especially powerful (Rus., *moshchnyĭ*) individual lama may bolster the authority of the sangha in the eyes of a layperson. Other times, it is the status of the sangha that ensures the reliability of individual lamas. The particular temple and organization affiliations are usually of secondary importance, if at all noticed. In Max Weber's (1978) terms, both charismatic and traditional authority are at play.

Moreover, the sangha is a pillar in the sense that lamas are seen in Buryatia as some of the main bearers of Buryat cultural heritage. To many Buryats, Buddhism embodies and represents a key part of Buryat culture. This is because of the enmeshment of religious and ethnic identity in the region and because the sangha members indeed are some of the main upholders of Buryat tradition, be it Buryat language, art, or conservative social norms. This is of great significance in the contemporary context, where many Buryats are worried about the impending and escalating "loss" of their culture and increasing Russification. Despite the antireligious repressions of the Soviet period and the continuing struggles over cultural sovereignty as an ethnoreligious minority in Russia, Buddhist institutions and communities have demonstrated their tenacity over decades and centuries, against all odds. This is especially striking given the difficulty in sustaining some of the other historical features of Buryat culture, such as nomadic pastoralism.

Indeed, the sangha aims at being a pillar not just in the religious sphere but in economic, political, and other matters as well, both on the levels of discourse and action (Jonutytė 2020c). One urban lama, for instance, shared a sentiment far from unique when he insisted that datsans should ideally be of immediate help to the laity: They should not just provide ritual support and counseling but also employ laypeople and establish businesses where others could work. In his opinion, it is the responsibility of the sangha to offer help (Rus., *okazyvat' pomoshch'*) to people in whatever ways it is needed. Lama Ayur, from the previous chapter, who had initially hoped to spread Buddhist teachings and philosophy among rural laity but largely cares for his laity in practical ways today, serves as another example of the sangha as a pillar sustaining local community.

The Buryat sangha, and the BTSR specifically, are proactive in implementing practical projects to cement the high esteem of the sangha through the maintenance of Buryat traditional culture. Examples of such efforts by the BTSR to offer "nonreligious" help to the laity, to name a few, are the Social Flock program that supports endemic sheep herding and projects to rehabilitate people with addictions, along with helping the homeless. But the Buryat language has been a particular focus of the BTSR at least since the 2010s.

Buddhist lamas of the BTSR and beyond are some of the main enthusiasts of the Buryat language today. During consultations and public rituals, lamas, especially those of an older age, often insist on using the Buryat language with laypeople and only rarely switch to Russian. The BTSR also reaches beyond the temples, having initiated several projects for the popularization of the Buryat language among the wider population. The first endeavor was a radio station launched in 2016. Apart from Buryat music, it also has deejays representing different dialects of Buryat and presenting shows about their regions. The second undertaking was a large-scale Buryat-language competition organized every few months. Divided into age groups and tasks—recitation, composition, vocabulary—children compete against other schools and regions. These competitions are very popular, and the endeavor is praised by the public, especially given the widespread decline of the knowledge of the Buryat language. Many Buryats, even some of the BTSR's critics, feel that the Khambo Lama works "for the people" by popularizing the Buryat language and exercises power beyond that of local politicians, who have done little for the cause. In this, he is contrasted to them as a caring leader who does what they should do, works without self-interest, and nurtures the future of Buryatia.

The positive appraisals of the ritual and practical support provided by the sangha are not limited to the dominant institution, the BTSR, but concern the Buryat Buddhist sangha as a whole. While the BTSR's efforts are often highly visible, other organizations and nonaffiliated lamas do important work to uphold Buryat traditions and communities. Laypeople are not always aware—and often do not care—whether a particular lama or temple is affiliated with the BTSR. Institutional bonds between individual lamas or temples and the BTSR can be rather vague in the urban context, and laypeople shift between various religious authorities and institutions—whether purposefully ignoring the distinctions or simply not caring much about them.

Also, for the most part, the BTSR does not impose a singular vision of Buddhism or its politico-religious affinities onto its lamas. It is in intimate religious settings like Buddhist counseling that this becomes especially visible, where lamas may draw on a host of personal experiences and views to diagnose and advise the laity. This is why Buddhist counseling constitutes an important infrapolitical field in Buryatia. In these settings, grievances can be aired and critiques of the dominant powers can be discussed. This can be done explicitly, for instance, through

FIGURE 15. A Buryat-language children's competition at Ivolginskiĭ datsan. A banner on the stage reads in Buryat, "Native language is our wealth." Ivolga, 2016. Photo by author.

attributing one's struggles in making a living to the policies of the Russian state or, implicitly, through seeking ways to avoid military conscription or trying to ensure a successful stint of labor migration. In these settings of religious intimacy, both the appearance of institutional, religio-political alliances and actual institutional affiliations tend to fade away, enabling exchanges stripped bare of officialities that seek to draw from the long-standing authority and efficacy of the Buryat sangha.

Buryat Buddhist authority, as shaped through the intimate interactions of Buddhist counseling, is a double-edged sword that, in the current situation, can save lives or place them in harm's way. Yet it provides a locally meaningful way of negotiating agency in a context where it is severely limited. Reviewing a broad range of consultations—from the seeking of a way to flee conscription to the securing of a successful stint of labor migration abroad—reveals Buddhist counseling to be a potent infrapolitical field wherein both the agency of laypeople and the authority of the sangha are reinforced and renegotiated, all within the overarching context of the precarious livelihoods of contemporary Ulan-Ude. With Buryat lives once again under threat from Russia, these intimate Buddhist interactions contrast sharply with the "public transcripts" of Russia's religious elites.

5

BUDDHIST IMPERFECTIONS
Religious Giving and Belonging

Buddhist counseling sessions are spaces of religious intimacy. Michael Herzfeld (2015) suggests this concept as a lens to think about sites that are essential to urban religious practice and identification yet not necessarily visible in the public field. It is an aspect of religion that is close to the heart and binds people inside the group but is invisible and unknowable to outsiders. Religious intimacy is a departure from doctrinal, formally promoted religious forms that is nonetheless recognized and accepted by a group of people. It is this very deviation and its loving admission that fosters mutuality among the practitioners. While monumental, grand religious contributions to the city typically capture the attention and imagination of outside observers, sites and practices of religious intimacy tend to be relatively neglected in the study of urban life.

To Herzfeld (2015, 33), religious intimacy is "an always-tolerated infraction against formal doctrine," be it in devotional practices or novel appropriations of urban space for makeshift shrines or processions. While practitioners are aware of the fact that their religion diverges from the officially promoted norm, there is comfort and mutuality in sharing this unsaid divergence. Such unofficial dissidence, however, may still threaten the dominant religious and state powers, as these "refractions of religiosity . . . imply a very different relationship between cosmos and community" (34). The adornment of neighborhoods with statuettes of the Madonna and their informal worshipping in Catholic Rome provides one such example of an informal religious community. Worshipping these Madonellas stands in contrast to the official ritual prescriptions of the Catholic church, yet it creates an implicit bond among practitioners (28–30).

In Buryatia, the practice of Buddhist counseling is also a site of religious intimacy. "Modernist" Buddhists, those with an active interest in Buddhist ethics and philosophy as well as an intense practice, typically look down on Buddhist counseling as an inferior religious form. While to them a strong presence of Buddhism in one's daily life is desirable, overreliance on religious professionals is problematic. This is a commonly repeated theme in Buddhist lectures by various lama and lay teachers in Ulan-Ude, where such overreliance on the sangha is mocked and criticized. As one Buddhist interlocutor put it, expressing a widespread sentiment: "Some people in Ulan-Ude ask a lama each time they have to use the bathroom!" But many laypeople who regularly resort to Buddhist counseling are themselves critical of it. In part self-critically and in part jokingly, my interlocutors called themselves "bad," "utilitarian," or "mechanical" Buddhists and other similar terms, referring to their heavy reliance on the sangha to solve their everyday problems (Jonutytė 2020b).

Laypeople express self-criticism for overreliance on the sangha and a lack of knowledge of Buddhist philosophy, rituals, and ethics, as well as inconsistent religious practice. Consider this excerpt from a vlog entry by a Buddhist laywoman, Ayuna:

> My attitude toward lamas . . . What attitude can someone who was raised in Soviet ideology have? Like all people of my generation today, in the last twenty years it was hammered into us that there exists something out there, that God [Rus., Bog] seems to exist. But in any case, we rely on ourselves more than on God. We start to put hope in God when we are in despair, even though it is a sin for religious people to fall into despair, because there is God, who will supposedly protect us all. In any case, when we are unwell, we remember God then. And we want to believe that he exists and that he will protect us. What else can we do if we do not rely on anyone and do not believe in anything? What then? . . . It would be good if faith was with us and we strive toward having faith within us. However, most likely it is not in our power to achieve that. Have hope in God, but act right yourself.[1]

In this excerpt, Ayuna grapples with her own Buddhist practice, which she recognizes as far from perfect. The value of religion has been "hammered" into her and others over the last couple of decades, but genuine faith is not there. However, upon facing difficulties in life, religion is still an important support that can keep one from despairing. Ayuna's reflections clearly demonstrate the tensions many lay Buddhists in Buryatia negotiate: They recognize the value of religion but do not necessarily feel immersed in faith; they feel they should be more persistent in their practice but turn to ritual as a strategy for problem-solving; they rely on themselves but also—when in need—on the divine. To many lay Buddhists like Ayuna, their lack of faith and religious expertise is a cause of frustration and a living proof of the violence exerted on Buryat traditions by the Soviet powers. This is usually dealt with by recourse to professional religious specialists, but in rarer instances, laypeople turn to self-education or join lay organizations to be better able to practice Buddhism.

Lama Erdem, a *geshe* monk educated in India, is a popular advanced lama in Ulan-Ude who regularly gave a course open to the public on the basics of Buddhism at the time of my fieldwork.[2] In his lectures, Lama Erdem would stress the importance of reading and thereby acquiring as well as critically evaluating knowledge of Buddhist philosophy and practice. He highlighted that while this is important for any practitioner, it is particularly needed in his native Buryatia. Having lived in India for a decade and a half, now based in Buryatia and regularly visiting Moscow, where he has a group of followers, Lama Erdem contrasted practitioners in the latter two places. A perfect Buddhist layperson, he argued, would be halfway between a Moscow Buddhist and a Buryat. While the former knows a lot and spends extensive hours reading texts and meditating, the latter has stronger faith and appreciates the value of ritual. While the former lacks genuine belief and does not understand ritual, the latter does not read at all and believes in everything uncritically (or has "blind faith"; Rus., *slepaĩa vera*). Even though Lama Erdem did not use the normative terms of "good" and "bad" Buddhist practice employed by many laypeople, his observations touch on similar key concepts: ritual, knowledge and faith, and the perceived skewed balance between them.

Shared—and permissible—religious imperfection is mutually recognized in a range of settings within and outside of Buddhist counseling. Seen through this lens, Buddhist counseling appears as a practice that is not officially promoted or entrenched in doctrine yet binds those who nonetheless engage in it into an imagined community of accepted divergence. The very practice itself can be considered religious intimacy, but it also provides a setting to share small infringements of religious prescription with coreligionists. One consultation I witnessed pertained to a young man's drinking problem. His wife and mother, agreeing on the severity of the problem, visited a lama together to find a solution. The young lama, a tall, strongly built man towering over the women, responded to their query in an unexpected way: "So what? There's no problem in drinking a little from time to time. I myself drink sometimes, too!" The lama laughed. The women, initially surprised by this reaction, tried to pinpoint the underlying issue: "But he drinks vodka. A lot!" The lama did not back down: "I drink vodka, too!" In this half-joking manner, the pair eventually homed in on the complex problems he was facing (joblessness, aggression, etc.) and the possible reasons behind it, discussing potential ritual and interpersonal interventions with the lama. The recognition of the shared imperfection of the lama and the layperson helped to assure the women that all was not lost—the situation might not be as dire as they had thought, since everyone, even a lama, might drink some vodka once in a while. It showed that the hardships Buddhists face are shared by others, as are their imperfect reactions to them. It also lessened the distance between the lama and the laity, implying a shared struggle toward gradually becoming better Buddhists and people, if pressed by the struggles of everyday urban life.

Buddhist Imperfections

Any discussion of Buddhist imperfections in Buryatia would have to include complaints about the shortcomings of the sangha. These have been prominent in public and private discussions on the state of Buddhism in Buryatia and a significant factor in the post-Soviet religious resurgence. These anticlerical critiques mainly focus on the background of Buryat lamas and their intentions, as well as on the anti-Tibetan parochialism discussed earlier.

Lamas in Buryatia today are mostly young and middle-aged men of rural background, although young urbanites are increasingly entering Buddhist education as well. The vast majority of lamas are not celibate monks but are married and reside outside of datsans with their families. Noncelibacy is partly a result of the Soviet disrobing of lamas and the destruction of the monastic system. At the same time, a nonmonastic tradition of nonstaff steppe lamas existed in the pre-Soviet period, too. In the mid-2010s, as several informed interlocutors estimated, there were likely only a handful of celibate lamas in Buryatia. Noncelibacy among lamas in Russia in the post-Soviet years has been openly criticized by the Fourteenth Dalai Lama and remains a contested issue today (see Abrahms-Kavunenko 2015 on a similar situation in Mongolia and Sinclair 2008 on Kalmykia). However, it remains accepted as a local tradition by many.

Tara Sinclair (2008) describes two kinds of Buddhism in Kalmykia in the early 2000s: "revival" (passed on by older generations) and "reform" (preached by newly arrived Tibetan monks). The two groups are "conceptually distinct but are entwined in practice" (242), each building on and dialectically coexisting with the other. While reform Buddhists consider celibacy a must, revival Buddhists view it with skepticism. As Sinclair puts it, "There is a widespread sense that monastic discipline is too restrictive, people want to have lovers, spouses and eventually children, which they cannot as ordained monks with vows of celibacy" (246). Buddhist specialists in Kalmykia, too, expect to lead a family life and typically disrobe as monastics when they want to marry, usually delighting their parents with the prospect of children.

Such expectations also exist in Buryatia. While monastics are highly esteemed and much respected, people do not necessarily see monasticism as an option for themselves and their loved ones. They hope to lead a regular family life, while also pursuing the path of a Buddhist lama. A young urban lama, Lama Daba, shared with me how difficult it had been to maintain strict Buddhist practice on returning to Buryatia after studying at a Tibetan monastery in India. While initially he had intended to hold to his monastic vows, he felt pressure from his parents to start a family since he was in his late twenties. In addition, he felt unable to keep up with his reading and meditation schedule, as being a lama in Buryatia typically means that most of the day is devoted to public khural rituals and individual lay consultations afterward.

Marriage and noncelibacy do not preclude one from being an esteemed lama in Buryatia, but some other transgressions do. Consuming alcohol, while widely accepted in moderation and outside of duty, is harshly judged while in service. A lay friend, Sayan, was left in shock and seriously offended by a lama who showed up drunk to his grandmother's funeral. They had been close, and her death was deeply upsetting to him as it was. Sayan was seriously angered by the disrespect that the drunk lama showed. To him, the lama came to represent the state of much of the Buryat clergy. Returning to Buryatia after years of studying and working abroad, and having lost several family members over recent years, Sayan had become a zealous Buddhist. With roots in a district in the south of Buryatia where shamanism was widespread, Sayan was part of a new urban Buddhist youth. They felt themselves to be heritage Buddhists—because they were Buryats—but were learning about the religion from an eclectic array of sources, including the internet, books, and various Buddhist lectures, as well as in traditional Buddhist settings, such as consultations and temple visits. While being proud of this heritage Buddhist identity, Sayan had a difficult—and in large part negative—experience when it came to encounters with local Buddhism. The lama at his grandmother's funeral was irresponsible and drunk, and some of the lamas he met in temples were annoyed by his questions on Buddhist philosophy and ethics and would turn him away. While Sayan did eventually find several Buryat lamas who became his teachers, the shortcomings of the local sangha were in his experience all too real. A few years later, Sayan moved abroad to devote himself to Buddhist education.

Lay Buddhists like Sayan are all too aware of their own religious shortcomings. Laypeople readily acknowledge their superficial knowledge of Buddhist philosophy and ethics and their reliance on the sangha for guidance as to what Buddhists should and should not be doing. This self-consciousness about practicing religion "correctly" was in fact an important methodological hindrance, as people were often reluctant to talk about Buddhism with me since they thought they did not know it well enough. They would refer me to lamas, but lamas would often say the same thing: "I am just a simple lama." I heard this time and again. To learn about Buddhism, they instructed me to read Buddhist texts and speak with high Buddhist teachers instead. While this self-consciousness about religious expertise is to some extent present in other contexts as well, it seems particularly pertinent in the postsocialist setting, where antireligious policies and repressions resulted in both a huge loss of knowledge, infrastructure, and expertise and a desire to reconnect with the past (Abrahms-Kavunenko 2012, 2015; Buyandelger 2013; Højer 2010; Humphrey 1992).

Saskia Abrahms-Kavunenko (2013) argues that religious ignorance in Ulaanbaatar constitutes a site of importance not just because of regret over religious loss but also because of its generative capacities. "Religious ignorance," she argues, "mobilises and is mobilised in a number of interacting ways the predominant effect of which has been the perceived proliferation of Buddhism as a site of possible knowing" (16).[3] While lack of knowledge can cause discomfort, it also facilitates a creative, explorative, and adaptive engagement with religion. The creative space that religious ignorance constitutes allows for an efflorescence of activities and forms that might appear less likely in a more formal religious setting, including open discussion of apprehensions toward religious institutions and actors, tapping into the potential of ritual to ameliorate dire socioeconomic conditions, and open and unapologetic religious syncretism. In the Buryat context, the perceived lack of Buddhist expertise gives rise to a vibrant, contested, and eclectic urban religious field.

Moral and Monetary Imperfections

An important focus in Buryatia is on the motivations of lamas and the corrupting influence of money. There is a widespread concern about lamas choosing the religious path out of desire to earn a good living. It is typically thought in Buryatia that lamas make an "average," "comfortable" wage, as my interlocutors put it. This is also considered appropriate. As one layman put it, lamas need to earn enough so that they do not have to worry about making ends meet, but luxury is a clear sign that a religious specialist is not primarily concerned with his spiritual pursuit.

The popular idea instead is that people should choose this path in life out of compassion for others and a wish—or, rather, an imperative urge—to help them. In fact, the very vocabulary used in talking about Buddhist specialists is fraught with the danger of blunder. While some Buddhists do casually use terms like "work" (Rus., *rabota*) or "profession" (Rus., *professiĩa*) to talk about what Buddhist specialists do, "office" (Rus., *ofis*) to indicate the spaces where they conduct consultations or "salary" (Rus., *zarplata*) to refer to their income, many others consider these terms inappropriate or even offensive. Talking to my Buryat interlocutors about the more practical aspects of their Buddhist practice thus sometimes became a laborious exercise to express what is typically unsaid, often with inelegant phrases like "the money we leave the lama" or "the place where the lama sees laypeople."

These concerns are especially prominent in the urban context. The urban environment is associated by many in Buryatia with immorality, crime, uncertainty, and lack of dignity. All kinds of temptations and pitfalls are thought to dwell there, with little of the guiding oversight of a close-knit community. In this uncontrolled and unscrupulous urban setting, wealth comes into focus as an issue of concern and debate. Since money concentrates in the city, urban lamas—at least in theory—have more access to it, and many in Buryatia are concerned that money has become the guiding motivation for urban lamas. It is not that wealth per se is seen as corrupting among Buryat Buddhists. Quite the opposite, wealthy people are well respected—so long as they contribute proportionately to the community and to its shared projects. Most of my interlocutors held the same to be true for lamas: While excessive wealth does pose a threat to a lama's virtue by way of concomitant temptations, it is not wealth itself that is harmful, and most laypeople expect lamas to lead a comfortable life.

This debate on the motivation of urban lamas can be seen as an iteration of the tension between the short-term and long-term cycles of exchange. As Jonathan Parry and Maurice Bloch (1989) have it, the short-term cycle refers to the economic activities of a person related to individual appropriation, enjoyment, luxury, and competition. In contrast, the long-term cycle of exchange is associated with the reproduction of the social body and shared values. Parry and Bloch argue that it is not the short-term cycle of exchange itself that is perceived as morally dubious but its domination over the long-term cycle. Normally, the two are intertwined and interdependent: Individual economic gains are harnessed not just to sustain the individual but also to contribute to socially productive ends. When the short-term cycle takes precedence, however, the related economic activities become "morally opprobrious" (1989, 28). Such concerns are active in debates around urban lamas: Their independence and greater opportunity for earning places their intentions and their role within the community under scrutiny. Hence, in the words of the rural abbot Lama Ayur mentioned earlier, urban lamas are "traitors." In the words of the Khambo Lama, they are "greedy for money."

This alleged greed, then, is part of what is locally often referred to as the commercialization (Rus., *kommertsializatsiia*) of Buddhism. Concerning lamas, this implies that money is the guiding motivation for their work, which is not just undesirable but also calls into question their skills and the efficacy of their ritual labor. On the part of the laity, this critique of commercialization points to excessive reliance on the sangha and on ritual intervention. Such a so-called consumerist (Rus., *potrebitel'skii*) approach by the laity is seen to transform not just Buddhist expertise, ritual activities, and divine help into commodities but also the health, wealth, and well-being that they bring into goods to be acquired. Consequently, the wealthier one is, the more benefits one will reap—a predicament far from desirable in the moral economy of Buryat Buddhism.

An important reason why consumerist approaches are harshly judged in Buryatia is the predominance of selfless giving in Buddhism. Jonathan Parry (1986) argues that disinterested generosity emerges as a virtue in societies where it is opposed to market exchange. An ethical imperative toward selfless giving emerges in societies where the economy is largely uncoupled from other spheres. That is, the promise of otherworldly benefits facilitates generous behavior in contexts where one needs an extra incentive to turn away from profits for oneself. Not only is selfless generosity seen in Buryatia as a virtue in general as well as a soteriological pursuit, but it is deemed especially desirable in a context where other political and economic actors appear to be guided by selfish and unvirtuous interests.

Disinterested generosity plays a crucial role in Vajrayana Buddhism, as it does in a number of other Indic religious traditions (see, for instance, Heim 2004; Ohnuma 2005). The *paramita* (a "perfection" or "virtue") of generosity is one of the key perfections that must be mastered to attain Buddhahood. Among these perfections a Buddhist seeks to develop through various practices and techniques, generosity is the first on the list and therefore the launching point for much of Buddhist endeavor. The perfection of generosity is significant to all traditions of Buddhism, but it plays a special role in Vajrayana and Mahayana Buddhism. Here, it is not one's own attainment of enlightenment that is the prime goal of a religious practitioner. Instead, one strives for enlightenment to be able to help all sentient beings to attain it as well. That is, the foremost ideal for a Vajrayana and Mahayana Buddhist practitioner is the bodhisattva, who strives toward enlightenment for the benefit of others. Awareness of the doctrinal reasoning behind this ideal and identification with it as a guiding principle vary greatly among Buryat Buddhists. However, the themes of giving and helping are widely present in Buryatia, both in formal Buddhist contexts, such as teachings, and in the more general consensus that Buddhism is largely about generosity and helping others.

Generosity without an expectation of return, known as *dāna* in Buddhism and other Indic religions, is a crucial Buddhist practice. Through it, a Buddhist seeks to transform themselves, achieving greater detachment from the mundane and purifying the mind. Importantly, this kind of giving generates karmic merit, resulting in favorable rebirth. In Buddhist doctrine, gifts should flow upward to bring most merit. They should be given, for instance, to honorable members of the sangha or to a bodhisattva (Ohnuma 2005, 114). The doctrinally grounded upward flow of Buddhist giving leads to a theoretical model of giving as the link between two distinct groups, the sangha and the laity. This is usually conceptualized as a system of exchange where the laity gives material support to the sangha, and the sangha gives ritual support and merit to the laity. According to Ivan Strenski (1983, 470), "Buddhist society was formed in the process of ritual giving. . . . Giving defines the very relationship between the sangha and lay society." He argues that in early Buddhism, it was this exchange with the laity that led to the "domestication" of the sangha, by which he means the sedentarization of the lives of previously wandering renouncers, as well as their entering into ritual, social, political, and economic relations with the laity.

In practice, however, things appear to be more complicated than in doctrine. Scholars have long debated whether *dāna* can ever be truly free, given the soteriological, social, and other benefits that it carries (e.g., Laidlaw 2000; Parry 1986; Rozenberg 2004). Moreover, many if not most Buddhists in fact conceptualize and practice truly virtuous, meritorious giving in a much broader sense than the oft-cited ideal of a disinterested upward-flowing "free" gift (see also Sihlé 2015). It is more diverse in settings of giving, its outcomes, as well as recipients, including beggars or others in need. Katherine Bowie (1998, 471), examining Thailand, puts it as follows:

> Contrary to the narrow doctrinal interpretation suggesting that only the sangha or Buddhist monkhood are appropriate recipients, most villagers have a broader conception of merit making which includes charity to the poor. Villagers generally use the phrase *tham bun* (to make merit) to refer to a wide range of good deeds or good actions occurring throughout everyday life, regardless of institutional setting. Acts ranging from helping villagers whose homes had burnt to giving fruit to anthropologists can be meritorious.

Similarly, in other Buddhist contexts, meritorious religious giving also appears much broader than doctrine would suggest. In Burma, humanitarian aid and devotional offerings to healers are also part of this field (Brac de la Perrière 2015). In Sri Lanka, organ donations are an important kind of Buddhist giving (Simpson 2004). Clearly, in a variety of Buddhist settings, it is not only giving to the sangha that constitutes virtuous giving.

Buddhist Giving in Practice

From the lay perspective, virtuous Buddhist giving can be directed at a broad range of receivers, and it can take a variety of forms. In Buryatia, as in other parts of the Buddhist world, charitable donations are part of the field of meritorious giving. One interlocutor, for instance, said that she tries to donate to a charity for orphans on the days of the Buddha of Medicine, when merit is multiplied. But remunerations for religious services are also considered a form of appropriate and virtuous giving, as they are in other Buddhist settings (Sihlé 2015).

In Buryatia, while some may call such remunerations to lamas a "payment" (Rus., *oplata*), many Buddhists are hesitant to use market-related terms for a religious transaction and prefer to call it terms like "donation" (Rus., *pozhertvovanie*), "offering" (Rus., *podnoshenie*), or to "thank [the lama] for" (Rus., *otblagodarit'*). Various strategies are employed to distinguish the money given for consultations from payments in market contexts. My interlocutors highlighted that it is important that the money is given in banknotes rather than coins.[4] Coins would imply a pittance, like alms given to beggars, and would therefore be disrespectful. People also do not ask for change—something that is common in market transactions but would be inappropriate in this context. Another factor that distinguishes these remunerations from payments is the etiquette around handling banknotes. People often straighten out the banknote before offering it. They then usually place it on the table without drawing attention to it, without mentioning it, and usually without the lama acknowledging it. Several informants told me that they hand the money directly to the lama because they find this more respectful—but use two hands to do it, in line with the Buryat-Mongolian etiquette of gift giving. In several cases, I saw people putting money on the table before the consultation rather than after, either with offerings needed for the ritual or on its own. In these cases, too, it was done in a discreet manner, arguably to negate the dynamic of a payment that follows a service, instead displaying the money as an offering and a sign of one's reverence to the lama upon entering, often together with bowing.

Such remunerations for rituals and consultations are not intended to generate merit. People do not conceptualize this giving as independent of the consultation, even though a strict service-payment relation also does not apply. Laypeople and lamas alike often explained to me that one does not have to leave a remuneration; it is wholly up to them. However, they invariably do. The reason for this is not only social convention but also—as my interlocutors explained—a shared understanding that lamas are professionals who have gained valuable education and possess unique skills that need to be sustained. Like other professionals, they should be compensated fairly for their labor. At the same time, many talked about remunerations as sustaining lamas and therefore enabling anyone in need to make use of Buddhist help, even if they do not have significant means. If one does have the means to remunerate for lamas' services appropriately, my interlocutors explained, they carry a responsibility to sustain this religious infrastructure that is available to all. To my knowledge, the only Ulan-Ude temple that had a set price list for different rituals rather than a system of voluntary remuneration was the "female" datsan (Zhenskiĭ datsan). Being rather marginalized in the Buryat Buddhist field, this seemed like a way of ensuring sufficient income with few lay visitors. At the same time, the price list itself became a cause of skepticism to some laypeople who considered a set price for rituals to be inappropriate and overly consumerist.

In consultations and rituals, lamas' everyday service to the laity is considered a form of giving to those in need. Lamas offer up their skill, expertise, care, advice, general knowledge, and experience, as well as their long-cultivated relationship with particular deities, for the benefit of the layperson. Sometimes, they even tap into their personal and professional networks to provide them with help. Moreover, some lamas explicitly frame their provision of such counseling to the laity as a sacrifice. Since it takes up much of the lama's day, they have less time and energy to pursue their own individual practices, such as meditation or reading. Some lamas spoke to me about Buddhist counseling as their service to the laity at the cost of their individual advancement along the Buddhist path. The Khambo Lama also frames the main role of the sangha as the giving of selfless help to the laity. In an address to lamas, he urged them: "Whether we [religious professionals] want this or not, we must take an active part in all spheres of life of the people. Otherwise, we move away from the people. . . . Give your every day after the morning khural to the believers, with as little concern for yourselves as possible, because caring about one's own well-being is a false path. And woe to the lama to whom laypeople do not come for consultations" (quoted in Makhachkeev 2013, 13–15).

Other kinds of Buddhist giving can be virtuous and impactful but far removed from the free gift ideal. A friend, Sayan, told me about his visit to Ivolginskiĭ datsan before an operation—a pilgrimage of sorts to ensure its success. He slowly circumambulated the grounds, spinning prayer wheels and repeating mantras, and walked into every temple, prostrating and leaving offerings of rice and coins. After a long and exhausting round, he entered the main temple and did the same. He also ordered prayers. The lama who collected donations for the new temple was busy with other people, so Sayan walked past him and left. As he was leaving, however, he started feeling guilty about not having donated money for the new temple and addressed the protector deities in his mind: Sayan pledged that if they made sure that the operation went well, he would make a large donation to the new temple. Later, as Sayan was recovering after the successful operation, he remembered his pledge but ignored it, thinking about all the other things he could do with the money. That night—as Sayan later recalled with laughter—he had terrible nightmares, and so he headed to the temple first thing in the morning, finally fulfilling his part of the bargain. The donation that Sayan made is therefore neither a free gift nor a payment or a remuneration but an act of conditional giving where both this-worldly and supernatural factors played a role: embarrassment in front of the fundraising lama, the wish for protection and help, the heightened, efficacious setting of a pilgrimage, Sayan's commitment to Buddhist practice, the obligation to reciprocate to the protectors as promised, and other factors.

An upward flow of Buddhist giving as purported ideal is also challenged by the many ways in which the sangha gives to the laity. Buddhist lamas give to the laity in the form of social engagement, such as the Social Flock project, where the Buddhist Traditional Sangha of Russia (BTSR) gives away sheep to the laity (Jonutytė 2020c), or the Buryat-language programs, such as the radio station and Buryat-language campaigns and festivals for children (Zhambalova 2021, 140). In a particularly striking instance, one prominent Buryat lama, Choidorzhi Budaev, "gifted" a temple to the laity.

Since the outset of the Buddhist revival in Buryatia in the late 1980s, over a dozen temples have been built in Ulan-Ude, a significant undertaking in terms of resources, time, and effort. While some were constructed on money raised during live TV fundraising shows (Rus., *telemarafon*), others relied on regional ties, door-to-door fundraising, and other networks for gathering funds, materials, and labor. One temple, however, stands out from the rest. It was built on a mortgage taken out by the founder, who is also its abbot. Lamrim Temple, named after a class of Tibetan Buddhist text that discusses the path to enlightenment, is a project of the middle-aged Buryat lama Choidorzhi Budaev. Starting off as a driver at a datsan, he went on to study at the Zanabazar Buddhist University in Ulaanbaatar in the 1980s, before returning to Buryatia to take on important positions in the local Buddhist administration. In 1993, he was elected the Khambo Lama but was soon removed, allegedly because of accusations of embezzlement.[5] Budaev then established his own local Buddhist organization, Lamrim, and later regional and federal Buddhist umbrella organizations, contributing to the changing institutional landscape of the previously centralized Buryat Buddhist administration. His efforts, however, have been somewhat marginal and have not undermined the prevalence of the BTSR, which runs most datsans in Buryatia.

In fact, Budaev embraces his marginal position in the local Buddhist hierarchy and uses it to criticize the current state of the sangha, which he sees as degenerate. As Budaev claimed in an interview, it was a wish to purify the sangha in Buryatia that was among the main reasons for building Lamrim Temple. Even though he had run several urban temples over the preceding two decades, the lamas there were just like elsewhere in Buryatia in terms of limited knowledge and noncelibacy. Budaev does not deem himself a role model: He does not lead a monastic life, while he often wears lama-like robes despite being a family man.[6] He admits to being beyond change as a result of the time when there were few opportunities for rigorous monasticism. Instead, he wants to be a facilitator, building a "proper" temple and bringing in well-educated Tibetan monks, a move he hopes will gradually help reform the Buryat sangha.

With this in mind, Budaev started the construction of Lamrim Temple in a quiet area not far from the city center in 2007. He later took out a private loan of RUB 45.5 million, opening a restaurant in the temple complex so that its profits would cover the loan payments. A hotel had also been planned but was never opened, and the whole temple complex, while open to the public, was still under construction when the economic crisis hit Russia in 2014. It became difficult for Budaev to keep up with loan payments, which had at times been RUB 1.2 million a month but fell that year to around 200,000.[7] The restaurant, with its fairly high prices and fancy interior, was not particularly popular, as it was out of the way and did not meet the standards of some of the well-off clientele that it targeted. After several unsuccessful attempts to restructure the debt, Lamrim Temple was put up for auction—an unprecedented event in Buryatia that was shocking to many. Unsurprisingly, no buyers volunteered, and Budaev was judged bankrupt in the summer of 2016. While a small group of lamas had split off from Budaev's organization over financial uncertainties half a year earlier, lamas who remained loyal were far from sure of a positive outcome and were considering various options for the future. In 2018, a gas company bought the datsan and transferred it to Budaev, but he continued to make payments to them to return the money for the purchase.[8]

The founder, Budaev, explained that the datsan was largely his gift to the people of Buryatia. The new temple with its envisioned "correct" Buddhist activities was to be an offering to both the Dalai Lama and the local people. The gift-like rhetoric around it focuses on two main points. One is giving local people an opportunity to practice what Budaev saw as a more authentic version of Buddhism, where monks would have completed substantial Buddhist education and would keep their vows. This would, in his opinion, not just provide laypeople with better and more varied ritual services and produce more merit but also inspire them to strive toward the Buddhist ideal, thus transforming their behavior and attitude toward life. While such correct Buddhism is, according to Budaev, very

FIGURE 16. Lamrim datsan's main temple, Ulan-Ude, 2016. Photo by author.

much needed in a socioeconomically depressed place like Ulan-Ude, it is not possible now due to the current deteriorated state of the Buryat sangha. Budaev therefore risked his own material well-being and took out a loan to provide this opportunity to the local laity.[9]

An important facet of the gift-like rhetoric is the fact that Budaev is building the temple using his own funds rather than gathering donations from laypeople. This rarely happens in temple building in Buryatia because donating toward such projects generates merit, and, as described earlier, people engage in it for a variety of reasons. Another Ulan-Ude lama shared a widespread sentiment when he told me that it seems not just odd but outright unfair not to accept lay donations for such a cause because this deprives laypeople of a merit-making opportunity. Even more, he carefully added, this implies motivations that are far from desirable in a lama: pride, a cry for acknowledgment, perhaps even narcissism. In contrast, Budaev highlights that he does not collect donations on moral grounds: People in Buryatia are poor, and he does not wish to burden them by asking for their money. Instead of stripping them of their last rubles, he argues, they themselves need support, which is what he is trying to achieve with the new temple. Many laypeople saw the good intentions in his undertaking but disapproved of his stubbornness. As a laywoman told me after a khural in Lamrim Temple, she did not see why he would not put a donation box in the temple or organize a TV fundraiser—while she personally could not give much, a large number of small contributions would still be substantial. However, even after the financial difficulties became public and seemingly overwhelming to Budaev, he continued to insist on not collecting lay donations.

Budaev—like some regulars I saw in his temple—highlighted his good intentions as being inscribed into the materiality of the temple. In many conversations, people pointed to the beautiful Buddhist art painted on the walls by a Tibetan artist, the quality furniture imported from Europe, and the imposing Buddha statue from Nepal. Taking journalists on a tour, Budaev lingered on the rubbish bins, windows, and bathroom tiles—of which he was proud because the temple was not built and furnished *kak papalo* (Rus., "randomly," "without sufficient attention") but was expensive and carefully thought through.[10] This quality was supposed to demonstrate Budaev's dedication to the project and to materialize his offering in a way that would be purifying and transformative. He had been active in Buryat Buddhism for over three decades, and this was to be his most significant contribution to its revival—in his words, a "pure" temple, where Buddhism could finally be "properly" practiced. To him, this would involve both material and immaterial forms: a temple that adheres more strictly to the canon in terms of physical space (for instance, through having monastic quarters within the precincts as well as a residence for the Dalai Lama in case he visits) and in terms of the kinds of people, knowledge, and practices present there.

In many ways, Budaev's gift to Buryat Buddhists is quite imperfect. His unwillingness to take donations and suspected pride was criticized by other Buddhists. His grand gesture appears less than grand in reality as the temple has not functioned as intended. Some Tibetan monks conduct rituals there but only on short trips and never in the form of a full monastic assembly. The temple itself has been a constant construction site, never completely finished. After the bankruptcy and temporary closures, it could be seen to be already falling apart, with the roof and walls in poor repair. Yet the Lamrim Temple remains important as a case of imperfect Buddhist giving, one that is religiously, socially, and politically consequential. In the context of a contemporary Russia marked by religiopolitical isolationism, everyday precarity, and declining minority cultural sovereignty, this grand temple dares to pursue a different kind of future for the Buryat Buddhist community.

An Ethical Community of Giving

Widening the lens to capture a broader range of meritorious Buddhist giving enables us to see how practices of giving, rather than distinguishing the laity from the sangha, instead create a sense of mutuality and local sociality. Through acts of care, support, and appropriate conduct, it creates a community of givers. Consider a passage from my interview with Sesegma, a Buryat woman in her early forties who comes from a remote district of Buryatia but has lived in Ulan-Ude for around two decades:

> KRISTINA: And have you donated to building a datsan?
> SESEGMA: Yes, of course. It wasn't huge sums of money—one thousand, two thousand, five hundred [roubles], something like that. I did it here [in Ulan-Ude] and in my home district as well. One has to lay bricks and all that. In [one of the Ulan-Ude datsans], Shėnėkhėn̄tsy [Buryats from Inner Mongolia, some of whom now live in Ulan-Ude] organized building a stupa; my family also contributed of course [Sesegma's family member is a Shėnėkhėn Buryat].
> KRISTINA: And why did you do it?
> SESEGMA: It was probably moral. And also, for the balance of the soul [Rus., *dushevnoe ravnovesie*]. If they ask you for money and you don't give it, you clench your money and only keep it to yourself, then you feel as if you're being egotistic. And when you give, you think, oh [sighs in relief], we make an effort for someone, for the people. You're not closed, like I don't want to give anything and so on. Even if we give little money, then the soul [Rus., *dusha*] is in balance.... How do I say this? Your soul is at peace then. So, when someone asks, I cannot say no; I cannot just walk by.... It's unpleasant to say no.

In fulfilling one's duty to give, one constitutes oneself as a moral person. More particularly, a moral person here is one who contributes to the collective, fulfills obligations, and is not led by egoism but rather by a concern for others.

A Buryat friend in his mid-twenties, Bair, grew up as a traditional Buddhist without particular intention or interest but had at the time of our acquaintance practiced, as he said, more "consciously" for a few years. He was an active participant in one of the international lay organizations in Ulan-Ude and dedicated much of his time and a significant part of his income to pursuing Buddhist practice. Knowing I was interested in religious giving, Bair often talked about it in relation to both Buddhist philosophy and its application. He stressed that while giving is a very basic Buddhist practice, it is also a very difficult one to develop, as most people's attachment to money and things is strong. He reflected on his own initial struggles with donating money and later feeling regret and on gradually developing a more spontaneous generosity, albeit always a work in progress. Donating money to his organization and making daily offerings to deities were some of the key aspects of Bair's dāna practice.

Bair stressed that his Buddhist practice of generosity extended beyond giving in strictly religious settings. Helping those in need was to Bair also part of his becoming a virtuous Buddhist. When he lends a friend money, Bair reflected, his generosity would lead the friend toward becoming a more generous person himself. When Bair gives someone good advice, this too will shape them into being a better person, which is to Bair synonymous with becoming a better Buddhist. In these instances of giving, Bair made reference to *upaya*, or "skillful means," which is the concept in Buddhism of spreading the teachings in adaptable, even unexpected ways so that they are more accessible to the recipient. After all, as Bair repeatedly explained to me, Buddhist teachings are the most precious gift, even if the recipient may not yet seek them. Since this gift is so valuable, it is seen as an obligation for an aspiring Buddhist to share it and spread it. The teaching, however, should not be forced upon the recipient, only transferred in moderate and appropriate ways.

A desired transformation of self, and that of others, is to Bair intimately intertwined with sharing knowledge and experience, as well as with the ontological interconnectedness present within tantric Buddhism.[11] However, well-read tantric Buddhists like Bair are few in number compared to more traditional lay Buddhists like Sesegma who spend less time and thought on their Buddhist practice. Duty and custom are important drivers behind both Bair's and Sesegma's acts of giving. The sense of duty is itself not uniform but of various shades and origins: social norms and obligations; a bond with one's home district; land and various human and nonhuman beings there; commitment to redeeming and upholding Buryat heritage, history, and tradition; a duty to contribute to "doing good" and thereby help others. In turn, following customs and fulfilling obligations are not just motivations to give; they also reinforce one's social relationships and are intimately linked to the cultivation of self.

While Sesegma's and Bair's approaches to Buddhist giving are different, both highlight the agency of the giver in cultivating self and others, as well as the embeddedness of the giver in social relations. In turn, these relations with others are key to the cultivation of a socially responsive self. I suggest that such mutuality of giving can be understood as an "ethical community," following Paul Anderson (2011). In a new reading of well-known studies of Muslim piety in Egypt (Mahmood 2005; Hirschkind 2006), Anderson suggests that newly pious urban Muslims are seeking not just self-transformation but also the transformation of others and of society at large. Through religious mutuality in their collective undertaking, pietists in Egypt seek to achieve a nonsecular society. Anderson (2011, 4) argues that, in this context, "piety is primarily constituted through social exchange and interaction" and suggests looking at the Egyptian piety movement as a gift economy where the gifts are "pious words," or teachings.

These "pious words" bind pietists into "ethical communities": They entail obligation and reciprocity, and they are inalienable from the giver (i.e., the speaker but also God, who is understood as the original giver), hence constituting a gift economy (Anderson 2011, 14). To Anderson (2011, 20), this ethical community "has emerged out of a felt need to maintain the community against the commodity economy of secularism. The pious gifts—the morally charged verbal exchanges—of *da'wa* [preachers] are the medium and process through which the ethical community comes into being."

In Buryatia, one enacts belonging to such an ethical community of giving both through conscious, laborious acts of giving and through simply doing what is expected of one in a particular situation. The latter can be referred to as "enaction," following David Sneath (2006). He argues that while many transfers are interpreted as transactions constituting exchange, some are in fact better explained as "enactions," or "the materialization of aspects of relations and persons that are more aptly described in terms of obligation and expectation" (89). Grounding his argument in examples from rural Mongolia, Sneath notes that in many transfers, the main impetus behind giving is following one's social role and performing what is customary or expected. The conventional hospitality of offering tea to a guest, for instance, "does not resemble Mauss's (1954) 'spirit of the gift'; the obligations to give and receive emerge from the social settings of host and guest, not the 'gifts' involved, and the transfer itself carries no obligations to reciprocate" (98–99).

What struck me in many of my interlocutors' reflections on giving was the customary nature of much of giving. There is little concern with why one makes offerings in certain situations; the fact that one does it and how it is done is more important. A Buryat friend, for instance, was amused by a question about why he leaves coins near prayer wheels: "No one will be able to answer this question. [He laughs.] . . . Simply, others do it; therefore, I do it." By performing appropriate acts of giving in particular situations, the person fulfills their role as, for instance, a correctly behaving layperson by remunerating a lama or a devout member of the sangha by providing help for other Buddhists.

Enactions of giving have a collective significance because the ideas concerning appropriate ways of giving are shared. Giving is often very public, and the gift is where "all [the] different eyes cross" (Ssorin-Chaikov 2006, 21–22). Through observing a "correct" giver, others recognize him or her as a fellow Buddhist. This is the case when, for instance, a person whose family member recently died makes ceremonial donations to every lama present in a khural service, and others present give approving looks and comments. This is also the case when a rich person donates to Buddhist projects proportionately, thereby maintaining the desired balance between the long- and short-term cycles of exchange. Moreover, people teach one another how to properly make an offering. People in temples often correct others who are, in their opinion, behaving inappropriately, for instance, those who circumambulate in the wrong direction or bring unsuitable offerings. In this way, in a context where many feel they do not practice Buddhism "correctly," such comments work to integrate one into a community of shared knowledge and norms. In an act of giving, the giver sees not only herself but also sees herself seen by others (Cross 2014, 139).

Buryat Buddhist givers constitute an ethical community, whereby one shapes the self through also shaping others via acts of giving. An ethical community forms not in a vacuum but in dialogue with societal processes, dominant values, and the surrounding socioeconomic and political context. The Cairo piety movement, for instance, positioned itself against secularization (Mahmood 2005, 48–57). Its members critiqued the fact that religion had come to be compartmentalized and reduced to a collection of discourses and practices—a separate domain of life that has little impact on everyday actions and decisions. Instead, they sought to return Islam to the fore and reintegrate it into every sphere of life as the grounding basis for all thought and action. Moreover, Anderson (2011, 3) adds, mosque movement participants constituted themselves in conscious opposition to the "commodity economy of goods, words and images experienced as morally and socially corrosive."

In Ulan-Ude, it is not the commodity economy per se that is seen as morally dubious and socially corrosive. What is critiqued—and what Buddhists seek to reform—is rather what is experienced as an ongoing degeneration of livelihoods and sociality in economic, social, and cultural terms: precarity and inequalities, mistrust, purported moral degradation, decline in Buryat language and traditions, and other problems. In Lama Erdem's well-attended lectures to laypeople, he often spoke of contemporary societal issues in Buryatia, such as alcoholism, high crime rates and violence, and indifference and enmity. He related them to the erosion of Buddhist values due to both Soviet atheism and post-Soviet "breakdown" (Rus., *razval*). While Buryats still consider themselves Buddhist, Lama Erdem argued, most of them are only nominal Buddhists, because a genuine mass following of the teachings would prevent such societal problems. He encouraged his followers to notice how their Buddhist practice gradually transforms them, allowing them to rise above the misery and crude condition of those around them. The Khambo Lama, too, sees his and the sangha's giving practices as being in opposition to dominant adverse trends in society: urbanization, alienation, and corruption. Those contributing to Buddhist projects, then, essentially partake in the building of an ethnical community positioned against the unvirtuous dominant structures that surround them. Practices of Buddhist giving serve as a substantial "tactic" to religious minority citizens in shaping their worlds, communities, and futures.

A prominent process in Buryatia that Buddhists are uniting against through their activities of giving is the experienced loss of Buryat culture and representation in contemporary Russia. Since Buddhism is closely linked with Buryat identity, increased Buddhist presence in the city adds to the visibility and value of Buryat representation in Ulan-Ude. At the same time, the visions for Buryat Buddhism embedded in these contributions differ greatly. To some, giving to Buryat Buddhism means bringing it closer to its Tibetan variant, considered more authentic and purer. To others, it means attempting to bring back Buryat traditional rural lifestyles and with them greater socioeconomic autonomy for the region. To still others, it means individual transformations toward more virtuous Buddhist living, through which the community and the region may also be transformed. Despite the differing visions, these imperfect forms of Buddhist giving work to strengthen shared Buryat Buddhist identity and cultural sovereignty, as well as social, political, and religious representation in the limited space available for their expression in contemporary Russia. Whether it is a laywoman donating money to a Buddhist building project to "lighten her soul," a lama giving his time to the laity for "utilitarian Buddhist" counseling, or a layman offering Buddhist advice to his friend, these imperfect acts of giving contribute "tactical" resources of an increasingly marginalized ethnic and religious minority.

Conclusion

"I feel like I have been robbed of my future. And the kids I don't even have yet are robbed of their future, too," my friend Zhambal told me as we were walking around a beautiful European park on a hot summer day. It was a year and a half since the outbreak of full-scale war in Ukraine. The sights could not have been more beautiful or the weather more pleasant, but there was little joy in our outing. Zhambal was able to secure a scholarship as a scholar at risk, enabling him to leave Russia when the military call-up took off. He was lucky—few opportunities were available to Russian citizens trying to leave the country as there were only a handful of countries accepting Russian emigrants. Only Kazakhstan, Kyrgyzstan, and Armenia allowed people with Russian domestic passports (Rus., *vnutrennii pasport*) to enter, while a few other countries, like Mongolia, accepted visitors with a regular Russian passport (Rus., *zagranpasport*) but no visa. Still, almost everywhere, visitors could only stay for a few months. To stay longer they had to find substantial grounds, such as a local job or studies. In most cases, these options were available only to the young and middle-aged, especially those with savings, knowledge of foreign languages, and who worked in particular professions, such as in the IT sector. The chances of a young scholar from the periphery of Russia being able to wait out this dangerous period in a safe European country were truly slim. In most academic and other programs, Russians, as citizens of the aggressor country, are not considered to be at risk.

Zhambal, in his early thirties, has always been truly passionate about Buryatia. He has been active in cultural and political circles his whole adult life and has always hoped to one day contribute to a different Buryatia, where Buryat language would dominate public life and Russians and Buryats alike would know and value Buryat history and culture. In Zhambal's lifetime, this had always seemed like a distant dream. But as the war in Ukraine continued unabated, it was now an image from the realm of fantasy. Zhambal was not able to return to Buryatia because of the military draft and because of the danger of cultural and political activists being arrested. At the same time, he was wary that spending this precarious time safely abroad would distance him from the lived realities of his fellow Buryats. He shared with me his worries that after the war, the returned soldiers would become the new elite, while those who spent this time abroad would be looked down upon as cowards and traitors. Thousands of disillusioned, traumatized, and violent men returning from the war could also potentially fuel new criminal structures and societal problems in the region.

When I spoke with him, Zhambal's vision of the future Buryatia was grim. He did not want to return to the kind of Buryatia he envisioned and had little hope for more positive developments. He also did not see a future for himself abroad, as his homeland had always been central to his hopes and dreams. Concerns like Zhambal's were very prominent in my conversations with Buryats who have fled Russia since the start of the war. Themes of new struggles for power, traumatized returning soldiers, deepening societal problems, and a substantial brain drain reoccurred. In October 2022, many had already noticed a great departure of professionals and those who were at all active in the oppositional political field. My interlocutors told me that the departure of men was so significant that it was even felt in Ulan-Ude through longer wait times for shuttle buses (Rus., *marshrutki*), the most popular means of local public transport, as many drivers fled the country. Even though a significant portion of these migrants did return to Russia over the coming months, the future seemed grim as a large proportion of professionals and active citizens remained abroad or were likely to leave again if possible.

Typically, Buddhism is not at the forefront of such considerations. There are more immediate problems of life and death, war and peace, exile and risk, on the minds of many Buryats today. Yet in these difficult circumstances, Buddhism continues to provide an important support system to many, aiding in making decisions, formulating courses of action, and making sense of the barely comprehensible situation many minority Russian citizens find themselves in today. Its everyday practice provides another source of tactics necessary in navigating contemporary Russia for those with few resources, as well as the basis of an alternative ethical community. Moreover, Buddhist lamas, while amply criticized by laypeople in the region, nonetheless remain a substantial authority, influence, and pillar of an alternative ethical community in Buryat society.

Looking at grand narratives and the official projection of Buryat Buddhism, one sees seamless Buddhist support of the Russian state and its war on Ukraine.

The Khambo Lama calls Buddhist participation on the Russian side of the war a "sacred debt," and in Buddhist Traditional Sangha of Russia's (BTSR) lamas' official speeches, Russia is the only motherland Buryats have. On the everyday level, the story is quite different. Lamas provide ritual help to those who mourn the loss of their relatives in war. They perform divination of the location and vicissitudes of soldiers who have lost contact with their close ones. Some lamas provide advice on how to flee the country or avoid conscription. Some refer to Buddhist philosophy and ethics to demonstrate to their followers that war is neither necessary nor good and that Ukrainians are people just like them.

Buddhism in Buryatia is rarely political in direct ways, other than the official demonstrations of loyalty to the Kremlin that are a condition of minority survival in contemporary Russia. Yet, as I have explored in this book, it constitutes an infrapolitical sphere: a field relating to identity, ethics, and collective action that amounts to a kind of politics in illiberal settings wherein the possibility of direct political action is heavily curtailed. Everyday religious interventions, from Buddhist consultations to religio-ethnic representations in urban space, are tactics available to a religious and ethnic minority in contemporary Russia and can be contrasted with the strategies available to the religious elites. This has been the case in Russia for many years, but the full-scale war in Ukraine has led to a further tightening of control over the public sphere. The ways in which everyday Buddhism enables the maintenance of a distinct personal and collective identity and contributes to the formation of alternative ethical frameworks and cultural orientations are socially and politically consequential.

While many Buryats feel insecure in their Buddhist practice amid the ongoing religious resurgence in the region, these Buddhist imperfections create a bond of religious intimacy among practitioners. Imperfect lamas guide an imperfect parish, all shaped by centuries of colonization and minoritization, as well as the extreme ethnic and religious repressions of the Soviet period. Post-Soviet Buddhist imperfections provide an opportunity for exploration and innovation both in terms of religious practice and communal—and, by extension, political—synergy. Particular strands of Buddhist history can and are being selectively highlighted, powerfully shaping continued religious and political identification. The post-Soviet moment provided newfound force to the historical synergy between Buryat Buddhist institutions and the Russian state, resacralizing this relationship and taking it to new heights. Yet this institutionalized alliance does not penetrate deep into everyday religion, which remains a powerful site of doubt, eclecticism, and possible resistance.

The urban setting provides an especially fruitful setting for such a Buddhist multiplicity. The city is more socially and economically diverse, marked by mobility and exchange. It hosts a varied selection of religious groups, both formal and informal, local and international, traditional and otherwise. Urban anonymity and a less watchful eye from the community enables religious explorations, divergence from the BTSR norm, and more diverse social and political underpinnings to Buddhism. The urban space also provides a visible arena for minority input and representation in a diverse—but Russian-majority—region.

The future of Buryatia, as of other minority regions in Russia, remains unclear. The full-scale invasion into Ukraine and especially the aggressive military draft have led to the surfacing of grievances with Russia. Among these are distress at the heavy losses of soldiers from Buryatia, as well as the seemingly disproportionate drafting of soldiers in the region. The externalities of the war, such as limited mobility and increased prices, do not go unnoticed. The current situation has also brought out and reinforced outrage with long-term injustices and inequalities in Russia. Online and abroad, Buryats have been sharing their stories of racial discrimination and violence experienced in Russian cities. They debate whether the depressed socioeconomic condition of the region represents a deliberate Russian policy to undermine ethnic regions. They condemn the policies leading to the rapid loss of minority languages, as well as the shrinking space for political participation.

Yet to many Buryats, Russia holds an important place in their lives and identities. Most of them grew up in Russia, speak Russian as their first language, and share a significant portion of their cultural and educational background with their fellow citizens from across the vast country. Their families and friends live in Russia; their careers are there. This has been the case for many generations. Such intertwinement of Buryats with Russia will not be seamlessly undone. At this point, many Buryats relate not just to Buryatia but also to Russia as their homeland.

Alongside those who do not doubt that the fate of their region is to be found within Russia are those who do see alternatives. Even before the Ukraine war, a small but substantial group of people in Buryatia saw the independence of Buryatia as necessary for the blossoming of the region and its people. The details of this vision vary, as historical Buryat lands extend well beyond the Republic of Buryatia itself, despite Buryats constituting a minority of the population across this region. Yet others, though few, see the future Buryatia forming a part of Mongolia, finally bringing the pan-Mongol vision to life. This is not an attractive vision to many due to the idea widespread in Russia that Mongolians are fundamentally "Asian" while Buryats and Russia are more "European" (Graber 2020, 37). Moreover, in Mongolia, Buryats continue to be labeled as more "Russified" and therefore fitting problematically into Khalkha-dominated Mongolian society (Bulag 1998). Finally, some of my interlocutors talked about other kinds of possible regional groupings Buryatia could be part of, such as entering into association with other Siberian peoples.

All these visions for the future of Buryatia remain blurry. Since the public sphere is extremely limited in Russia, and has been so for decades, genuine and open debates about these issues cannot be held. Alternative visions to the official Russia-centric one are outlawed and unable to effectively organize, and in the rare instances when they achieve visibility, they are immediately denounced as radical and separatist. At this time, all forms of local belonging and distinct identity are in themselves a political, not just a cultural, achievement. Urban Buryat Buddhism is one such form of belonging, best reflected not in official representations of political synergy, but in local practices of everyday religion. These constitute a meaningful field whose influence extends far into Buryat society and may one day contribute to the blossoming of a future Buryatia.

Acknowledgments

This book would not have been possible without the help and support of many people and institutions.

First and foremost, I feel eternally indebted to friends, colleagues, and research participants in Buryatia. From before my arrival in Ulan-Ude through to the very end of writing this book, so many of them have kindly shared their invaluable time, knowledge, and care with me without hesitation and despite the unfavorable conditions for our companionship. In the context of the already tense political climate at the time of my research, their acts of kindness are particularly meaningful. Given the extremely hostile sociopolitical environment in Russia as I sit to write this, I will refrain from mentioning the people who have supported and befriended me by name. I hope that I will be able to visit Buryatia again one day and give my thanks to them in person.

My research in Buryatia, including the bulk of the fieldwork for this book, started at the Max Planck Institute for Social Anthropology in Halle, Germany. There, I am especially grateful to my mentor Christoph Brumann, who spent countless hours patiently reading and discussing my work, all the while being a positive, supportive, and generous colleague. I also extend thanks to Saskia Abrahms-Kavunenko, Hannah Klepeis, and Beata Świtek for their friendship as well as their extensive engagement with my research and thinking process. I appreciate the many anthropology discussions, often extending late into the night, I shared with Ceren Deniz, Laura Hornig, Katerina Ivanova, Elzyata Kuberlinova, Giuseppe Tateo, Darya Tereshina, Diána Vonnák, and many others in Halle. I am grateful to many colleagues there for providing useful feedback for my work, including Elisa Kohl-Garrity, Patrice Ladwig, Dittmar Schorkowitz, and Asta Vonderau. I thank the Max Planck Society and the then codirector of MPI Halle, Chris Hann, for their generous support of my research.

In Lithuania, I have benefited from a great circle of colleagues for discussions concerning research, for mutual support, and for the liveliness of a small but enthusiastic anthropology community. At Vilnius University, I am especially grateful to Konstantinas Andrijauskas, Donatas Brandišauskas, Victor de Munck, Kristina Garalytė, Aivaras Jefanovas, and Deimantas Valančiūnas; at Vytautas Magnus University, to Jurga Bučaitė-Vilkė, Vytis Čiubrinskas, Eugenijus Liutkevičius, and Kristina Šliavaitė. I thank the administrative staff at the Faculty of Philosophy and especially the Institute of Asian and Transcultural Studies at Vilnius University, who have always been swift and thorough in providing assistance to my research.

Many colleagues have provided insightful feedback, having read through parts of this book or discussed my research in other settings. For this, I thank Ganchimeg Altangerel, Marjorie Mandelstam Balzer, Anya Bernstein, Trine Brox, Uradyn Bulag, Isabelle Charleux, Tatiana Chudakova, Tsypylma Darieva, Rebecca Empson, Peter Finke, Valeria Gazizova, Kathryn Graber, Caroline Humphrey, Jeanna Kormina, Stefan Krist, Smadar Lavie, Sayana Namsaraeva, Jeronim Perović, Justine Buck Quijada, Jesko Schmoller, Manja Stephan, Nikolai Tsyrempilov, and Ayur Zhanaev. I am grateful to various audiences for engaging with my work and providing astute comments during my presentations at the Groupe Sociétés, Religions, Laïcités, École pratique des hautes études; Seoul National University; the University of Cambridge; the University of Copenhagen; and the University of St. Andrews, as well as numerous conferences.

I had the pleasure of working through the material for this book and writing and presenting parts of it in the comfort of several research stays within vibrant academic environments. These include the Mongolia and Inner Asia Studies Unit at the University of Cambridge, the Center for Eastern European Studies at the University of Zurich, Alexanteri Institute at the University of Helsinki, and the Central Asian Seminar at Humboldt University of Berlin. I am grateful for their financial and administrative support as well as for the feedback and academic exchanges I shared with colleagues and other visiting fellows.

I am grateful to the language editor of this book, Shultz Abrahms-Kavunenko, for his excellent improvements of the text. I thank Jutta Turner for designing and allowing me to use two maps. I thank Cornell University Press editors Jim Lance and Bethany Wasik for their support in the publishing process. I also extend my thanks to the two anonymous reviewers who provided helpful feedback that much improved the final version of this book. Any shortcomings in the text are of course my own.

Finally, I could not have written this book without the warm support of my family and friends. I owe a special mention here to Artem Moskalev from whom I first heard about the esteemed monk Itigelov, a serendipity that led me to my interest in Buryat Buddhism.

My husband Vladimir has been there for me throughout the years of completing this book, shouldering together the challenges of fieldwork and the bumps in the writing process but also sharing the joy of learning about the rich Buryat Buddhist world. My daughters, Elena and Ona, have witnessed parts of the writing process and will hopefully forgive me for the long hours spent at my desk.

ACKNOWLEDGMENTS

Writing the draft manuscript for this book as well as part of the Mongolian fieldwork received funding from the European Social Fund under grant agreement with the Research Council of Lithuania (LMTLT), under the project "Urban Religion and Spatiality in Multiethnic Postsocialist Ulan-Ude," 2021–2023 (project no. 09.3.3-LMT-K-712-19-0059). Parts of the fieldwork in Buryatia were funded by the Max Planck Society, the Frederick Williamson Memorial Fund, and in Mongolia by the Research Promotion Fund of Vilnius University.

Notes

INTRODUCTION

1. I use the term *lama* (Rus., *lama*; Bur., *lama*), in general, to refer to a Buddhist professional religious specialist in Buryatia. With only few exceptions, lamas in Buryatia are men, noncelibate, and they generally reside outside of Buddhist temple complexes. The term derives from Tibetan (*bla ma*) but, unlike in Tibetan use, does not have to denote a venerated spiritual leader. There are several female lamas in Buryatia, too, but they remain marginalized and are deemed unorthodox in the Buryat Buddhist milieu.

2. Here and throughout the book, non-English online links are presented in endnotes. An article on the Russian Forbes site, October 4, 2022: https://www.forbes.ru/society/478827-rossiu-posle-21-sentabra-pokinuli-okolo-700-000-grazdan (accessed May 30, 2023).

3. An article on a Mongolian site Ikon, October 21, 2022: https://ikon.mn/n/2pbb (accessed July 10, 2025).

4. Joseph Kabzon, a Soviet pop singer from Donbas, had a long political career in the Aga Buryat Autonomous Okrug in the 1990s and the early 2000s. He was elected as a representative of this autonomous okrug to the Russian State Duma several times and is overall very well known and liked in the region.

5. An article on the Russian site *Komsomol'skai͡a Pravda*, March 3, 2022: https://www.kp.ru/daily/27371/4553876/ (accessed June 3, 2023).

6. That is, Buryats constitute approximately 0.7–1.0 percent of the Russian army, while Buryats constitute 0.34 percent of the Russian population. Here and throughout the book, social media sources are presented in endnotes. https://www.facebook.com/freeburyatia foundation/photos/a.119150370802487/200054992712024/ (accessed June 3, 2023).

7. On March 10, 2023, there were 55.6 deaths from the Republic of Buryatia for every 100,000 of the population, while there were 0.9 deaths from Moscow for every 100,000. Note, however, that this refers to not just Buryats but all soldiers from Buryatia. https://www.facebook.com/photo?fbid=206489685401888&set=pcb.206489755401881 (accessed June 3, 2023).

8. *Datsan* (Bur., *dasan*) is a local word in Russian to refer to a Buddhist temple complex in Buryatia. I use the local word instead of *monastery* because lamas in Buryatia usually do not reside in datsans or uphold other aspects of monastic life. Datsan may also be used to refer to single temples (which are also called *dugan* in both local Russian and Buryat, as well as *khram* in Russian). Datsan derives from Tibetan (*grwa tshang*), although unlike in Tibet, in Buryatia a datsan does not have to have a Buddhist university component.

9. The full name of the organization is the Buddhist Traditional Sangha of Russia (Rus., Buddiĭskai͡a traditsionnai͡a Sangkha Rossii). A more detailed discussion of this organization follows in chapter 2. The Khambo Lama (full title, the Pandito Khambo Lama; Bur., Bandida Khamba lama) is the commonly recognized highest position of Buddhist leadership among Buryats and the head of the Buddhist Traditional Sangha of Russia.

10. The term *sangha* can refer to the Buddhist monastic order, but in Buryatia, it is used as a collective term to refer to all Buddhist religious professionals.

11. https://www.facebook.com/photo/?fbid=1643468866045924&set=pcb.164346909 6045901 (accessed July 10, 2025).

12. Bur. and local Rus., *khural*. Khural is a Buddhist religious service in Buryat. Literally, khural means a "gathering" in Buryat, in this case, a ritual assembly of lamas.

13. Institute of Religion and Policy. 2022. "The Abbot of the Datsan 'Damba Braibunling': Their Lama in Donbass." April 26, 2022. https://irp.news/nastojatel-dacana-damba-brajbunling-ih-lama-na-donbasse/.

14. https://www.chita.ru/text/religion/2022/04/26/71284517 (accessed September 11, 2025).

15. https://vk.com/wall-482671_33966 (accessed May 30, 2023).

16. Victory Day (Rus., Den' Pobedy) marks the end of the Second World War and is celebrated on May 9 in Russia. In Putin's Russia, it has become a very important national holiday, complete with military parades and processions commemorating the "immortal regiment" (Rus., *bessmertnii polk*) by carrying pictures of family members or others who were war veterans or were otherwise affected by the Second World War. This holiday is often seen as "the breeding ground for state propaganda and glorifying military conflicts" (Pakhomova 2024, 14) and as being used "to cultivate a 'domestic brand of fascism'" (Pakhomova 2024, 14, quoting Zygar 2023, 225).

17. For an overview, see Jerryson and Juergensmeyer 2010.

18. The Buryat population has also shrunk since the 2010 census: from 461,389 to 460,053 (Rosstat 2021).

19. An all too narrow understanding of civil society as an associational, organized, NGO-like format functioning outside of state institutions has previously been critiqued by anthropologists, especially in relation to postsocialist Eurasia (Hann 1996). It is in such a narrow view of civil society that these authors and many others define it as "underdeveloped." As Chris Hann (1992, 20) has it, civil society is more productively defined "*positively* in the context of ideas and practices through which cooperation and trust are established in social life" (emphasis in the original).

20. VKontakte is the most popular social media platform in Russia.

21. Cf. Humphrey 1999 on such connectivities of urban shamanism in Buryatia in the 1990s. I explore this connection further in chapter 3.

22. In 1958, the name of the republic was changed to the Buryat Autonomous Soviet Socialist Republic, arguably to curb its connections with Mongolia and further remove Buryat ethnic identity from Mongolian.

23. Buryatia statistics data from *BurStat: Chislennost' naseleniia Respubliki Buriatiia v razreze raionov*. http://burstat.gks.ru/wps/wcm/connect/rosstat_ts/burstat/ru/statistics/population/ (accessed August 28, 2018).

24. Buryatia statistics data from *BurStat: Chislennost' naseleniia Respubliki Buriatiia v razreze raionov* (1.1.1). http://burstat.gks.ru/wps/wcm/connect/rosstat_ts/burstat/ru/statistics/population/ (accessed November 5, 2016).

25. An article on the news site Baikal-Daily, February 17, 2025: https://www.baikal-daily.ru/news/15/494832/ (accessed July 10, 2025).

26. An article on the RIA Novosti site. October 31, 2025: https://ria.ru/20221031/reyting_prestupnost-1827922290.html (accessed on June 3, 2023).

27. Note that this does not indicate fluency, only some knowledge.

28. *Pribalt* is a commonly used word in Russia to refer to someone from the three Baltic countries: Lithuania, Latvia, and Estonia. Outside Russia, many consider it an inappropriate, offensive term due to the comical or negative portrayals of people from the Baltics typically associated with this word.

1. BURYATS IN RUSSIA

1. These are Indigenous "small-numbered peoples" (Rus., *malochislennye narody*), a Russian classification of Indigenous peoples assigned to those ethnic groups with fewer

than fifty thousand people, living in the Russian Far North, Siberia, and the Russian Far East. In the 1920s, twenty-six ethnic groups were counted in this category.

2. With a brief unsuccessful attempt at introducing a Latin script in the 1930s.

3. Based on preliminary data from the first two weeks of mobilization, Buryatia was the third-hardest-hit region of Russia by drafting. The number of those mobilized exceeded the official plan from mobilization by more the three times. In contrast, in both Moscow and St. Petersburg, mobilization rates are well below average across Russia (respectively 73% and 83% of the national average). https://istories.media/stories/2022/10/05/kakie-regioni-otdali-bolshe-vsego-muzhchin-na-voinu/ (accessed May 18, 2023).

4. The process even resulted in a new Russian word, *obnulit'sia* (to return oneself to zero), used specifically for this process.

5. See Graber 2020 on the complex negotiations of belonging in Buryat-language media. While Buryat-language media maintains a minority-language public and upkeeps a particular kind of identity related to it, it also is largely state-sponsored, and as such it reproduces positions supporting the Russian state-sponsored dominating discourses. Minority-language media in Russia has also become a niche field of "cultural" expressions, as people typically consume Russian-language news for political, economic, and other relevant news.

6. See Humphrey 2011 on reactions to racial violence in Moscow and St. Petersburg in Buryatia.

7. An article on the SOVA website, January 25, 2023: https://www.sova-center.ru/racism-xenophobia/publications/2023/01/d47521/ (accessed May 21, 2023).

8. An article on the website Indigenous Russia, May 8, 2022: https://indigenous-russia.com/archives/21116 (accessed July 11, 2025).

9. The video is posted on the YouTube channel of the NGO Free Buryatia Foundation: https://www.youtube.com/watch?v=_aPBrWOwNhU (accessed May 22, 2023).

10. An article on TASS website, May 19, 2023: https://tass.ru/politika/17792949 (accessed May 22, 2023).

11. I was not able to find any scientific publications that followed from this research. The BTSR, which guards Itigelov's body, deems that this research was sufficient and has not allowed further studies.

12. The price for the ticket in 2016 was RUB 350. This system is, however, flexible, and non-Asians are sometimes turned down on the grounds that they are not Buddhists.

13. It is not quite clear why that particular year was chosen and not, for instance, 2002, when Itigelov was unearthed.

14. These are yearly collective rituals that take place in the summer, usually in June, in sites on hilltops demarcated by cairns. These rituals are held to give offerings to local master spirits and deities and are usually followed by a festive gathering.

15. Otherwise known as Vajrapani, Ochirvani is a protector bodhisattva who is associated with the Buddha's power but also more generally with strength and might.

2. BURYAT BUDDHISM

1. This also led to the phenomenon of "steppe lamas" (Rus., *stepnye lamy*), that is, lamas who were not registered and resided outside of monasteries.

2. While it is widespread knowledge reinforced by the BTSR itself that Empress Catherine the Great conferred this title upon Zayaev, it is likely that Zayaev himself initiated the process (Tsyrempilov 2013, 77).

3. Rus., TSentral'noe dukhovnoe upravlenie buddistov SSSR.

4. Sesegma Zhambalova (2011, 89) also notes the increased role of laywomen in Buryat Buddhism as a result of the Soviet period.

5. https://twitter.com/GLandsbergis/status/1650430549998092288 (accessed June 5, 2023).

6. Rus., TSentral'noe dukhovnoe upravlenie buddistov.

7. It is a widespread practice to think of a wish or ask a question and communicate it to Itigelov either in one's mind or on a piece of paper. If this is done properly and sincerely, many believe that Itigelov will respond (see also Quijada 2012).

8. See, e.g., Lee Myers (2002).

9. An example from March 3, 2017. "A woman says: 'I was told to carry an image of the Green Tara'. She looks at the various images of the deity that are for sale. Khambo Lama Itigelov advises: 'One must treat the teachings of Buddha carefully and scrupulously.'" This message is published in Russian and Buryat, and an interpretation by Khambo Lama Ayusheev is provided. It suggests that one should not handle sacred images carelessly. http://sangharussia.ru/content/detail.php?ID=658 (accessed April 3, 2017).

10. Among other prominent Buddhist sites today that enable the status and legitimation of the BTSR is the Zandan Zhuu statue. It is a statue of Shakyamuni Buddha, claimed to have been produced at the time of his life, that is, around the fifth century BC. As the story goes, it was moved between India, China, Tibet, and Mongolia before it was taken (many claim stolen) from Beijing by Buryat Cossacks in the early twentieth century and transported to Buryatia. Since 1991, it has been kept in the main temple of Ėgituĭskiĭ datsan in the east of Buryatia, open to visitors. The authenticity of Zandan Zhuu is not recognized internationally, but within Buryatia, its history is rarely questioned. Another important site is the self-arisen image of the goddess Yanzhima, which appeared on a stone in a forest in Barguzinskiĭ District in the north of Buryatia in 2005. The image is said to have appeared as a result of the intense efforts of an advanced tantric practitioner, Lama Soodoĭ, who had lived in Barguzinskiĭ Monastery nearby over a century earlier. The stone of Yanzhima now attracts believers from both within the region and outside of it, including from abroad. As worshipping Yanzhima is said to help in matters of love and fertility, it is predominantly women and occasionally couples who visit the site.

11. An article on RG.ru website. August 24, 2009: http://www.rg.ru/2009/08/24/medvedev-buddisty-anons.html (accessed February 16, 2017).

12. This is a local variation of the dichotomy of "ours" (Rus., *nash*) versus "not ours" (Rus., *ne nash*) behind various forms of social inclusion and exclusion in everyday life in Russia (see Pesmen 2000; Caldwell 2002).

13. This is true for Buryat, Kalmyk, Tuvan, Altaian, Tibetan, and Mongolian lamas, but many of my interlocutors expressed doubts about ethnic Russian or other European lamas, of whom there are several in Buryatia.

14. Samsara is the world of endless rebirth, defined by desire and suffering. This contrasts with the state of nirvana, where one is free from suffering and able to recognize things as they are.

15. "The Social Flock" (Rus., *sotsial'naia otara*) is a social engagement project of the BTSR aimed at supporting traditional Buryat sheep herding and popularizing an endemic breed of sheep.

16. An article on the *Mezhreligioznyĭ Sovet Rossii* website. March 27, 2023: https://interreligious.ru/news/news-council/news-council_645.html (accessed on July 10, 2025).

17. An article on the news site *Gazeta Nomer Odin*. No. 39, 2022: https://gazeta-n1.ru/archive/detail.php?ID=115713 (accessed July 11, 2025).

18. https://www.facebook.com/photo/?fbid=23947168751536915&set=a.469596499720804 (accessed May 28, 2023).

19. An article on the site *Sibir' Realii*. February 20, 2025: https://www.sibreal.org/a/buddizm-putinskogo-rezhima/32276081.html (accessed May 28, 2023).

3. URBAN BUDDHISM IN BURYATIA

1. For the relevant nonhuman beings in the region, see also Galdanova et al. 1983, 119–82, for Buryatia; and Swancutt 2012, 49–99, for Buryats in Mongolia.

2. Buryats therefore tend to avoid cemeteries, and people of mixed ethnic or religious backgrounds sometimes experience special tensions there. An interlocutor told me about her friend, an Orthodox Christian Buryat from Irkutsk Oblast who is also part Buddhist, who was told by a Christian priest to visit the graves of her family members. However, according to the Buddhist horoscope, that year was a time of increased danger when visiting cemeteries, and she had to avoid them at all costs. She did eventually go to the cemetery but went to a Buddhist temple immediately afterward to perform rituals to ameliorate potential adverse effects.

3. Stupas (Bur. and local Rus., *suburgan*) are a kind of Buddhist sacred architecture and usually contain relics. They are built for the purposes of commemorating persons or events, for the subdual and sanctification of territory, or to earn merit that leads to the growth of positive karma.

4. After the Tibetan Palden Drepung Tashi Gomang monastery.

5. Since there are no institutional structures for women to undergo Buddhist education in Buryatia, women who work in Zhenskiĭ datsan have typically studied in Mongolia.

6. Interestingly, a religious situation elsewhere in Russia, in Dagestan, is comparable: There exists a discursive separation of "traditional" and "modernist" branches of Islam, but they appear intertwined in practice (Kaliszewska 2023, 76–78).

7. This eventually fell through, as later in 2016 there were again financial and administrative problems that even resulted in discussions of potentially erecting the monument in the neighbouring city Chita. An article on the site UlanMedia. November 5, 2016: http://ulanmedia.ru/news/543438/ (accessed November 17, 2017).

8. An article on the site UlanMedia. December 25, 2015: https://ulanmedia.ru/news/480535/ (accessed June 16, 2023).

4. BEING A PILLAR

1. A *biznes-tsentr* in Russia is a mixture of a shopping mall and an office building.

2. People who come to consult a lama are called *prikhozhane* (lit., "those who come") in Russian. It can be loosely translated as "laypeople" or "parishioners," but these terms imply a level of commitment to the temple or the lama, which is not always present in the context of Buddhist consultations.

3. Divinatory Buryat is often more of an everyday spoken language than literary Buryat, incorporating many Russian words and phrases. For instance, *goorod* (Buryatized version of Russian *gorod*) was used here instead of *khoto* for "city," IUzhna-Koreeĭa (Rus., IUzhnaĭa Koreĭa) instead of Solongo for South Korea.

4. The new year usually starts sometime in February, according to the Buryat-Mongolian lunar calendar. It is customary to see a lama before or just after it to receive an astrological prognosis for the year. This horoscope is based on Tibetan, Mongolian, and/or Buryat Buddhist astrological traditions and is related to the Tibetan Tsi astrology.

5. My impression was that this extra money was an additional demonstration of gratefulness, although it also could have been remuneration for what was a relatively lengthy consultation.

6. Usually referred to in Russian as *priëm u lamy* (lama's reception) or *konsul'tatsiia*. People also refer to the practice as *pogovorit' s lamoĭ* (talk to a lama) and *posovetovat'sia s lamoĭ* (to get advice from a lama).

7. This is not to say that ritual is a one-sided form of communication but simply to highlight that this exchange happens in a very direct way in consultations.

8. Some locally refer to these spaces as "offices" (Rus., *ofisy, kontory*), while others avoid the term because of its market connotations.

9. In some temples, lamas keep all income they gain in consultations, while in others part of it goes to the temple.

10. For a discussion of shamanic consultations among Buryats in Mongolia, see Buyandelger 2013; among Buryats in Inner and Outer Mongolia, see Swancutt 2012; for Tuva, see Lindquist 2005.

11. While from an emic point of view Buddhist and shamanic consultations may seem very similar, both their diagnostics and their approaches significantly differ: Shamans tend to relate issues to one's ancestors, to local spirits, or to one's social relations, while lamas pay more attention to karma and Buddhist ethics.

12. In a conversation, a shaman told me about how he instructed a friend of mine to call a lama to exorcise his new flat. When I asked why he felt that a lama should do it, the shaman saw the question as an excessive concern with detail: It did not matter who was to perform it, as long as the person could control the spirits.

13. He cited Gyushi texts ("The Four Tantras") in Tibetan medicine as the basis of his practice.

14. Cf. Chudakova (2021, 117) for a similar effect in traditional healing.

15. This is, however, different from consultations with mediums and psychics as discussed by Wooffitt (2006), which are also interactionally coproduced. In the course of a consultation, psychics essentially utter statements or questions that are then fully or partially confirmed or denied by the sitter. This opens space for the psychic to move the consultation forward and make further propositions and predictions, thereby demonstrating their skill and access to paranormal cognition and further establishing their authority.

16. Evans-Pritchard ([1937] 1968), too, writes of certain ways in which various actors shape the outcome of poison oracle consultations. For instance, inquirers may formulate questions in particular ways to increase the likelihood of their desired outcome, or observers may urge the operator to apply more poison to a chicken, which is used in divination.

5. BUDDHIST IMPERFECTIONS

1. https://www.youtube.com/watch?v=lRtb-Q7SR1Q&t=1s (accessed February 10, 2025).

2. Geshe is a high academic degree in Gelug monastic education, conferred to those who have completed the full curriculum (which usually takes between twelve and twenty years) and passed an exam.

3. See also Højer (2009) for an exploration of "the procreative aspects of absent knowledge" and how they facilitate the efficacy of certain religious forms and practices.

4. The largest denomination of coins is RUB 10, and the smallest of banknotes is RUB 50 (RUB 10 notes exist but are rare). A remuneration of RUB 50 in five coins of RUB 10 would be considered inappropriate.

5. An alternative local version is that those charges were falsely laid in the subsequent Khambo Lama's struggle for power.

6. These are clothes in a shade of red, often traditional Mongol or Chinese style. Many lamas in Buryatia wear such clothes instead of actual lama robes because the Dalai Lama criticized nonmonastics wearing robes.

7. An article on the website *Gazeta Nomer Odin*. November 25, 2015: http://gazeta-n1.ru/news/37962/?sphrase_id=117790 (accessed February 8, 2018).

8. An article on the website *Gazeta Nomer Odin*. No. 1, 2019: https://gazeta-n1.ru/archive/2019/1/70913/ (accessed June 14, 2023).

9. Of course, it is entirely possible that not just religious considerations influenced Budaev's gift. By building Lamrim Temple with his own funds, Budaev presents himself as a successful businessman, which is a very respected image throughout post-Soviet Russia (Yurchak 2003).

10. https://vk.com/lamrimdatsan?z=video-107680664_171420662%2F306a487f99b78831a0%2Fpl_wall_-107680664 (accessed February 8, 2018).

11. Cf. Coleman's (2004) discussion on the "spiritual gift" of Swedish Christians, who, through various kinds of giving, seek to extend the self and affect others. See also Strathern (1991) on extending the self through gifts.

References

Abrahms-Kavunenko, Saskia. 2012. "Religious 'Revival' after Socialism? Eclecticism and Globalisation amongst Lay Buddhists in Ulaanbaatar." *Inner Asia* 14 (2): 279–97.
Abrahms-Kavunenko, Saskia. 2013. "The Blossoming of Ignorance: Uncertainty, Power and Syncretism amongst Mongolian Buddhists." *Ethnos* 80 (3): 346–63.
Abrahms-Kavunenko, Saskia. 2015. "Paying for Prayers: Perspectives on Giving in Postsocialist Ulaanbaatar." *Religion, State and Society* 43 (4): 327–41.
Abrahms-Kavunenko, Saskia. 2016. "Spiritually Enmeshed, Socially Enmeshed: Shamanism and Belonging in Ulaanbaatar." *Social Analysis* 60 (3): 1–16.
Abrahms-Kavunenko, Saskia. 2018. "Tenuous Blessings: The Materiality of Doubt in a Mongolian Buddhist Wealth Calling Ceremony." *Journal of Material Culture* 25 (2): 153–66.
Abu-Lughod, Lila. 1990. "The Romance of Resistance: Tracing Transformations of Power through Bedouin Women." *American Ethnologist* 17 (1): 41–55.
Adorno, Theodor W. 1957. "The Stars Down to Earth: The *Los Angeles Times* Astrology Column: A Study in Secondary Superstition." *Jahrbuch für Amerikastudien* 2:19–88.
Ahmed, Syed Jamil. 2009. "Performing and Supplicating Mānik Pīr: Infrapolitics in the Domain of Popular Islam." *TDR: The Drama Review* 53 (2): 51–76.
Al-Hlou, Yousur, Masha Froliak, Dmitriy Khavin, Christoph Koettl, Haley Willis, Alexander Cardia, Natalie Reneau, and Malachy Browne. 2022. "Caught on Camera, Traced by Phone: The Russian Military Unit that Killed Dozens in Bucha." *The New York Times*, December 22. https://www.nytimes.com/2022/12/22/video/russia-ukraine-bucha-massacre-takeaways.html.
Alexander, Catherine, and Victor Buchli. 2007. "Introduction." In *Urban Life in Post-Soviet Asia*, edited by Catherine Alexander, Victor Buchli, and Caroline Humphrey, 1–39. University College London Press.
American Magazine. 2022. "Exclusive: Pope Francis Discusses Ukraine, U.S. Bishops and More." November 28. https://www.americamagazine.org/faith/2022/11/28/pope-francis-interview-america-244225.
Ammerman, Nancy T. 2007. *Everyday Religion: Observing Modern Religious Lives*. Oxford University Press.
Amogolonova, Darima. 2018. "Early Soviet Policy towards Buddhism." *Inner Asia* 20 (2): 242–60.
Anderson, Paul. 2011. "'The Piety of the Gift': Selfhood and Sociality in the Egyptian Mosque Movement." *Anthropological Theory* 11 (1): 3–21.
Arnold, Richard. 2015. "Systematic Racist Violence in Russia between 'Hate Crime' and 'Ethnic Conflict.'" *Theoretical Criminology* 19 (2): 239–56.
Atwood, Christopher P. 2004. *Encyclopedia of Mongolia and the Mongol Empire*. Facts on File.
Badmatsyrenov, Timur B., and Sanzhida A. Dansarunova. 2015. "Vosproizvodstvo religioznogo soobshchestva: sovremennyĭ gorodskoĭ shamanizm g. Ulan-Ude." *Religiovedenie* 3:50–55.

REFERENCES

Bailey, Greg, and Ian Mabbett. 2003. *The Sociology of Early Buddhism*. Cambridge University Press.

Baldano, Marina N., Victor I. Dyatlov, and Svetlana V. Kirichenko. 2020. "Buryat Migrations and Diasporas in Historical Space and Time (20th–21st Centuries)." *Journal of Siberian Federal University: Humanities and Social Sciences* 13 (5): 716–27.

Balmforth, Tom. 2016. "Hate Crimes Said down in Russia as Kremlin Cracks Down on Nationalist Critics." Radio Free Europe Radio Liberty, February 19, 2016. https://www.rferl.org/a/russia-sova-hate-crimes-down-nationalist-crackdown/27562759.html.

Balzer, Marjorie Mandelstam. 2000. *The Tenacity of Ethnicity: A Siberian Saga in Global Perspective*. Princeton University Press.

Balzer, Marjorie Mandelstam. 2022. *Galvanizing Nostalgia? Indigeneity and Sovereignty in Siberia*. Cornell University Press.

Balzer, Marjorie Mandelstam. 2023. "Siberia, Protest, and Politics: Shaman Alexander in Context." *Focaal—Journal of Global and Historical Anthropology* 95:30–45.

Baranova, Vlada. 2024. "The Linguistic Landscape of the War: Minority Languages, Language Activism, and Contesting Identities in Russia." *Linguistic Landscape* 10 (1): 55–78.

Baranova, Vlada, and Tsypylma Darieva. 2023. "Russia's Ethnic Minorities in the Struggle against Cultural Imperialism." ZOiS Spotlight, July 2023. https://www.zois-berlin.de/en/publications/zois-spotlight/russias-ethnic-minorities-in-the-struggle-against-cultural-imperialism.

Batomunkuev, Sergei. 2003. "Buryat Urbanisation and Modernisation: A Theoretical Model Based on the Example of Ulan-Ude." *Inner Asia* 5 (1): 3–16.

Batomunkuev, Bair M., L. R. Budatarova, L. P. Dashiev, and V. N. Tsydypova. 2004. *Buddiĭskai͡a traditsionnai͡a Sangha Rossii. Dat͡san "Baldan-Breĭbun"*. Dominoprint.

Bazarov, Boris V. 2011. *Istorii͡a Buri͡atii. XVII – Nachalo XX v.* Vol. 2. Izdatelʹstvo BNTS SO RAN.

Bell, Catherine. 1992. *Ritual Theory, Ritual Practice*. Oxford University Press.

Bernstein, Anya. 2009. "Pilgrims, Fieldworkers and Secret Agents: Buryat Buddhologists and the History of an Eurasian Imaginary." *Inner Asia* 11 (1): 23–45.

Bernstein, Anya. 2013. *Religious Bodies Politic: Rituals of Sovereignty in Buryat Buddhism*. University of Chicago Press.

Bigg, Claire, and Ilya Kizirov. 2015. "Banished Tibetan Lama Says He Was Warned By Russian Authorities." Radio Free Europe Radio Liberty. October 15. https://www.rferl.org/a/russia-tibetan-lama-expelled-shiwalha-rinpoche/27308604.html

Blakkisrud, Helge. 2016. "Blurring the Boundary Between Civic and Ethnic: The Kremlin's New Approach to National Identity Under Putin's Third Term." In *The New Russian Nationalism: Imperialism, Ethnicity and Authoritarianism 2000-15*, edited by Pål Kolstø and Helge Blakkisrud, 249-274. Edinburgh University Press.

Blom Hansen, Thomas. 2014. "Religion." In *A Companion to Urban Anthropology*, edited by Donald M. Nonini, 364–80. John Wiley & Sons.

Bowie, Katherine. A. 1998. "The Alchemy of Charity: Of Class and Buddhism in Northern Thailand." *American Anthropologist* 100 (2): 469–81.

Brac de la Perrière, Bénédicte. 2015. "Religious Donations, Ritual Offerings, and Humanitarian Aid: Fields of Practice according to Forms of Giving in Burma." *Religion Compass* 9 (11): 386–403.

Bräker, Hans. 1983. "Buddhism in the Soviet Union: Annihilation or Survival?" *Religion in Communist Lands* 11 (1): 36–48.

Breslavsky, Anatoly S. 2012a. *Postsovetskiĭ Ulan-Udė: Kulʹturnoe prostranstvo i obrazy goroda (1991–2011 gg.)*. BGU Izdatelʹstvo.

Breslavsky, Anatoly S. 2012b. "Post-Soviet Ulan-Ude: Content and Meaning of a New Urban Idea." *Inner Asia* 14 (2): 299–317.
Breslavsky, Anatoly S. 2014. *Nezaplanirovannye prigorody: Sel'sko-gorodskai͡a migrat͡sii͡a i rost Ulan-Udė v postsovetskiĭ period*. Izdatel'stvo BNTS SO RAN.
Bulag, Uradyn, E. 1998. *Nationalism and Hybridity in Mongolia*. Clarendon.
Burchardt, Marian, and Irene Becci. 2013. "Introduction: Religion Takes Place: Producing Urban Locality." In *Topographies of Faith*, edited by Irene Becci, Marian Burchardt, and José Casanova, 1–21. Brill.
Buyandelger, Manduhai. 2013. *Tragic Spirits: Shamanism, Memory, and Gender in Contemporary Mongolia*. University of Chicago Press.
Buyandelgeriyn, Manduhai. 2007. "Dealing with Uncertainty: Shamans, Marginal Capitalism, and the Remaking of History in Postsocialist Mongolia." *American Ethnologist* 34 (1): 127–47.
Caldwell, Melissa. L. 2002. "The Taste of Nationalism: Food Politics in Postsocialist Moscow." *Ethnos* 67 (3): 295–319.
Campi, Alicia. 2006. "The Rise of Cities in Nomadic Mongolia." In *Mongols from Country to City: Floating Boundaries, Pastoralism and City Life in the Mongol Lands*, edited by Ole Bruun and Li Narangoa, 21–55. NIAS.
Červinková, Hana. 2012. "Postcolonialism, Postsocialism and the Anthropology of East-Central Europe." *Journal of Postcolonial Writing* 48 (2): 155–63.
Chakars, Melissa. 2014. *The Socialist Way of Life in Siberia: Transformation in Buryatia*. Central European University Press.
Chakars, Melissa. 2020. "The All-Buryat Congress for the Spiritual Rebirth and Consolidation of the Nation: Siberian Politics in the Final Year of the USSR." *Journal of Eurasian Studies* 11 (1): 62–71.
Chari, Sharad, and Katherine Verdery. 2009. "Thinking between the Posts: Postcolonialism, Postsocialism, and Ethnography after the Cold War." *Comparative Studies in Society and History* 51 (1): 6–34.
Chatterjee, Partha. 2004. *The Politics of the Governed: Reflections on Popular Politics in Most of the World*. Columbia University Press.
Cheng, Sealing. 2022. "Feeding Hungry Ghosts: Grief, Gender, and Protest in Hong Kong." *Critical Asian Studies* 54 (3): 327–47.
Chimitdorzhiev, Shirap. B. 2001. *Khozhdenie khori-buri͡at k Sagaan Khanu (belomu t͡sariu): Ocherki po istorii khori buri͡at. Srednevekov'e i novoe vremi͡a*. Buri͡atskoe knizhnoe izdatel'stvo.
Chudakova, Tatiana. 2021. *Mixing Medicines: Ecologies of Care in Buddhist Siberia*. Fordham University Press.
Chumachenko, Tatiana A. 2002. *Church and State in Soviet Russia: Russian Orthodoxy from World War II to the Khrushchev Years*. Translated by E. E. Rosolf. Routledge.
Coalson, Robert. 2023. "Russia's 2021 Census Results Raise Red Flags Among Experts And Ethnic-Minority Activists." Radio Free Europe Radio Liberty. February 5. https://www.rferl.org/a/russia-census-ethnic-minorities-undercounted/32256506.html
Coleman, Simon. 2004. "The Charismatic Gift." *Journal of the Royal Anthropological Institute* 10 (2): 421–42.
Collier, Stephen J. 2011. *Post-Soviet Social: Neoliberalism, Social Modernity, Biopolitics*. Princeton University Press.
Contursi, Janet A. 1989. "Militant Hindus and Buddhist Dalits: Hegemony and Resistance in an Indian Slum." *American Ethnologist* 16 (3): 441–57.
Crews, Robert D. 2006. *For Prophet and Tsar: Islam and Empire in Russia and Central Asia*. Harvard University Press.

Cross, Jamie. 2014. "The Coming of the Corporate Gift." *Theory, Culture and Society* 31 (2/3): 121–45.
de Certeau, Michel. 1984. *The Practice of Everyday Life.* Translated by Steven F. Rendall. University of California Press.
Derrick, Matthew. 2009. "The Merging of Russia's Regions as Applied Nationality Policy: A Suggested Rationale." *Caucasian Review of International Affairs* 3 (3): 317–23.
Dollbaum, Jan M. 2023. "Protest and Opposition." In *Routledge Handbook of Russian Politics and Society,* 2nd ed., edited by Graeme Gill, 216–26. Routledge.
Dolyaev, Erentsen, and Radjana Dugar-DePonte. 2023. "'Free Nations League': A Political Platform for Independence." *Inner Asia* 25 (1): 137–47.
Dragadze, Tamara. 1993. "The Domestication of Religion under Soviet Communism." In *Socialism: Ideals, Ideologies and Local Practice,* edited by Chris M. Hann, 148–57. Routledge.
Dugarova, Esuna. 2023. "Buddhism, Power, Identity: The Transnational Buryat Buddhist Living Tradition." *Europe-Asia Studies* 75 (10): 1744–74.
Dyrkheeva, Galina A. 2015. "Buri͡aty i burīatskiĭ ͡iazyk v zerkale statistiki (po rezul'tatam perepisi naseleniī͡a)." *Acta Linguistica Petropolitana: Trudy Instituta Lingvisticheskikh Issledovaniĭ* 11 (3): 158–66.
Elverskog, Johan. 2006. "Two Buddhisms in Contemporary Mongolia." *Contemporary Buddhism* 7 (1): 29–46.
Evans-Pritchard, Edward E. (1937) 1968. *Witchcraft, Oracles and Magic among the Azande.* Oxford University Press.
Fisher, Gareth. 2008. "The Spiritual Land Rush: Merit and Morality in the New Chinese Buddhist Temple Construction." *Journal of Asian Studies* 67 (1): 143–70.
Fisher, Gareth. (2008) 2014. *From Comrades to Bodhisattvas.* University of Hawai'i Press.
Forsyth, James. 1992. *A History of the Peoples of Siberia: Russia's North Asian Colony, 1581–1990.* Cambridge University Press.
Fröhlich, Christian, and Kerstin Jacobsson. 2019. "Performing Resistance: Liminality, Infrapolitics, and Spatial Contestation in Contemporary Russia." *Antipode* 51 (4): 1146–65.
Fuller, Paul. 2021. *An Introduction to Engaged Buddhism.* Bloomsbury.
Gale, Richard. 2004. "The Multicultural City and the Politics of Religious Architecture: Urban Planning, Mosques and Meaning-Making in Birmingham, UK." *Built Environment* 30 (1): 30–44.
Galdanova, Galina R., Ksenya M. Gerasimova, D. B. Dashiev, and G. C. Mitupov. 1983. *Lamaizm v Burīatii XVIII-nachalo XX veka. Struktura i sot͡sial'na͡ia rol' kul'tovoy sistemy.* Nauka.
Garri, Irina R. 2014. "Tibetskiĭ buddizm i tibetska͡ia obshchina v religioznoĭ kul'ture buri͡at." *Ėtnograficheskoe Sibirevedenie* 6:64–79.
Gazizova, Valeriya. 2022. "Exclusion, Secrecy, and the (Under)ground: Dynamics of Female Religious and Ritual Agency in Kalmykia." In *Laughter, Creativity, and Perseverance: Female Agency in Buddhism and Hinduism,* edited by Ute Hüsken, 23–43. Oxford University Press.
Gel'man, Vladimir. 2023. "The Putin Era." In *Routledge Handbook of Russian Politics and Society,* 2nd ed., edited by Graeme Gill, 22–32. Routledge.
Gerasimova, Ksenya M. 1957. *Lamaizm i nat͡sional'no-kolonial'na͡ia politika t͡sarizma v Zabaĭkal'e v XIX-nachale XX vekov.* Buryat-Mongol'skiĭ nauchno-issledovatel'skiĭ institut kul'turi.
Gombrich, Richard F., and Gananath Obeyesekere. 1990. *Buddhism Transformed: Religious Change in Sri Lanka.* Motilal Banarsidass.

Goossaert, Vincent. 2015. "Territorial Cults and the Urbanization of the Chinese World: A Case Study of Suzhou." In *Handbook of Religion and the Asian City: Aspiration and Urbanization in the Twenty-First Century*, edited by Peter van der Veer, 52–68. University of California Press.
Graber, Kathryn E. 2017. "The Kitchen, the Cat, and the Table: Domestic Affairs in Minority-Language Politics." *Journal of Linguistic Anthropology* 27 (2): 151–70.
Graber, Kathryn E. 2020. *Mixed Messages: Mediating Native Belonging in Asian Russia*. Cornell University Press.
Graber, Kathryn E., and Joseph Long. 2009. "The Dissolution of the Buryat Autonomous Okrugs in Siberia: Notes from the Field." *Inner Asia* 11 (1): 147–55.
Gravers, Mikael. 2012. "Monks, Morality and Military. The Struggle for Moral Power in Burma—and Buddhism's Uneasy Relation with Lay Power." *Contemporary Buddhism* 13 (1): 1–33.
Graw, Knut. 2006. "Locating *Nganiyo*: Divination as Intentional Space." *Journal of Religion in Africa* 36 (1): 78–119.
Graw, Knut. 2012. "Divination and Islam: Existential Perspectives in the Study of Ritual and Religious Praxis in Senegal and Gambia." In *Ordinary Lives and Grand Schemes: An Anthropology of Everyday Religion*, edited by Samuli Schielke and Liza Debevec, 17–32. Berghahn.
Hale, Lindsay L. 2008. "Preto Velho: Resistance, Redemption, and Engendered Representations of Slavery in a Brazilian Possession-Trance Religion." *American Ethnologist* 24 (2): 392–414.
Hamayon, Roberte N. 1998. "Shamanism, Buddhism and Epic Hero-ism: Which Supports the Identity of the Post-Soviet Buryats?" *Central Asian Survey* 17 (1): 51–67.
Hancock, Mary, and Smriti Srinivas. 2008. "Spaces of Modernity: Religion and the Urban in Asia and Africa." *International Journal of Urban and Regional Research* 32 (3): 617–30.
Hann, Chris. 2000. "Problems with the (De)Privatization of Religion." *Anthropology Today* 16 (6): 14–20.
Hann, Chris. 2005. "Introduction: Political Society and Civil Anthropology." In *Civil Society: Challenging Western Models*, edited by Chris Hann and Elizabeth Dunn, 1–26. Routledge.
Hann, Chris. 2006. *"Not the Horse We Wanted!": Postsocialism, Neoliberalism, and Eurasia*. LIT.
Hann, Chris, Caroline Humphrey, and Katherine Verdery. 2002. "Introduction: Postsocialism as a Topic of Anthropological Investigation." In *Postsocialism: Ideals, Ideologies and Practices in Eurasia*, edited by Chris Hann, 13–40. Routledge.
Heim, Maria. 2004. *Theories of the Gift in South Asia: Hindu, Buddhist, and Jain Reflections on Dana*. Routledge.
Herzfeld, Michael. 2015. "Practical Piety: Intimate Devotions in Urban Space." *Journal of Religious and Political Practice* 1 (1): 22–38.
Herzfeld, Michael. 2016. "The Intimate Solidarities of Religion in the City." *History and Anthropology* 27 (3): 265–72.
Hirschkind, Charles. 2006. *The Ethical Soundscape: Cassette Sermons and Islamic Counterpublics*. Columbia University Press.
Hobsbawm, Eric. 1983. "Introduction: Inventing Traditions." In *The Invention of Tradition*, edited by Eric Hobsbawm and Terence Ranger, 1–14. Cambridge University Press.
Højer, Lars. 2009. "Absent Powers: Magic and Loss in Post-Socialist Mongolia." *Journal of the Royal Anthropological Institute* 15 (3): 575–91.

REFERENCES

Holland, Edward C. 2014. "Buddhism in Russia: Challenges and Choices in the Post-Soviet Period." *Religion, State and Society* 42 (4): 389–402.
Humphrey, Caroline. 1983. *Karl Marx Collective: Economy, Society and Religion in a Siberian Collective Farm*. Cambridge University Press.
Humphrey, Caroline. 1992. "The Moral Authority of the Past in Post-Socialist Mongolia." *Religion, State and Society* 20 (3–4): 375–89.
Humphrey, Caroline. 1999. "Shamans in the City." *Anthropology Today* 15 (3): 3–10.
Humphrey, Caroline. 2002. "Stalin and the Blue Elephant: Paranoia and Complicity in Postcommunist Metahistories." *Diogenes* 49 (194): 26–34.
Humphrey, Caroline. 2003. "Rethinking Infrastructure: Siberian Cities and the Great Freeze of January 2001." In *Wounded Cities: Destruction and Reconstruction in a Globalized World*, edited by Jane Schneider and Ida Susser, 91–107. Berg.
Humphrey, Caroline. 2007. "New Subjects and Situated Interdependence: After Privatization in Ulan-Ude." In *Urban Life in Post-Soviet Asia*, edited by Catherine Alexander, Victor Buchli, and Caroline Humphrey, 175–207. UCL Press.
Humphrey, Caroline. 2011. "Politicheskaia logika protivostoianiia rasizmu: Diskurs buriatskikh internet-forumov." In *Antropologiia sotsial'nykh peremen*, edited by El'za-Bair Guchinova and G. Komarova, 655–82. Rosspen.
Humphrey, Caroline, and Hürelbaatar Ujeed. 2013. *A Monastery in Time: The Making of Mongolian Buddhism*. Chicago: The University of Chicago Press.
Hürelbaatar, Altanhuu. 2007. "The Creation and Revitalisation of Ethnic Sacred Sites in Ulan-Ude since the 1990s." In *Urban Life in Post-Soviet Asia*, edited by Catherine Alexander, Victor Buchli, and Caroline Humphrey, 136–56. UCL Press.
Inglis, Kenneth. 1963. *Churches and the Working Classes in Victorian England*. Routledge and Kegan Paul.
Jackson, Peter A. 1989. *Buddhism, Legitimation, and Conflict: The Political Functions of Urban Thai Buddhism*. Institute of Southeast Asian Studies.
Jerryson, Michael. 2010a. "Militarizing Buddhism: Violence in Southern Thailand." In *Buddhist Warfare*, edited by Michael Jerryson and Mark Jurgensmeyer, 179–209. Oxford University Press.
Jerryson, Michael. 2010b. "Introduction." In *Buddhist Warfare*, edited by Michael Jerryson and Mark Jurgensmeyer, 3–18. Oxford University Press.
Jerryson, Michael, and Mark Juergensmeyer, eds. 2010. *Buddhist Warfare*. Oxford University Press.
Jonutytė, Kristina. 2020a. "Shamanism, Sanity and Remoteness in Russia." *Anthropology Today* 36 (2): 3–7.
Jonutytė, Kristina. 2020b. "Beyond 'Bad' Buddhism: Conceptualizing Buddhist Counseling in Ulan-Ude, Buryatia." *Journal of Global Buddhism* 21:261–76.
Jonutytė, Kristina. 2020c. "Bez ovech'eĭ otary dostoĭnoĭ zhizni ne budet": Ustanovlenie granitsy religii v kontekste sotsial'no vovlechënnogo buddizma v Buriatii." *Gosudarstvo, religiia, tserkov' v Rossii i za rubezhom* 38 (1): 106–22.
Jonutytė, Kristina. 2022. "The Post-Soviet City as a Communal Apartment: Spatialized Belonging in Ulan-Ude." *Nationalities Papers* 50 (5): 1022–36.
Jonutytė, Kristina. 2024. "Taming the City: Unfinished Religious Expansion in Buryatia." *Ethnos* 89 (5): 907–25.
Kaliszewska, Iwona. 2023. *For Putin and for Sharia: Dagestani Muslims and the Islamic State*. Northern Illinois University Press.
Kappeler, Andreas. (2001) 2013. *The Russian Empire: A Multi-Ethnic History*. Translated by Alfred Clayton. Routledge.
Karbainov, Nikolay I. 2007. "'Nakhalovki' Ulan-Ude: 'Ogorazhivanie prigorodnoĭ zemli." *Sotsiologicheskie issledovaniia* 11:136–40.

Karis, Timothy. 2013. "Unofficial Hanoians: Migration, Native Place and Urban Citizenship in Vietnam." *Asia Pacific Journal of Anthropology* 14 (3): 256–73.
Kent, Daniel W. 2010. "Onward Buddhist Soldiers: Preaching to the Sri Lankan Army." In *Buddhist Warfare*, edited by Michael Jerryson and Mark Jurgensmeyer, 157–77. Oxford University Press.
Keyes, Charles F. 1987. *Thailand: Buddhist Kingdom as Modern Nation-State*. Routledge.
Khamutayev, Vladimir A. 2005. *Buriatskoe natsional'noe dvizhenie 1980–2000-e gg.* Izdatel'stvo Buriatskogo nauchnogo tsentra SO RAN.
Khamutayev, Vladimir A. 2011. *Vkhozhdenie Buriatii v sostav Rossii: Istoriia, pravo, politika*. Izdatel'stvo Buriatskogo nauchnogo tsentra SO RAN.
Khilkhanova, Erzhen V. 2007. *Faktory kollektivnogo vybora iazyka i ėtnokul'turnaia identichnost' u sovremennykh Buriat (diskurs-analiticheskiĭ podkhod)*. FGOU VPO VSGAKI.
Khodarkovsky, Michael. 1997. "'Ignoble Savages and Unfaithful Subjects': Constructing Non-Christian Identities in Early Modern Russia." In *Russia's Orient: Imperial Borderlands and Peoples, 1700–1917*, edited by Daniel. R. Brower and Edward J. Lazzerini, 9–26. Indiana University Press.
Khodarkovsky, Michael. 2001. "The Conversion of Non-Christians in Early Modern Russia." In *Of Religion and Empire: Missions, Conversion, and Tolerance in Tsarist Russia*, edited by Robert. P. Geraci and Michael Khodarkovsky, 115–43. Cornell University Press.
Khovalyg, Dankhaiaa. 2023. "On 'New Tuva' Anti-War Movement." *Inner Asia* 25 (1): 118–25.
King, Sally B. 2009. *Socially Engaged Buddhism*. University of Hawaii Press.
Kleinman, Arthur. (1980) 2003. *Patients and Healers in the Context of Culture: An Exploration of the Borderland between Anthropology, Medicine and Psychiatry*. University of California Press.
Klumbytė, Neringa. 2022. "Radical Sovereignty." Hot Spots, Fieldsights, March 28, 2022. https://culanth.org/fieldsights/radical-sovereignty.
Kormina, Jeanne. "'The Church Should Know Its Place': The Passions and the Interests of Urban Struggle in Post-Atheist Russia." *History and Anthropology* 32 (5): 574–95.
Krist, Stefan. 2004. "Where Going Back Is a Step Forward: The Re-traditionalising of Sport Games in Post-Soviet Buryatia." *Sibirica* 4 (1): 104–15.
Kuvaev, Sergey Y. 2020. "'Stepnye lamy' v Rossii i Mongolii v XIX-nachale XX v." In *Buddizm Vadzhraiany v Rossii: Aktual'naia istoriia i sotsiokul'turnaia analitika*, 99–106. Almaznyĭ put'.
Kuznetsova, Irina, and John Round. 2019. "Postcolonial Migrations in Russia: The Racism, Informality and Discrimination Nexus." *International Journal of Sociology and Social Policy* 39 (1/2): 52–67.
Laidlaw, James. 2000. "A Free Gift Makes No Friends." *Journal of the Royal Anthropological Institute* 6 (4): 617–34.
Laszczkowski, Mateusz. 2011. "Building the Future." *Focaal* 60:77–92.
Ledeneva, Alena V. 1998. *Russia's Economy of Favours: Blat, Networking and Informal Exchange*. Cambridge University Press.
Lee Myers, Steven. 2002. "Ivolginsk Journal; A Russian Lama's Body, and His Faith, Defy Time." *New York Times*. October 1. https://www.nytimes.com/2002/10/01/world/ivolginsk-journal-a-russian-lama-s-body-and-his-faith-defy-time.html.
Light, Felix. 2022. "Desperation on Russia's Borders as Draft-Eligible Men Flee." Reuters. September 27. https://www.reuters.com/world/europe/desperation-russias-borders-draft-eligible-men-flee-2022-09-27/.

Lindquist, Galina. 2005. "Healers, Leaders and Entrepreneurs: Shamanic Revival in Southern Siberia." *Culture and Religion* 6 (2): 263–85.
Lindquist, Galina. 2006. *Conjuring Hope: Healing and Magic in Contemporary Russia.* Berghahn.
Lindquist, Galina, and Simon Coleman. 2008. "Introduction: Against Belief?" *Social Analysis* 52 (1): 1–18.
Luehrmann, Sonja. 2005. "Recycling Cultural Construction: Desecularisation in Postsoviet Mari El." *Religion, State and Society* 33 (1): 35–56.
Mack, Jennifer. 2019. "An Awkward Technocracy: Mosques, Churches, and Urban Planners in Neoliberal Sweden." *American Ethnologist* 46 (1): 89–104.
Mahmood, Saba. 2005. *The Politics of Piety: The Islamic Revival and the Feminist Subject.* Princeton University Press.
Makhachkeev, Aleksandr. 2013. *Khambo Lama. Mysli Naedine.* Novaprint.
Manzanova, Galina. 2007. "City of Migrants: Contemporary Ulan-Ude in the Context of Russian Migration." In *Urban Life in Post-Soviet Asia,* edited by Catherine Alexander, Victor Buchli, and Caroline Humphrey, 137–47. University College London Press.
Martin, Bradford G. 1969. "Muslim Politics and Resistance to Colonial Rule: Shaykh Uways B. Muhammad Al-Barawi and the Qadiriya Brotherhood in East." *Journal of African History* 10 (3): 471–86.
Martin, Terry. 2001. *The Affirmative Action Empire: Nations and Nationalisms in the Soviet Union, 1923–1939.* Cornell University Press.
Mauss, Marcel. 1954. *The Gift: Forms and Functions of Exchange in Archaic Society.* Cohen & West.
Miazhevich, Galina. 2023. "Media and Culture in Putin's Russia." In *Routledge Handbook of Russian Politics and Society,* 2nd ed., edited by Graeme Gill, 354–63. Routledge.
McGuire, Meredith B. 2008. *Lived Religion: Faith and Practice in Everyday Life.* Oxford University Press.
McMahan, David L. 2008. *The Making of Buddhist Modernism.* Oxford University Press.
Mills, Martin A. 2003. *Identity, Ritual and State in Tibetan Buddhism: The Foundations of Authority in Gelukpa Monasticism.* Routledge Curzon.
Minert, Liudvig K. 1983. *Arkhitektura Ulan-Ude.* Buriatskoe Knizhnoe Izdatel'stvo.
Mittermaier, Amira. 2014. "Bread, Freedom, Social Justice: The Egyptian Uprising and a Sufi Khidma." *Cultural Anthropology* 29 (1): 54–79.
Mittermaier, Amira. 2019. *Giving to God: Islamic Charity in Revolutionary Times.* University of California Press.
Morris, Jeremy, Andrei Semenov, and Regina Smyth. 2023. "Everyday Activism: Tracking the Evolution of Russian State and Society Relations." In *Varieties of Russian Activism: State-Society Contestation in Everyday Life,* edited by Jeremy Morris, Andrei Semenov, and Regina Smyth, 1–27. Indiana University Press.
Morris, Jeremy, Andrei Semenov, and Regina Smyth, eds. 2023. *Varieties of Russian Activism: State-Society Contestation in Everyday Life.* Indiana University Press.
The Moscow Times. 2019. "Siberian Shamans Revive Ancient Camel-Burning Rite 'to Help Russia.'" February 22. https://www.themoscowtimes.com/2019/02/22/siberian-shamans-revive-ancient-camel-burning-rite-help-russia-a64593.
Mumford, Stan R. 1989. *Himalayan Dialogues: Tibetan Lamas and Gurung Shamans in Nepal.* University of Wisconsin Press.
Murray, Jesse D. 2012. *Building Empire among the Buryats: Conversion Encounters in Russia's Baikal Region, 1860s–1917.* PhD diss., University of Illinois at Urbana-Champaign.
Müller, Martin. 2019. "Goodbye, Postsocialism!" *Europe-Asia Studies* 71 (4): 533–50.

Namsaraeva, Sayana. 2012. "Ritual, Memory and the Buriad Diaspora Notion of Home." In *Frontier Encounters: Knowledge and Practice at the Russian, Chinese and Mongolian Border*, edited by Franck Billé, Grégory Delaplace, and Caroline Humphrey, 137–63. Open Book.

Namsaraeva, Sayana. 2024. "'Haunted by Ukrainian Ghosts': Three Stories of Ethnic-Military Relationships in Buryatia during the Russia-Ukraine War Crisis." *Inner Asia* 26:109–41.

Nowicka, Ewa, and Ayur Zhanaev. 2017. "Life on the Borderland: Buryats in Russia, Mongolia and China." *Ethnologia Polona* 37:121–32.

Obadare, Ebenezer. 2009. "The Uses of Ridicule: Humour, 'Infrapolitics' and Civil Society in Nigeria." *African Affairs* 108 (431): 241–61.

Ohnuma, Reiko. 2005. "Gift." In *Critical Terms for the Study of Buddhism*, edited by Donald S. Lopez Jr., 103–123. University of Chicago Press.

Oliker, Olga, ed. 2018. *Religion and Violence in Russia: Context, Manifestations, and Policy*. Rowman & Littlefield.

Orsi, Robert A., ed. 1999. *Gods of the City: Religion and the American Urban Landscape*. Indiana University Press.

Oushakine, Serguie A. 2009. *The Patriotism of Despair: Nation, War, and Loss in Russia*. Cornell University Press.

Pakhomova, Evgeniya. 2024. "Victory Day in Russia: Performative Patriotism and State Discourse." *Anthropology Today* 40 (5): 14–18.

Parry, Jonathan. 1986. "'The Gift, the Indian Gift and the 'Indian Gift.'" *Man (N. S.)* 21 (3): 453–73.

Parry, Jonathan, and Maurice Bloch. 1989. "Introduction: Money and the Morality of Exchange." In *Money and the Morality of Exchange*, edited by Jonathan Parry and Maurice Bloch, 1–32. Cambridge University Press.

Pedersen, Morten A. 2011. *Not Quite Shamans: Spirit Worlds and Political Lives in Northern Mongolia*. Cornell University Press.

Pesmen, Dale. 2000. *Russia and Soul: An Exploration*. Cornell University Press.

Prina, Federica. 2015. *National Minorities in Putin's Russia: Diversity and Assimilation*. Routledge.

Prina, Federica. 2018. "National in Form, Putinist in Content: Minority Institutions 'Outside Politics.'" *Europe-Asia Studies* 70 (8): 1236–63.

Prina, Federica. 2021. "Constructing Ethnic Diversity as a Security Threat: What It Means to Russia's Minorities." *International Journal on Minority and Group Rights* 28 (1): 1–35.

Queen, Christopher S. 1996. "Introduction: The Shapes and Sources of Engaged Buddhism." In *Engaged Buddhism: Buddhist Liberation Movements in Asia*, edited by Christopher S. Queen and Sally B. King, 1–44. State University of New York Press.

Quijada, Justine Buck. 2019. *Buddhists, Shamans, and Soviets: Rituals of History in Post-Soviet Buryatia*. Oxford University Press.

Redfield, Robert. 1956. *Peasant Society and Culture: An Anthropological Approach to Civilization*. University of Chicago Press.

Richters, Katja. 2013. *The Post-Soviet Russian Orthodox Church: Politics, Culture and Greater Russia*. Routledge.

Ringel Felix. 2022. "The Time of Post-Socialism: On the Future of an Anthropological Concept." *Critique of Anthropology* 42 (2): 191–208.

Rosstat. 2021. Predvaritel'nye itogi Vserossiĭskoĭ perepisi naseleniia 2020 goda (na datu perepisi 01.10.2021 g.). https://rosstat.gov.ru/storage/mediabank/pred_vpn_2010-2020.xlsx

Rozenberg, Guillaume. 2004. "How Giving Sanctifies: The Birthday of Thamanya Hsayadaw in Burma." *Journal of the Royal Anthropological Institute* 10 (3): 495–515.

Rubin, Eli. 2016. *Amnesiopolis: Modernity, Space, and Memory in East Germany*. Oxford University Press.

Rupen, Robert A. 1956. "The Buriat Intelligentsia." *Journal of Asian Studies* 15 (3): 383–98.

Russell, John. 2011. "Kadyrov's Chechnya—Template, Test or Trouble for Russia's Regional Policy?" *Europe-Asia Studies* 63 (3): 509–28.

Rüpke, Jörg. 2020. *Urban Religion: A Historical Approach to Urban Growth and Religious Change*. de Gruyter.

Sablin, Ivan. 2016. *Governing Post-Imperial Siberia and Mongolia, 1911–1924: Buddhism, Socialism, and Nationalism in State and Autonomy Building*. Routledge.

Sablin, Ivan. 2017. "Making Baikal Russian: Imperial Politics at the Russian-Qing Border." *Europe-Asia Studies* 69 (3): 401–25.

Sassen, Saskia. 2007. *Sociology of Globalization*. W. W. Norton.

Schober, Juliane. 2017. *Modern Buddhist Conjunctures in Myanmar: Cultural Narratives, Colonial Legacies, and Civil Society*. University of Hawaii Press.

Schorkowitz, Dittmar. 2001a. "The Orthodox Church, Lamaism, and Shamanism among the Buriats and Kalmyks, 1825–1925." In *Of Religion and Empire: Missions, Conversion, and Tolerance in Tsarist Russia*, edited by Robert. P. Geraci and Michael Khodarkovsky, 201–25. Cornell University Press.

Schorkowitz, Dittmar. 2001b. *Staat und Nationalitäten in Rußland: Der Integrationsprozeß der Burjaten und Kalmücken, 1822–1925*. Franz Steiner.

Schwenkel, Christina. 2015. "Spectacular Infrastructure and Its Breakdown in Socialist Vietnam." *American Ethnologist* 42 (3): 520–34.

Scott, James C. 1990. *Domination and the Arts of Resistance: Hidden Transcripts*. Yale University Press.

Scott, James C. 1998. *Seeing Like a State: How Certain Schemes to Improve the Human Condition Have Failed*. Yale University Press.

Scott, Rachelle M. 2009. *Nirvana for Sale? Buddhism, Wealth, and the Dhammakaya Temple in Contemporary Thailand*. State University of New York Press.

Shaglanova, Ol'ga. 2012. "Buriat Urban Shamanism as a Phenomenon." *Anthropology and Archaeology of Eurasia* 51 (3): 76–88.

Sharafutdinova, Gulnaz. 2013. "Gestalt Switch in Russian Federalism: The Decline in Regional Power under Putin." *Comparative Politics* 45 (3): 357–76.

Sharafutdinova, Gulnaz. 2019. "Was There a 'Simple Soviet' Person? Debating the Politics and Sociology of 'Homo Sovieticus.'" *Slavic Review* 78 (1): 173–95.

Shevchenko, Olga. 2009. *Crisis and the Everyday in Postsocialist Moscow*. Indiana University Press.

Sihlé, Nicolas. 2015. "Towards a Comparative Anthropology of the Buddhist Gift (and Other Transfers)." *Religion Compass* 9 (11): 352–85.

Simmel, Georg. 1950. *The Sociology of Georg Simmel*. Translated by K. Wolff. Free Press.

Simpson, Bob. 2004. "Impossible Gifts: Bodies, Buddhism and Bioethics in Contemporary Sri Lanka." *Journal of the Royal Anthropological Institute* 10 (4): 839–59.

Sinclair, Tara. 2008. "Tibetan Reform and the Kalmyk Revival of Buddhism." *Inner Asia* 10 (2): 241–59.

Sinitsyn, Fedor L. 2013. *Krasnaīa burīa: Sovetskoe gosudarstvo i buddizm v 1917–1946 gg*. Andrey Terentev and Save Tibet Foundation.

Slezkine, Yuri. 1994a. "The USSR as a Communal Apartment, or How a Socialist State Promoted Ethnic Particularism." *Slavic Review* 53 (2): 414–52.

Slezkine, Yuri. 1994b. *Arctic Mirrors: Russia and the Small Peoples of the North.* Cornell University Press.
Slocum, John W. 1998. "Who, and When, Were the *Inorodtsy*? The Evolution of the Category of 'Aliens' in Imperial Russia." *Russian Review* 57 (2): 173–90.
Sneath, David. 2006. "Transacting and Enacting: Corruption, Obligation and the Use of Monies in Mongolia." *Ethnos* 71 (1): 89–112.
Sneath, David. 2014. "Nationalising Civilisational Resources: Sacred Mountains and Cosmopolitical Ritual in Mongolia." *Asian Ethnicity* 15 (4): 458–72.
Snelling, John. 1993. *Buddhism in Russia: The Story of Agvan Dorzhiev, Lhasa's Emissary to the Tsar.* Element Books.
Spiro, Melford. (1970) 1982. *Buddhism and Society: A Great Tradition and Its Burmese Vicissitudes.* University of California Press.
Spivak, Gayatari C., Nancy Condee, Harsha Ram, and Vitaly Chernetsky. 2006. "Are We Postcolonial? Post-Soviet Space." *PMLA* 121 (3): 828–36.
Ssorin-Chaikov, Nikolai. 2006. *Dary Vozhdyam: Gifts to Soviet Leaders.* Pinakoteka.
Stenning, Alison, and Kathrin Hörschelmann. 2008. "History, Geography and Difference in the Post-Socialist World: or, Do We Still Need Post-Socialism?" *Antipode* 40 (2): 312–35.
Stephan-Emmrich, Manja, and Abdullah Mirzoev. 2016. "The Manufacturing of Islamic Lifestyles in Tajikistan through the Prism of Dushanbe's Bazaars." *Central Asian Survey* 35 (2): 157–77.
Stewart, Katie L. 2023. "Cultural Production as Activism." In *Varieties of Russian Activism: State-Society Contestation in Everyday Life*, edited by Jeremy Morris, Andrei Semenov, and Regina Smyth, 31–50. Indiana University Press.
Strathern, Marilyn. 1991. 'Partners and Consumers: Making Relations Visible', *New Literary History* 22(3): 581-601.
Strenski, Ivan. 1983. "On Generalized Exchange and the Domestication of the Sangha." *Man (N. S.)* 18:463–77.
Subtelny, Maria E. 1989. "The Cult of Holy Places: Religious Practices among Soviet Muslims." *Middle East Journal* 43 (4): 593–604.
Suchland, Jennifer. 2011. "Is There a Postsocialist Critique?" *Lichnost'. Kul'tura. Obshchestvo* 13 (3): 103–14.
Swancutt, Katherine. 2012. *Fortune and the Cursed: The Sliding Scale of Time in Mongolian Divination.* Berghahn.
Tambiah, Stanley J. 1979. "A Performative Approach to Ritual." *Proceedings of the British Academy* 65:113–69.
Tateo, Giuseppe. 2020. *Under the Sign of the Cross: The People's Salvation Cathedral and the Church-Building Industry in Postsocialist Romania.* Berghahn Books.
Taylor, James L. 1993. *Forest Monks and the Nation-State: The Anthropological and Historical Study in Northeastern Thailand.* Institute of Southeast Asian Studies.
Tlostanova, Madina. 2017. *Postcolonialism and Postsocialism in Fiction and Art.* Palgrave Macmillan.
Tsyrempilov, Nikolay. 2009. "For Holy Dharma and White Tsar: Russian Empire through the Eyes of Buriat Buddhists in the Eighteenth–Early Twentieth Centuries." *Ab Imperio* 2:105–30.
Tsyrempilov, Nikolay. 2012. "'Alien' Lamas: Russian Policy toward Foreign Buddhist Clergy in the Eighteenth to Early Twentieth Centuries." *Inner Asia* 14 (2): 245–55.
Tsyrempilov, Nikolay. 2013. *Buddizm i imperiia: buriatskaia buddiiskaia obshchina v Rossii (XVIII-nach. XX B.).* IMBIT SO RAN / Buriaad-Mongol Nom.

Tsyrempilov, Nikolay. 2015. "Konstitutsionnai︠a︡ teokratii︠a︡ Lubsan-Samdan T︠S︡ydenova: Popytka sozdanii︠a︡ buddiĭskogo gosudarstva v Zabaĭkal'e (1918–1922)." *Gosudarstvo, religii︠a︡, t︠s︡erkov v Rossii i za rubezhom* 33 (4): 318–46.

Tsyrempilov, Nikolay. 2021. *Under the Shadow of White Tara: Buriat Buddhists in Imperial Russia*. Ferdinand von Schoeningh.

Van der Veer, Peter, ed. 2015a. *Handbook of Religion and the Asian City: Aspiration and Urbanization in the Twenty-First Century*. University of California Press.

Van der Veer, Peter. 2015b. "Introduction: Urban Theory, Asia, and Religion." In *Handbook of Religion and the Asian City: Aspiration and Urbanization in the Twenty-First Century*, edited by Peter van der Veer, 1–17. University of California Press.

Victoria, Brian Daizen. 2006. *Zen at War*. Rowman & Littlefield.

Von Schnitzler, Antina. 2013. "Traveling Technologies: Infrastructure, Ethical Regimes, and the Materiality of Politics in South Africa." *Cultural Anthropology* 28 (4): 670–93.

Vrijhof, Pieter H., and Jacques Waardenburg. 1979. *Official and Popular Religion: Analysis of a Theme for Religious Studies*. DeGruyter Mouton.

Vyushkova, Mariya, and Evgeny Sherkhonov. 2023. "Russia's Ethnic Minority Casualties of the 2022 Invasion of Ukraine." *Inner Asia* 25 (1): 126–36.

Wanner, Catherine. 2018. "Public Religions after Socialism: Redefining Norms of Difference." *Religion, State and Society* 46 (2): 88–95.

Weber, Max. 1978. *Economy and Society: An Outline of Interpretive Sociology*. Edited by Guenter Roth and Claus Wittich. University of California Press.

Weber, Max. (1916) 2009. "India: Hinduism and Buddhism." In *The Protestant Ethic and the Spirit of Capitalism with Other Writings on the Rise of the West*. Translated by S. Kalberg. Oxford University Press.

Werth, Paul. 2002. *At the Margins of Orthodoxy: Mission, Governance, and Confessional Politics in Russia's Volga-Kama Region, 1827–1905*. Cornell University Press.

Werth, Paul. 2014. *The Tsar's Foreign Faiths: Toleration and the Fate of Religious Freedom in Imperial Russia*. Oxford University Press.

Whalen-Bridge, John, and Pattana Kitiarsa. 2013. "Introduction: 'Buddhist Politics' as Emptiness; History and the Forms of Engagement in Asia." In *Buddhism, Modernity, and the State in Asia: Forms of Engagement*, edited by John Whalen-Bridge and Pattana Kitiarsa, 1–14. Springer.

Wickham, Ted 1969. *Church and People in an Industrial City*. Lutterworth.

Williams, Raymond. 1975. *The Country and the City*. Oxford University Press.

Wirth, Louis. 1938. "Urbanism as a Way of Life." *American Journal of Sociology* 44 (1): 1–24.

Wooffitt, Robin. 2006. *The Language of Mediums and Psychics: The Social Organization of Everyday Miracles*. Ashgate.

Yangulbaev, Abubakar. 2023. "Russia's Invasions: From Chechnya to Ukraine." *Inner Asia* 25 (1): 148–57.

Yudin, Greg. 2020. "Governing through Polls: Politics of Representation and Presidential Support in Putin's Russia." *Javnost—the Public* 27 (1): 1–19.

Yurchak, Alexei. 2000. "Privatize Your Name: Symbolic Work in a Post-Soviet Linguistic Market." *Journal of Sociolinguistics* 4 (3): 406–34.

Yurchak, Alexei. 2003. "Russian Neoliberal: The Entrepreneurial Ethic and the Spirit of 'True Careerism.'" *Russian Review* 62 (1): 72–90.

Yusupova, Guzel. 2021. "How Does the Politics of Fear in Russia Work? The Case of Social Mobilisation in Support of Minority Languages." *Europe-Asia Studies* 74 (4): 620–41.

Yusupova, Guzel. 2023. "The Promotion of Minority Languages in Russia's Ethnic Republics." In *Varieties of Russian Activism: State-Society Contestation in Everyday Life*, edited by Jeremy Morris, Andrei Semenov, and Regina Smyth, 51–69. Indiana University Press.

Zakharov, Nikolay. 2015. *Race and Racism in Russia*. Springer.

Zeitlyn, David. 2012. "Divinatory Logics: Diagnoses and Predictions Mediating Outcomes." *Current Anthropology* 53 (5): 525–46.

Zhambalova, Sesegma G. 2011. "O narodnom buddizme v sovremennoĭ Burī͡atii." *Gumanitarnyĭ Vektor* 2: 87–93.

Zhambalova, Sesegma G. 2014. "Narodnyĭ buddizm i sangaril u burī͡at." *Gumanitarnyĭ Vektor. Serī͡a: Filosofī͡a, kulʹturologī͡a* 2 (38): 116–25.

Zhambalova, Sesegma G. 2021. "Ėtnokulʹturnye processy v Burī͡atii v 2010-e gg.: Problemy sokhranenī͡a burī͡atskogo ī͡azyka (po materialam SMI)." *Oriental Studies* 14 (1): 134–43.

Zhanaev, Ayur. 2021. "Reading a 1908 Buryat Schoolbook on Buddhism in the Light of Its Socio-cultural Setting." *Adeptus* 18:1–25.

Zhanaev, Ayur, and Kristina Jonutytė. 2023. "The Voices of Russia's Minorities on the Invasion of Ukraine: Introduction." *Inner Asia* 25 (1): 111–17.

Zhimbiev, Balzhan. 2000. *History of the Urbanisation of a Siberian City Ulan-Ude*. White Horse.

Index

Page numbers followed by letter "f" refer to figures.

Abrahms-Kavunenko, Saskia, 66, 69, 134
Abu-Lughod, Lila, 73
Adorno, Theodor, 119
Aga Buryat Autonomous Okrug, 13, 43, 49, 98
agency, laypeople's: in Buddhist counseling, 121–25, 128; in Buddhist giving, 145
Aginskiĭ datsan, 65
Aĭtmatov, Chingiz, 4
Amgalan, Lama, 88, 107–11, 113, 118, 119, 121, 123–24
Amogolonova, Darima, 64–65
Anderson, Paul, 145–46, 147
Atsagatskiĭ datsan, 79f
Autonomous Soviet Socialist Republic(s) (ASSRs), 41; Buryat-Mongolian, 30, 31, 41, 180n22; in Russian Federation, 46–47
Ayur, Lama, 83–84, 85, 126, 135
Ayusheev, Damba (Khambo Lama): background, 57; on Buryat Buddhist history, 72; and Buryat language, 127; on consultations with lamas, 112; criticism of, 7, 10, 58, 73, 76, 125; on day of Itigelov's worship, 56; election, 69; on giving practices, 139, 147; interpretation of Itigelov's messages, 162n9; interview, 57, 71, 84–85; position on war in Ukraine, 7, 8, 9–10, 75–76, 151; and Putin, 74–75; residence, 93; sexist attitudes, 93; and traditional sports, 57–58; on urban Buddhism, 84–85, 135

Badmatsyrenov, Timur, 114
Baikal, Lake, 13, 14f, 38
Bailey, Greg, 89
Baldan Breĭbun (TSongol'skiĭ datsan), 83
Balzer, Marjorie Mandelstam, 23
Bardamov, Lev, 104
Bayar, Lama, 4–6
Becci, Irene, 27, 81
Bernstein, Anya, 70, 72, 73, 85
Blakkisrud, Helge, 46
Bloch, Maurice, 135
Bogdanov, Mikhail, 40

Bowie, Katherine, 137
Budaev, Choĭdorzhi, 140–43
Buddhism/Buddhists: and Buryat identity/culture, 58, 79, 126; high vs. low forms, 18; knowledge of, need to acquire and critically evaluate, 131; mediation between rural powers and urban settings, 89–90; modernist and traditional strands, 34–35, 71, 94–95; in postsocialist settings, 68, 69, 94; Russia's isolationist foreign policy and, 71–73; selfless giving in, 19, 136–48; social and political engagement of, 59–60; and war, participation in, 6–7, 10–11. *See also* Buryat Buddhism; rural Buddhism; urban Buddhism
Buddhist Traditional Sangha of Russia (BTSR), 69–70, 159n9; and Buddhist sites, 9, 28, 79, 162n10; and Buryat language, 34, 127, 140; criticism of, 7, 10, 71, 72, 76, 91, 125; influence on regional level, 55; institutionalization, 69, 71; loyalty to Kremlin, 29, 74–76, 151; practical projects, 74, 126–27, 140, 162n15; support for war in Ukraine, 9–10, 19, 59, 60, 75–76, 151
Burchardt, Marian, 27, 81
Buryat(s), 11; centrality of Buddhism for, 58, 126; colonization of, xi, 13, 38–40, 103–4; complex identity, 38–48, 43, 45–46, 79; lands, 13, 38; migration to China and Mongolia, 41; as "model minority," 42; as Mongol ethnic group, 2, 11, 13; in Mongolia, attitudes toward, 45, 152; nomadic background, 13, 30, 38, 39–40, 43, 61, 78; oppositional organizations, 53–54; overrepresentation in Russian army/casualties in war in Ukraine, 3–4, 45–46, 120, 159n6–7, 161n3; percentage of population of Buryatia, 11, 43; percentage of population of Russia, 2; percentage of population of Ulan-Ude, 30, 32; racism against, 51, 52, 152; and Russia, intertwinement with, x, 6, 45–48,

181

Buryat(s) (*continued*)
152; Soviet policies and, 42–43; war in Ukraine and, ix, x–xii, 1–6, 152
Buryat Buddhism/Buryat Buddhists: changing religious topographies, 91; double bind, 6, 7, 74; ethical community, 143–48, 150, 151; everyday religion, 19–20, 120–21, 150, 151, 153; foreign connections, 72–74; golden age, 64; imperfections, 131–35, 143, 151; as infrapolitical field, 20, 105, 106, 112, 151; main spiritual authority, 19, 73; vs. Moscow Buddhism, 131; in post-Soviet period, 68–71; practitioners' insecurity in talking about, 36; revival, 70–71, 95; rural, 78–81; and Russian state, 8, 11, 15, 17f, 18–19, 60–65, 74–76, 77, 150–51; in Soviet period, 64–66; Tibetan and Mongolian origins of, denial of, 72, 73; and urban aspirations, 98–99. *See also* rural Buddhism; urban Buddhism
Buryat Buddhist *sangha*: critiques, 125, 132–35, 141; institutionalization, 61–62; and lay society, 137; as pillar of Buryat society, 112, 123, 125–28, 150; selfless giving by, 139, 140. *See also* Buddhist Traditional Sangha of Russia (BTSR); lama(s)
Buryatia, Republic of, 11, 12f, 14f; Buryat population, 11, 43; cultural revival during perestroika, 44; diversity, 11, 32; establishment, 30–31; future, 150, 152–53; migration and urbanization, 31; Putin's visit, 74; quality of life, 32–33; Soviet policies, 41–44; urban-rural relations, 31–32, 33
Buryat language: BTSR's efforts to popularize, 34, 127, 140; Buryat intellectuals promoting, 40; children's competitions, 127, 128f; decline in later Soviet period, 42, 43; decline under Putin, 50; divinations in, 163n3; everyday use, 33–34; media in, 181n5
Buryat-Mongolian Autonomous Soviet Socialist Republic (BMASSR), 30, 31, 41, 43, 180n22
Buyandelger, Manduhai, 68

Catherine the Great (Empress of Russia), 62
Central Spiritual Board of Buddhists of the USSR, 65, 69
Chakars, Melissa, 42
chakravartin (Buddhist concept), 60
Chatterjee, Partha, 20–21
Chechnya/Chechens, 3, 47

Chimit, Lama, 4, 6–7, 8
China: Buryat migration/population, 13, 41; divine territoriality, 81; lay Buddhist preaching, 18; temple building, 105–6
Chubais, Anatoly, 70
consultations with lamas (Buddhist counseling), 19, 35, 107–25; at datsans, 100; dialogic nature, 121–23, 164n16; divination, 109, 110–11, 116, 119, 121, 122; impetus behind, 112–13, 116, 123–24; as infrapolitical field, 127–28; Khambo Lama on, 112; vs. *khural* ritual, 112; on labor migration, 109, 116–17; laypeople's agency, 121–25, 128; and learning about Buddhism, 118–19; on military service, 119–20; "normal human need" met by, 100; in "offices," 113; as practical pillar for society, 118, 119–20, 121; queuing for, 107–9, 114f; range of questions, 114–15, 120, 125, 128; and religious intimacy, 128, 129–32; remuneration, 109, 110, 113, 118, 138–39, 164n9; terms, 163n6; war in Ukraine and, 5–6, 111, 116, 120, 151
consultations with shamans, 114–15
Crews, Robert, 63

Daba, Lama, 118–19
Dalai Lama: Buryat lamas criticized by, 70, 132; Khambo Lama compared to, 62; as spiritual authority for Buryat Buddhists, 19, 73; and Ulan-Ude datsans, 85, 92; visits to Russia, 72
Dansarunova, Sanzhida, 114
datsan(s), Buryat Buddhist, 159n8; Buryat language in, 34, 128f; counseling at, 100; funding for construction, 101–2; ritual services at, 97f, 99–100; rural, 78–79, 79f, 81, 82–83; sports at, 56, 57–58; state support, 74, 100–101, 103; urban, 28–29, 29f, 85, 91–92, 92f, 93–94, 97f, 99–100, 107, 108f; *zemliāchestvo*, 32, 86–87. *See also specific datsans*
Datsan na Verkhneĭ Berëzovke (Khambyn Khurê datsan), 28, 85, 87, 93, 97f
de Certeau, Michel, 16, 19
Dharmapāla, Anagārika, 94
Diamond Way Buddhism, 70
divinations: Buryat language, 163n3; consultations with lamas and, 109, 110–11, 116, 119, 121, 122; egalitarian dynamics, 121–22; Senegambian, 124–25; war in Ukraine and, 151

INDEX 183

Dorzhiev, Agvan, 28, 62, 64
Dragadze, Tamara, 65

Ėgituiskiĭ datsan, 162n10
Elverskog, Johan, 68
enaction, concept of, 146
Erdem, Lama, 131, 147
ethnic groups *(natsional'nosti)*, 48; and religion, 54. *See also* minorities
Evans-Pritchard, E. E., 164n16
Evenki ethnic group, 95
everyday religion, 16, 77; Buryat Buddhist, 19–20, 120–21, 150, 151; studies of, 17–18

Fisher, Gareth, 18, 105–6
Foucault, Michel, 73
Francis, Pope, 3
Free Buryatia Foundation, 3, 53
Fröhlich, Christian, 22
Fuller, Paul, 60

Gabyshev, Alexander, 47–48, 61
Gazizova, Valeria, 65–66
geshe monk, 131, 164n2
giving (generosity), Buddhist, 19, 136–48; agency, 145; duty and custom, 144–45, 146; enactions, 146; ethical community, 143–48; merit making, 137; remuneration, 138–39; temple building, 142, 144; upward flow, 137, 140–43; virtue *(paramita)*, 136–37; without expectation of return *(dāna)*, 137, 144
Gomboev, Zhambal Dorzho, 10
Gombrich, Richard, 94
Gorbachev, Mikhail, 44
Graw, Knut, 17–18, 124–25
Gunzėnchoĭnėĭ datsan, St. Petersburg, 28
guru lama, 114

Hansen, Thomas Blom, 27
Herzfeld, Michael, 18, 129
Højer, Lars, 66
Humphrey, Caroline, 43, 66, 90

India: Buddhism in, 89; Buryat lamas studying in, 83, 85, 96, 101, 131, 133
indigenization *(korenizatsiia)*, 30, 41–42
indigenous groups *(korennye narody)*, 48
infrapolitics, 20–23; Buddhist counseling and, 127–28; Buryat Buddhism and, 20, 105, 106, 112, 151; social ties and, 22
inorodtsy (aliens), Buryats as, 38, 39
Irkutsk Oblast, 13, 14f, 49

Islam: in Dagestan, traditional vs. modernist, 163n6; giving practices in Egypt (Cairo piety movement), 18, 145–46, 147; in Russian Empire, 63
Itigelov, Dashi-Dorzho (Khambo Lama), 8–9; daily messages, 8, 9, 162n9; day of worshipping, 55–56, 58; incorruptible body, 9, 54–55, 68, 70; and revival of Buryat Buddhism, 70–71; unearthing, 70
Ivolginskiĭ datsan, 9, 56f, 93; Buryat-language children's competition, 128f; construction, 65, 70; Itigelov's body at, 9, 54–55; lamas studying at, 86; pilgrimage to, 54–58; Putin and, 74; secret group prayers at, 66

Jackson, Peter, 26–27
Jacobsson, Kerstin, 22
Japanese militarism, Zen Buddhism and, 10–11
Jebdzundamba, authority in Mongolia, 62
Jerryson, Michael, 11

Kalmyk(s), 13
Kalmyk Buddhism/Kalmyk Buddhists: in post-Soviet period, 68–69; "revival" vs. "reform," 132–33; in Soviet period, 66; Tibetan Buddhist institutions and, 72, 73; war in Ukraine and, 76–77
Kalmykia, Republic of, 46
karma: participation in war in Ukraine and, 6; selfless giving and, 137
Khambo Lama(s), 7, 15, 159n9; Budaev as, 140; institutionalization of position, 62; Itigelov as, 8, 58; during Soviet period, 65; Zayaev as, 62, 72. *See also* Ayusheev
Khambyn Khurė datsan. *See* Datsan na Verkhneĭ Berëzovke
khural(s) (rituals), 81, 160n12; vs. Buddhist counseling, 112; at datsans, 97f, 99–100; local products used in, 87–88; war in Ukraine and, 9
Kitigawa, Joseph, 59
Kleinman, Arthur, 115
Klumbytė, Neringa, x
Kobzon, Joseph, 3, 159n4
Kyakhta, Treaty of, 13, 38, 61

labor migration, Buryat, 116; Buddhist counseling regarding, 109, 116–17
lama(s), Buryat Buddhist, 159n1; alcohol consumption, 131–32, 133; and Buryat cultural heritage, 126; critiques, 69–70,

lama(s) *(continued)*
  91, 96, 125, 132–35, 141; expertise, 118;
  income, 109, 110, 113, 118, 134–35,
  138–39, 164n9; interviews, 35;
  involvement in war in Ukraine, 8; vs.
  magi, 123; noncelibacy, 70, 132, 133;
  participation in World War II, 10;
  regional ties, 32; robes, 141, 164n6;
  rural, 82, 83–84, 85; rural background,
  34; sexist attitudes, 93; vs. shamans, 115;
  staff *(shtatnye)*, 62, 79, 84; steppe, 63,
  79, 84–85, 132, 161n1; study in India,
  83, 85, 96, 101, 131, 133; temple-based,
  counseling by, 113, 164n9; urban, 83,
  85–86, 93; women, 92, 163n5; *zemliak*, 87,
  109–10, 114, 119. *See also* consultations
  with lamas; Khambo Lama(s)
lama(s), Tibetan, in Buryatia, 72–73
Lamrim Temple, 140–43, 142f
languages, minority: and covert political
  action, 23; Putin's policies and, 50; Soviet
  policy of indigenization *(korenizatsiia)*
  and, 42. *See also* Buryat language
League of Free Nations, 53
Lenin, Vladimir, 61
Lindquist, Galina, 123
Lithuania: and post-Soviet label, 67; response
  to Russia's war on Ukraine, ix–x
Lovtsov, Gavril, 104
Luehrmann, Sonja, 67

Mabbett, Ian, 89
Markhaev, Vyacheslav, 50
Mauss, Marcel, 146
McMahan, David, 94
media/social media: in Buryat language,
  181n5; exoticized portrayals of Russia's
  minorities, 21; oppositional, elimination
  under Putin, 50; on war in Ukraine,
  Buryat/Buddhist participation in, 2–3, 8
Medvedev, Dmitrii, 70
Mergen, Lama, 117
military draft avoidance, 1–2, 36, 45, 149–50;
  consultations with lamas, 119–20
Mills, Martin, 115
minorities, Russia's: complex identities, 45,
  46; contradictory experiences in empire,
  42–43, 44; exoticized portrayals, 21;
  indigenization *(korenizatsiia)* and, 30,
  41–42; overrepresentation in soldiers/
  casualties in war in Ukraine, 3–4, 53,
  159n6–7; Putin's policies, 49–51; racism,
  51–52, 152; repression during Soviet
  period, 15–16; in Russian Empire, 13–15,
  38, 39, 63–64; in Russian Federation,
  46–48; Soviet project of nation-building,
  31, 41–42; Stalin's policies, 42, 43; support
  for Russia's politics, 21–22, 51; war in
  Ukraine and issue of decolonization,
  53–54. *See also* languages, minority;
  specific groups
Mittermaier, Amira, 18
monasteries, Buryat Buddhist. *See* datsan(s)
Mongolia: attitudes toward Buryats, 45, 152;
  Buddhism and shamanism, 68, 69, 80;
  Buddhism reconceptualized as "national
  heritage," 60; Buryat Buddhists as
  mediators for Russian Empire, 62; Buryat
  migration/population, 13, 41; selfless
  giving, 146. *See also* Ulaanbaatar
Morris, Jeremy, 22
Moscow: Buddhism in, vs. Buryat Buddhism,
  131; early post-Soviet, magical practice
  in, 123; racist violence against Buryats
  in, 51
Müller, Martin, 67

Nicholas II (Tsar of Russia), 28
nirvana, 162n14
nomadism, Buryat, 13, 30, 38, 39, 61, 78;
  forced sedentarization and, 39–40, 43
Nydahl, Ole, 70

Obeyesekere, Gananath, 94
oboo ritual(s), 72, 80; urban, 88, 89f
Orthodox Christianity: missionary activity in
  Buryat lands, 40; in Ulan-Ude, 93, 94

pan-Mongolist movement, 40–41, 152
Parry, Jonathan, 135, 136
political participation: activism in post-Soviet
  period, 47–48; alternative modes, 20–23;
  limited venues in contemporary Russia,
  21; social ties as building blocks of, 22.
  See also infrapolitics
postsocialism (term), critiques of, 67
postsocialist settings: ambient presence of
  religion in, 77; Buddhism in, 68, 69,
  94; self-consciousness about religious
  expertise in, 134; shifting topographies of
  faith in, 81, 105; urban aspirations in, 98
post-Soviet (label), debates on, 67
post-Soviet Russia. *See* Russia, contemporary
prayer wheel *(khurdė)*, in Ulan-Ude,
  101–3, 102f
Prina, Federica, 50–51, 105

propaganda, Russian, 21–22; effectiveness of, 6, 36–37
Putin, Vladimir: ethnic minority policies, 49–51; as incarnation of White Tara, 61, 75; and invasion of Ukraine, 52; on issue of decolonization in Russia, 54; and Khambo Lama, 74–75; minorities' support for policies of, 21–22; on minority soldiers in war on Ukraine, 3; and partial military draft, 1; rise to power, 48; visits to Buryat Buddhist temples, 70, 74

Quijada, Justine Buck, 66, 68

racism, in contemporary Russia, 51–52, 152
Razin, Albert, 50
religion: and ethnicity, close link in Russia, 54; everyday, 16, 17–18, 77; lack of knowledge and creative engagement with, 134; and management of minority populations in Russian Empire, 13–15; minority agency through, 23; official vs. popular, 18; and politics, deep enmeshment in Russia, 16; in postsocialist settings, 77, 105; in post-Soviet Russia, 66–67, 68, 69; Soviet repression of, 15–16, 64–66; Toleration Edict of 1905 and, 15, 40; and urban aspirations, 98–99. *See also specific religions*
religious intimacy, 129; Buddhist counseling and, 128, 129–32
Rinchino, El'bekdorji, 40
Rinpoche Bagsha datsan, 28–29, 93
rituals, Buddhist: during consultations with lamas, 113; new genre during Soviet period *(sangaril)*, 66; performative aspects of, 117–18; as problem-solving strategy, 130; remuneration for, 138. *See also khural(s); oboo* ritual(s)
Rupen, Robert, 40
rural Buddhism, in Buryatia, 78–81; continuing relevance of, 90; and urban Buddhism, 24, 82, 86–91
rural datsan(s), 78–79, 79f, 82–83; urbanization and challenges for, 81
rural lamas, 82, 83–84, 85
Russia, contemporary: Buryats' intertwinement with, x, 6, 45–48, 152; isolationist policies, 71; limited venues for direct political participation in, 21; as multiethnic federation, 46–48; racist violence in, 51–52, 152; religion in, 66–67, 68, 69. *See also* Russian state

Russian Cossacks: colonization of Siberia, 30, 38, 40; statue in Ulan-Ude, 103–4, 105
Russian Empire: colonization of Buryats, xi, 13, 38–40; management of minority populations, 13–15, 38, 39, 63–64
Russian state: Buryat Buddhists' relationship with, 8, 11, 15, 17f, 18–19, 60–65, 74–76, 77, 150–51; uncaring/incapable, and consultations with lamas, 112–13, 116, 123–24
Russian studies, war in Ukraine and, xii

Samdan, Lama, 101–2
samsara, 162n14
sangaril (ritual), 66
sangha, 159n10. *See also* Buryat Buddhist *sangha*
Sassen, Saskia, 25
Schorkowitz, Dittmar, 62
Scott, James, 20, 21–22
Semenov, Andrei, 22
shamanism/shamans: organizations' loyalty to Russian state, 61; in post-Soviet period, 68; Russian Empire's attempts to convert, 63, 64; in Soviet period, 66; in Ulan-Ude, 93, 114–15; urban, 90
Shambhala war, Soviet power interpreted as sign of, 64
Shėnėkhėn Buryats, 95, 144
Shiwalha Rinpoche, 72
Shutenkov, Igor, 50
Siberia, colonization of, 30, 38, 39–40
Simmel, Georg, 24–25
Sinclair, Tara, 68, 132
Slocum, John, 39
Smyth, Regina, 22
Sneath, David, 146
Social Flock program, 74, 127, 140, 162n15
Soodoĭ, Lama, 162n10
SOVA Center for Information and Analysis, 51, 52
Soviet Union: antireligious campaign in, 15–16, 64–66; Buryat Buddhism in, 64–66; "fractality" of power in, 43; Gorbachev's policies in, 44; indigenization *(korenizatsiia)* policy in, 30, 41–42; Kalmyk Buddhism in, 66; modernization and urbanization in, 44
spirits (nonhuman beings): in cemeteries, fear of, 80, 163n2; concerns with taming and harnessing power of, 79–80, 81; consultations with shamans regarding, 115
sports ("masculine games"), at Buryat Buddhist temples, 56, 57–58

staff lamas *(shtatnye)*, 62, 79, 84
Stalin, Joseph: Buryat Buddhists and, 61; ethnic minority policies, 42, 43; religion policies, 65
steppe lamas, 63, 79, 84–85, 132, 161n1
Stewart, Katie L., 22
St. Petersburg: Buryat Buddhist temple in (Datsan Gunzėnchoĭneĭ), 28; racist violence against Buryats in, 51
Strenski, Ivan, 137
stupas *(suburgan)*, 82, 163n3
Swancutt, Katherine, 122

tactics: employed by Buddhist laity, 19; minority subjects and, 43; vs. strategies, 16–17
Taiwan, religious counseling in, 115
Tatarstan, in Russian Federation, 47
Telo Tulku Rinpoche, 76–77
temples, Buryat Buddhist. *See* datsan(s)
Thailand: ascetic forest monks in, 89; merit making in, 137; religion and statehood in, 60; southern, "military monks" in, 11; urban Buddhism in, 25, 26–27
Thurman, Robert, 70
Tibet, Buryat Buddhists as mediators in, 62
Tibetan Buddhism: links to Buryat Buddhism, official denial of, 72, 73; transnational nature of, 71. *See also* Dalai Lama
Tibetan lamas, in Buryatia, 72–73, 143
Tinlay, Geshe Jampa, 95
Toleration Edict of 1905, 15, 40
Trans-Siberian Railway, 30, 39, 95
T͡Songolʹskiĭ datsan (Baldan Breibun), 83
Tsyrempilov, Nikolay, 62

Udmurt people, protests by, 50
Ukraine, Russia's war on: booming religious market following, 100; Buddhist counseling related to issues of, 5–6, 111, 116, 120, 151; Buddhist images in media coverage of, 8; Buryats as symbol of minority participation in, 2–3; impact on Buryats, ix, x–xii, 1–6, 152; impact on Russia's ethnic minorities, 53–54; Khambo Lama's/BTSR's position on, 7, 8, 9–10, 59, 60, 151; and limited political expression, 21; Lithuania's response to, ix–x; minority soldiers'/Buryats' overrepresentation and casualties in, 3–4, 45–46, 120, 152, 159n6–7, 161n3; official pretext for, 52; rethinking of research and interpretations in context of, xii–xiii; Russian citizens (Buryats) fleeing military conscription for, 1–2, 36, 45, 149–50; soldiers returning from, concerns regarding, 150

Ulaanbaatar: Buddhism in, 34; graffiti supporting Buryat independence in, 5f; Mongolian material culture in, 102; origins of, 25, 78; religious ignorance in, 134; Russian citizens fleeing military conscription in, 1–2, 36, 45

Ulan-Ude: Buddhist counseling in, 100, 107–25; Buddhist datsans in, 28–29, 29f, 85, 91–92, 92f, 93–94, 97f, 99–100, 107, 108f, 140–43, 142f; Buryats "taming," 33; ceremonial scarves tied to trees in, 17f; contemporary, social and economic problems in, 32–33, 113; demography of, 30, 32; eclectic religious practices in, 93–97, 114–15; "female" datsan *(zhenskiĭ datsan)* in, 92, 139, 163n5; future of Buryat culture and Buddhism in, visions of, 91; growth in Soviet period, 69; international lay Buddhist dharma centers in, 34, 96, 144; mayoral elections in 2019, 50; *oboo* ritual in, 88, 89f; origins of, 30–31; Orthodox churches in, 93, 94; prayer wheel *(khurdė)* in, 101–3, 102f; relations with surrounding countryside, 31–32; shamanism in, 93, 114–15; squatter settlements *(nakhalovki)* in, 33, 98; statue of Cossack founders of, 103–4, 105; Tibetan temples in, 91; *zemli͡achestvo* temples in, 86–87

urban aspirations, 97–98; religion and, 98–99
urban Buddhism, in Buryatia: and destabilization of state-sangha alliance, 26–27; diverse sources of power in, 91–97, 151–52; globalization and, 27; Khambo Lama's criticism of, 84–85; "normal human needs" met by, 99–100; and rural Buddhism, 24, 82, 86–91; and shift in local religious topographies, 81–82; as space for innovation and resistance, 24, 27, 29–30, 153
urban datsan(s), 28–29, 29f, 85, 91–92, 92f, 93–94, 97f, 99–100, 107, 108f; rural datsans compared to, 81
urban lamas, 83, 85–86, 93; criticism of, 91, 135; retreats in countryside, 88
urban religion: characteristics of urban space and, 81; diversity, 25–26; eclecticism, 98–99; infrapolitical facets, 23–24; scholarship on, 24–27, 81

urban shamans, in Buryatia, 90
Ust'-Orda Buryat Autonomous Okrug, 13, 43, 49

Vajrayana Buddhism, 71, 81, 94, 136
van der Veer, Peter, 25, 97–98
Victory Day, 10, 160n16
VKontakte (social media platform), 24, 160n20
von Schnitzler, Antina, 21

Wanner, Catherine, 77
war: Buddhist participation in, 6–7, 10–11. See also Ukraine, Russia's war on
Weber, Max, 120, 126
Werth, Paul, 15, 63
White Tara (Buddhist deity), incarnation of: Putin as, 61, 75; Russian tsar as, 60–61
Wirth, Louis, 25
women: increased role in Buryat Buddhism, 66, 161n4; lamas, 92, 163n5; lamas'/Khambo Lama's sexist attitudes toward, 93; Yanzhima worship by, 162n10

World War II, Buryat monks fighting in, 10
wrestling tournament, Buryat *(bükhe barildaan)*, 56, 57, 58

Yanzhima (goddess), stone of, 162n10
Yelo Rinpoche, 28, 93, 95
Yeltsin, Boris, 47
Yusupova, Guzel, 23

Zabaykalsky Krai, 2, 13, 14f, 49, 98
Zandan Zhuu statue, 162n10
Zangskar, Buddhist consultations in, 115
Zayaev, Damba-Darzha (Khambo Lama), 62, 72
Zeitlyn, David, 112
zemliachestvo (regional network), and Buddhist temples, 32, 86–87
zemliak lama(s), 87, 109–10, 114, 119
Zen Buddhists, Japanese militarism and, 10–11
Zhambalova, Sesegma, 161n4
Zhamtsarano, Tsyben, 40
Zhimbiev, Balzhan, 30, 31

www.ingramcontent.com/pod-product-compliance
Lightning Source LLC
Chambersburg PA
CBHW052215240426
43670CB00037B/614